Into—and
Out of—THE GAP

Into—and
Out of—**THE GAP**

A Cautionary Account of an American Retailer

LOUIS E.V. NEVAER

QUORUM BOOKS
Westport, Connecticut • London

Library of Congress Cataloging-in-Publication Data

Nevaer, Louis E.V.
    Into—and out of—The Gap : a cautionary account of an American retailer / Louis
E.V. Nevaer.
      p. cm.
    Includes bibliographical refererences and index.
    ISBN 1–56720–438–4 (alk. paper)
    1. GAP, Inc.—History. 2. Retail trade—United States. 3. Clothing and dress—
United States—Marketing. I. Title.
    HF5429.N4184 2001
    381′.45687′0973—dc21   2001019590

British Library Cataloguing in Publication Data is available.

Library of Congress Catalog Card Number: 2001019590
ISBN: 1-56720–438–4

First published in 2001

Quorum Books, 88 Post Road West, Westport, CT 06881
An imprint of Greenwood Publishing Group, Inc.
www.quorumbooks.com

Printed in the United States of America

The paper used in this book complies with the
Permanent Paper Standard issued by the National
Information Standards Organization (Z39.48–1984).

10 9 8 7 6 5 4 3

Copyright Acknowledgments

This book is dedicated to the new generation:
Marcus D'Avignon
Isabel and Liam Cullinane
Sarah and Natalie Deck
Carter and Laird Eitreim
Balvenie Swope Emma
Arthur John, Margaret and Thomas Golder
Benjamin and Rebecca Gucciardi
Andrew and Michael Hnilo
Chelsea, Haley and John Meskunas
Emerson, Gardner, Malcolm and William Reed
Cheyenne, Jay and Mickey Reynolds
Catherine and Timothy Ring
Lydia Sensenhauser
Sarah and Zachary Shaya

CONTENTS

PREFACE

"GAP" is a corporate brand, the image of which is highly coveted by Gap, Inc. This book is based on over 60 interviews conducted with former and current employees of Gap, Banana Republic, Old Navy and Gap Kids. I also interviewed fashion writers, editors, financial analysts, industry observers, socialites and Gap, Inc. customers of all ages. It is also based on my own personal experiences as a Gap-watcher, which date back to the seventies when I first met Donald Fisher, and my own observations and conclusions about the trends in the clothing industry.

I attended all the store locations and public events described in detail in this book. Gap employees who spoke to me on the condition of anonymity are quoted throughout the text. I have attempted to verify facts by contacting other individuals who were present when certain conversations are quoted, or who have contemporaneous knowledge of them. When no independent confirmations have been possible, the sentence is written in the conditional and quotation marks are not used. Because Gap, Inc. had no editorial control over the discussion presented, Gap, Inc. refused to cooperate officially with this book. Officials of Gap, Inc., however, on two different occasions were extended the courtesy of reviewing certain chapters in their entirety prior to publication in a good faith effort to exercise due diligence. Gap, Inc. declined to review the material for accuracy. Its General Counsel, however, expressed "absolute and unqualified concerns" about the contents, but did not indicate a single error of fact.[1] Donald Fisher and other top executives declined being interviewed for this book.

The story of the Gap is a success story, one that has had broad social and cultural impact on American society. In the interest of providing an accurate and fair historical record of this admirable enterprise, however, it is necessary to present different sides of the story in a responsible manner. Social commentary and a cultural context are provided to help the reader understand the place of the Gap in the history of American consumerism and the evolution of merchandising at the conclusion of the twentieth century. All the opinions expressed are my own. If there are any errors of fact, then these are unintentional and will be corrected in future editions. For the sake of full disclosure, I own no stock in Gap, Inc. or in any other apparel manufacturer, whether publicly traded or privately held. I do not shop at any of the Gap's divisions.

This book is divided into ten chapters that trace chronologically the history of the Gap within the cultural context of American life as the twentieth century came to a close. Chapters 1 and 2 detail the beginnings of the Gap, from the Summer of Love in San Francisco and the opening of the first store through the trial-and-error approach adopted by Donald Fisher that led to his refining his unique approach to the science of merchandising clothes. In the process, Donald Fisher launched a revolution in retailing that resulted in the Gap becoming the largest retailer of Levi's® jeans in the world, and the Gap's easy-going marriage between retailing and pop culture made America eagerly, "fall into the Gap."

Chapter 3 finds the Gap growing steadily through the seventies. The year 1976, however, proved to be a defining moment, one that would shape how the Gap's business model evolved over the next quarter century. In 1976 not only did the Gap go public, but then in 1978 the Federal Trade Commission ruled Levi Strauss could no longer dictate retail prices of its jeans, squeezing profit margins at the Gap. Donald Fisher then resolved to integrate his company "vertically," a decision that fundamentally altered the Gap's relationship with Levi Strauss & Co.

The following three chapters detail the Gap's expansion into other chains. The acquisition of Banana Republic in 1983, the same year Mickey Drexler came aboard in order to integrate the company vertically, moved the Gap into the area of fashion. The turbulent incorporation of Banana Republic into Gap, Inc.'s corporate culture proved to be a dramatic and sad experience for all involved. That the Gap's own experiment in the high-end retail market had been shunned by both Seventh Avenue and consumers alike further exacerbated the pressure for Banana Republic to perform. When that division did not meet expectations and there were philosophical differences, Donald Fisher replaced Banana Republic founders Mel and Patricia Ziegler. Stunned by the failure of Hemisphere, another division, the Gap retreated entirely from "fashion." Chapter 5 explains how "simplicity"— a euphemism for a basic line of classic clothes—became the guiding principle for the Gap.

The eighties found the Gap enjoying phenomenal growth as its "antifashion" philosophy to dressing found resonance among the baby boomers and members of Generation X. As the Gap would find out in the early nineties, only when its core business strayed from its proven no-frills, no-fashion approach did it encounter problems. The only exception would be Banana Republic, which, in the wake of the openness precipitated by the AIDS crisis, became highly profitable, in part, by tapping the mainstreaming of gay urban aesthetics in the United States in the mid-nineties. Jeanne Jackson, lured to Banana Republic from Victoria's Secret, was able to translate her provocative approach to retailing by marketing an ambiance as distinct as the image Banana Republic cultivated for itself.

The maturing of the core business and Banana Republic's successful presence in high-end retailing, however, presented the Gap with a crisis. As more and more Americans flocked to discounters, such as Wal-Mart and Target, the lower-end market resisted the Gap's prices. The solution—opening twenty-five Gap Warehouses that later became Old Navy Clothing Company—led Donald Fisher and Mickey Drexler to stumble into a highly profitable business. Old Navy's mission to "revolutionize" the experience of shopping for discounts proved, perhaps, to be too successful as it began to eat away at the Gap's core business. This cannibalism is examined in chapter 7; it was clear that the Gap as a brand held little intrinsic value to consumers, who were willing to abandon the Gap if the price was right somewhere else.

As the nineties progressed, it became obvious that the problems the Gap was experiencing were not due entirely to pressures from Old Navy's success. The Gap had misunderstood the psychology of Generation Y. The Gap's effortless courting of Generation X had given it a false sense of security. Chapter 8 discusses the reasons why Generation Y—a generation almost twice the size of Generation X—did not identify with the Gap. This failure to seduce the new generation of American consumers was compounded when Global Exchange targeted the Gap to protest labor abuses at sweatshops abroad. The politicized members of Generation Y, as chapter 9 discusses, identified both Nike and the Gap as "villains" to be resisted. The Gap, which is a portrait of America as a pocket T-shirt, now confronted itself being vilified by Youth Culture.

It was not without irony that the uniform of American Youth Culture—jeans, T-shirts and sneakers—would be closely identified with corporate giants depicted as oppressors of women and children in impoverished countries around the world. These campaigns, coupled with the nature of youthful rebellion, rendered the Gap as "uncool" by a generation of Americans raised with Internet chat rooms, cell phones and MTV. The Gap, to Generation Y, appeared too quaint and ancient—and politically incorrect. Chapter 10 explores precisely how—and why—America's thirty-year love affair with the Gap may be coming to an end. This public repudiation of the

Gap suffused the culture as the twenty-first century began. From music videos and television commercials that ridiculed the Gap to op-ed essays in the *New York Times* that lampooned the Gap's idea of "fashion," the Gap was associated with the status quo, a status quo against which American youth would rebel.

A NOTE ON LANGUAGE

While this book uses Standard Written English (SWE), there are instances in which, in a bold affirmation of identity by the lesbian, gay, bisexual, transgender, queer (LGBTQ) community, words and expressions that comprise value-neutral terms in common usage in Standard Queer English (SQE) are used.

ACKNOWLEDGMENTS

Alison Lurie, under whom I studied at Cornell University, generously allowed me to interrupt her vacation in Key West to grant me permission to quote from her book. Alexandra Close has given me unfettered access to all the talented members of Generation Y at Pacific News Service and *Youth Outlook*, for which I am thankful. Angela Cuevas offered intriguing insights and comments that helped me understand more precisely the corporate culture of Gap, Inc. Leila Salazar was generous in providing information about Global Exchange's efforts to educate the public about the Gap's labor practices around the world. Carl Croft, Steve Fletcher and Delwin Rimbey of Dandelion Tampopo in San Francisco offered insights into the Matures generation, which proved instructive in understanding the cultural forces against which Youth Culture in the sixties rebelled. Wally Sharp and Donald Huber were gracious enough to offer valuable criticism on my take of New York fashionistas at the end of the twentieth century. Glen and Abby Weisberg offered invaluable feedback while observing shoppers up and down Magnificent Mile. John Hook tremendously facilitated my research in Chicago. Alain Giberstein in Mexico City generously shared his observations on the seismic shift between Generations X and Y. Mark Schurmann of New York and San Francisco made observations that helped me understand the subtle differences among those members of Generation Y who live in New York and those who live in California. Milton White in New York and David Stork in Los Angeles both patiently read through portions of the manuscript while in its roughest draft stage. Eric Valentine, as always, remains as delightful an editor as any writer could be fortunate to have. Jean Paul Gaultier and the late Gianni Versace offered their take on the state of fashion in the second half of the twentieth century. Santiago Balducci in Milan broadened my understanding of the European perspective on American fashion, as had the late Diana Vreeland years before him. Ed Hardy of Ed Hardy Antiques offered generous encouragement during the development of this book. Amy Rennert offered wise advice on how the story of the Gap could best be told. Anonymous current and former employees in San Francisco, New York, Los Angeles, Chicago and Miami Beach shared their own experiences of working for the Gap, offering splendid anecdotes and, on several occasions, allowed me to make observations at the stores in order to test certain theories. Laura Handman of Davis, Wright & Tremaine provided authoritative legal advice in the writing of this book. Her effort is most appreciated. Special thanks are in order to Robert Brenner in New York, Robert Coleman in San Francisco and Robert Lawrence in Miami. This book could not have been written without any of these men and women. I have nothing but sincere gratitude and steadfast affection for each and every one.

Into—and
Out of—THE GAP

INTRODUCTION: IN THE STREETS OF SAN FRANCISCO

On a glorious California summer day in June 1999, dozens of police officers began to assemble near Three Embarcadero Center in the financial district of downtown San Francisco. The police officers arrived on foot, in patrol cars and on horseback. Blue wooden barricades were positioned around the streets and along the sidewalks flanking Three Embarcadero where the pedestrian-level shops are located. Police officers were stationed in front of the entrances to one of the more popular shops, the Gap. They also stood guard in front of the store's floor-to-ceiling glass walls, partially obstructing the slogans on the oversized posters invoking "Everybody . . . in cords," which was the campaign on billboards, in magazines and flooding the airwaves on MTV.

In a matter of moments, from around the corner and down the street where they had assembled in front of the Hyatt Hotel at Five Embarcadero on Drum Street, hundreds of protesters suddenly came into view. They began their march toward the Gap. The spectacle resembled an apparition out of an Italian Renaissance painting: hundreds of pilgrims, in a festive—and noisy—procession, bearing witness to their compelling faith. In this case, it was a public repudiation of the materialism that the Gap embodied, a warning to us all, to these activist members of Youth Culture, of the apocalyptic moral depravity Gap, Inc. had now unleashed upon the world.

Amid the whistles being blown, the chants that mocked Gap's current marketing campaign—"Everybody . . . in cords! Everybody . . . in leather!"—became on that summer day "Everybody the *same!* Everybody *insane!*" as they rose high above the protesting multitudes of the outraged.

The police officers stood stoically. The startled horses whined, and passersby and tourists alike stopped in their tracks, taken by surprise. Business as usual paused for a few moments.

In the midst of this festive demonstration, a vision on the horizon above the streets of San Francisco surprisingly came into view. For there, carried aloft as the devout protesters marched from east to west, not unlike a gigantic Indonesian shadow puppet, looming over all this assembled humanity was the effigy of a nondescript, balding and bespeckled man: Donald Fisher, the founder and chairman of Gap, Inc.

A demonstration against the Gap? Such an uproar over Gap's Donald Fisher, the man who revolutionized the mass merchandising of a $12.50 pocket T-shirt?

If Donald Fisher thought that 1999 would be a time when he could celebrate with abandon the thirtieth anniversary of the founding of Gap, Inc., which in 2000 sold almost $13 billion at its 3,500 stores throughout the world, then he was in for a stunning surprise.

As the protesters wound their noisy way under police escort toward Grant Avenue and Sutter Street, where the flagship Banana Republic store is located, leaving the streets in their wake littered with paper, flyers, confetti and police horse excrement, something of greater consequence was taking place.

Gap, Inc., a publicly traded New York Stock Exchange company, was the firm that had launched America's antifashion revolution with one new store opening every day throughout 1998. However, it was now confronting repudiation in its own hometown—and by the very young people it had successfully courted, celebrated and bewitched for more than a quarter century.

How could this be? The antifashion philosophy Gap initiated in 1983 began when Donald Fisher acquired Banana Republic and hired Mickey Drexler, the former president of Ann Taylor, to run the Gap stores. Gap's approach to clothing—defying the changes that "fashion" mandates from season to season by focusing on a collection of casual clothes that, by being able to be worn season after season, year after year, would constitute a basic wardrobe—was characterized as "antifashion" by Teri Agins, a journalist who covers fashion for the *Wall Street Journal*. That antifashion philosophy had met with singular and spectacular success and was the envy of the retailing world. Possessed by marketing magic, in sixteen years the Fisher-Drexler strategy had revolutionized the mass merchandising of clothes in the United States.

Those protesters shouting louder and louder as they marched toward the flagship Banana Republic store, however, demonstrated that consumer attitudes were changing in ways no one had anticipated.[1] The Gap's success at bringing baby boomers and Generation X-ers into the stores had in the nineties created a retailing sensation without parallel in American history. The Gap's credibility with the American consumer, who kept coming back to the stores for more no-frills basics, was—suddenly—crumbling to the most savvy consumers the world has ever known: Generation Y.

Generation Y consists of the 70 million people born after 1978, who command an estimated $200 billion in consumer spending. For Generation Y-ers the Gap was in a free fall in the vital category of "coolness"—whatever that elusive idea may be in fact.[2] Indeed, had it not been for the advent of Old Navy, there would have been a net loss in the overall "coolness" factor of Gap, Inc. among young people.[3] But with or without Old Navy, the imaginations of America's youth had been seduced by other clothes, ones that did not rely on mass merchandising.

One only had to turn the television on to see the rebellion against, and targeting of, the Gap unfold with breathtaking speed. There, on MTV of all places, the handsome young men of the pop group LFO performed in a sexy and stylish video singing their runaway Top Ten hit, "Summer Girls," a song that praised young women for wearing clothes from Abercrombie & Fitch. The boys made it clear that they liked girls who "wear Abercrombie & Fitch."

A few video plays later on the popular *TRL Hour* (*Total Request Line Hour*) was none other than Blink 182 singing "What's My Age Again?" This video included three handsome young men running naked (and doing somersaults) through a scathing send-up of a Gap commercial.[4] And between these videos—one celebrating the Gap's rival and the other mocking the Gap itself—were, of course, the Gap commercials themselves, only now they were being seen in a different light by America's youth, as objects of derision, alienating, androgynous and completely uncool.[5]

Whereas the droll approach the Gap had favored in its commercials—disinterested teenagers ruefully reciting the words to old songs, such as Madonna's "Dress You Up"—had been the hallmark of a hip nineties antifashion stance, this was suddenly transformed into one of unintended irony: the Material Girl, to Generation Y, was now the "Immaterial Icon."

To the millions of Generation Y-ers tuned into MTV, the coolest of the cool were ignoring the Gap—or worse yet, they were ridiculing it. Indeed, for American youth weaned on the visual and musical immediacy of MTV, the members of Generation Y are wary of the hard sell, and they recognize corporate mass merchandising when they see it. Unlike their less sophisticated predecessors of decades past, Generation Y-ers are more jaded and smarter in stunning ways. More than recoiling from anything that smacked of parental approval—their parents, after all, were those baby boomers uncool enough to have been seduced by the hard sell pioneered by the splendid mutuality of the Gap's complementary brands—their loyalty could not be taken for granted by anyone.[6]

Their parents' allegiance to a mass-merchandised brand has not been inherited by Generation Y, a generation whose *de rigueur* look found inspiration in the understated retro bowling shirts favored by the members of Sugar Ray, the guayabera-inspired shirts worn by Santana and Rob Thomas, the muted orange Hawaiian-inspired print shirts and button-front woven shirts of Smash Mouth's band members, the Giorgio Armani wardrobe of Ricky Martin, the urban street styles of Jennifer Lopez, the hip-hop flair of TLC and the calculated stylishness of the Backstreet Boys.

The Gap had miscalculated terribly in the spring and summer of 1999. Its attempt to invoke the notorious Madonna song in its commercials in the summer of 1999, for instance, was to Generation Y-ers hard sell at its most jaded and offensive.[7] And it had the unintended effect of dating the store— and the Gap brand—all the way back to the irrelevant pre-Internet pre-his- toric age of the eighties, when the members of Generation Y were wearing diapers and playing with crayons, just like MTV itself was back then.

The Gap, by the fall of 1999, was to Generation Y the height of the uncool. Its decline accelerated throughout 2000, which saw its stock value drop by half as it missed sales goal after sales goal, quarter after quarter. This was an ominous beginning to the new century to be sure.

One only had to consider that the Gap's Old Navy, despite its enormous marketing muscle and budget, had stumbled with its drawstring pants campaign. While Banana Republic and Old Navy were expanding with daunting speed in the nineties, for instance, the impact of the antifashion philosophy on American society had begun to raise eyebrows. "Have We Become a Nation of Slobs?" *Newsweek* asked in its February 20, 1995, issue. No . . . but we all shop at the Gap.

The Gap itself likewise fared poorly with its "Everybody . . . in vests." Both campaigns—vests and drawstring pants—were so short-lived neither one could be considered anything but a "flash fad." Gap had failed to un- derstand the powerful influence of the statements about style inculcated by forces such as Surf and Ska music from southern California and how Latin style from San Juan via New York was suffusing popular culture, capturing the imagination of the young and transforming how the members of Gen- eration Y thought about their self-image—and how dress defined that im- age for themselves and each other. For the Gap this was a critical lapse in judgment that represented a stunning miscalculation.

If the Gap had once been lauded for its ability to turn to gold everything it wove into the fabric of its corporate enterprise, then the magic had van- ished in the time it takes to play a music video. To the casual observer it was as if the world beyond the fog enveloping the San Francisco Bay area no longer mattered.

The Gap was now drifting toward one urban reality (Manhattan), one aesthetic (homosexual) and one technological medium (MTV) upon which its vision of itself and the world was defined—and then projected unto the world. This represented a monumental failure. Whether one of hubris or myopia, as if it made a difference, it was evident that the Gap, founded to bridge the generational gap, was now failing to connect with the newest generation of consumers. Why would a seventeen year old think that that ancient song sung by a woman more than twice his age had anything to say to the members of his generation? Why would a song that was now best suited for an occasional appearance on VH1's *Pop-Up Video* be taken seriously?[8]

It's like, as if . . .

Worse than having the city of San Francisco, where Gap, Inc. has its worldwide headquarters, issue permits for demonstrations against the Gap in the middle of a busy work week was the realization that throughout the world, the Gap's antifashion revolution was now being dismissed by Generation Y, a generation that found the new clothing brands, such as Phat Farm, Marc Ecko, FUBU, Mecca, P.N.B. Nation and Sean John, the vanguard of what is truly cool. What stung more was the public rebuke of having Global Exchange, a social and political organization of activists that galvanized Generation Y's youthful idealism, which is also based in San Francisco, launch a multiyear anti-Gap campaign.

After a five-year campaign against the Gap, its impact was clear for all to see: sales at the Gap's core business, which includes Gap Kids and Baby Gap, faltered throughout 1999 culminating when Robert Fisher, Donald Fisher's son, stepped down as president of the Gap stores, and, by the middle of the year 2000, Old Navy failed to meet sales projections, sending prices for the firm's stocks into a free fall. Those Generation Y-ers who dissed the Gap were wreaking catastrophic damage on the bottom line, simply because they were the first generation of American consumers who refused to be seduced by the Gap.

For the Gap the late nineties were certainly different from the late eighties. The seductive appeal of the "Individual of style," in striking black-and-white ads that featured Dizzy Gillespie in a Gap mock turtleneck and Kim Basinger in a white Gap men's shirt, so successful in the eighties with baby boomers, was ancient history to these young consumers. The vintage photographs that featured the compelling statements, such as "Humphrey Bogart wore khakis," had hit the right buttons with Generation X in the early 1990s. But as the century ended, however, Generation X-ers were now old, as irrelevant and ancient as Neanderthals.

The importance of demographics now becomes clear: Generation X is defined as roughly the 45 million people born between 1965 and 1978, while Generation Y consists of the new kids, almost twice as many, who are as much in the malls throughout the country as they are in the chat rooms on-line. As the nineties drew to a close the Gap was losing its resonance and currency with Generation Y.

To exacerbate the implications from a marketing perspective, even the campaigns that had been successful in the past were now being co-opted in a fresher, smarter formula by the Gap's competitors. Levi Strauss & Co., for instance, was struggling to jump-start its campaign to put itself on the road back, attempting to court Generation Y. Sugar Ray's Mark McGrath, Christina Aguilera and Lauryn Hill both reinvigorated and reintroduced Levi's® to Generation Y, those skeptical kids wary of the Gap's antifashion philosophy. Levi Strauss & Co.'s advertising spreads began to appear in the cool magazines, including *Revolution*, *Wallpaper* and *Details*. Its television commercials, launched in the fall of 2000, featured the music of Marvin Gaye and were directed by Spike Jonze, best known for his music videos and film direction. One was titled "Dressing Room" and attempted to leverage the veteran brand to the alienated young men.[9] Its print ads showcased Levi's Dockers K-1 khakis, featuring stunning young models with the arresting tagline, "Created thirty-five years before the advent of the gentle cycle."

Or of the Gap, for that matter.

There was something rather unsettling that sunny summer day on the litter-strewn streets of San Francisco. It was the realization that for Generation Y, it had come down to this draconian assessment: Gap clothes are what your grandparents buy you to make you think they are hip; Old Navy is what you buy yourself when you are desperately broke; Banana Republic is just too queer for words; and Gap Kids and Baby Gap don't even register the faintest of blips on the radar screen of your life.

How did one pop group of three young men get kudos for streaking through a mock Gap commercial in one video, and another group of young men send girls screaming by revealing that their dream girls wear Abercrombie & Fitch in a second one?

The spring of 1999, in fact, was the first time in its history that the Gap was identified as "uncool." The antifashion explosion the Gap had so masterfully engineered had begun to turn on its master. It was a simple matter for the Embarcadero Center's maintenance staff to hose the sidewalks clean after the protest was spent, but that the Gap had now been christened as "uncool" was shocking collateral damage no one had anticipated.

Anyone, however, could have seen this backlash coming. In the same way that in the corporate world, "casual Fridays" were now beginning to raise eyebrows as more and more people wandered down the corridors dressed as "slobs," masquerading in "casual" attire, young people throughout the country began to rebel against living their lives as if they were freshmen who had run out of clean clothes and the washing machines were out of order back at their dorms.[10]

The backlash in the corporate world was one of belittling amusement. *Worth* magazine published in September 1999, "The New Paradigm," with a mocking invitation for the reader to "meet some people who aren't afraid to say no—to khakis, to tee shirts, to wrinkles." Generation Y-ers offered their own corresponding defiance in the world of MTV videos, where stylish clothes were once again a powerful force; getting dates was easier if one didn't walk around dressed like a bum.

How people dress impacts not only their self-esteem, but also how others interact with them, of course. For the members of Generation Y, the one way to break out from under the shadow of the baby boomers and Generation X was to adopt the frivolity of fashion. Walking around in a pastel-colored T-shirt, wrinkled khakis and white tube socks had become blasé; it was the kind of thing your father did at his office, and no one wanted to go there.[11]

Generation Y-ers (and to a lesser degree Generation X-ers who preceded them) had minds of their own, and they didn't like the dictates of the antifashion establishment. Witness the failure of certain "trends" to catch on in the early nineties: the "grunge" phenomenon never caught on among young men, and neither had the "waif" look among young women.[12]

In a few seasons, the more dressed-up look of Tommy Hilfiger and the athletic brilliance of Abercrombie & Fitch and J. Crew were the happening looks. These entrants were able to connect with young people, forging a connection based on the glamour inherent in the idea of fashion. Generation Y, confounded at being lost in the wake of Generation X, was becoming confident that the Gap was not its own.

There were other brands—and other chain stores—that allowed them to stand apart and stand out. Generation Y-ers had physically differentiated themselves: when Blink 182 ran naked in its videos, their tattoos were still visible. For Generation Y, for whose members body modification, temporary or otherwise, was now ubiquitous, the Gap was repudiated because in the Gap, "Everybody the *same!*"

Indeed, none of the models featured in the Gap or Banana Republic advertisements displayed a single tattoo—to say nothing of body piercing. To many self-respecting members of Generation Y intent on pushing the envelope, "Individuals of style" meant a tattoo over one's pierced left nipple and not a pastel T-shirt uniform. To succumb to a predetermined corporate prêt-à-porter would be a betrayal, nothing less than "Everybody *insane!*"

To *dis* the Gap?[13] How had it come to this?

The Gap has never won accolades from the fashionistas on Seventh Avenue. The Gap never held fashion shows, had no high-concept designs. Its greatest intellectual achievement was the $12.50 pocket T-shirt. In fact, nothing in any of its stores revealed a sophisticated take on fashion, or introduced an innovation that created the buzz and splash on which the fashion world thrives. The fashion editors had nothing to crave or remark upon as they walked past a Gap store. The fashion-forward elite stood aghast as the nondescript pocket T-shirt adorned the pages of magazines including *Vanity Fair*, *Vogue* and *Esquire*, and quickly flipped on to something not so mundane or dull. The Gap's billboards throughout the urban landscapes of

America were regarded by those gifted with fashion sensibilities to be nothing but urban blight.

If the Gap was snubbed for lacking "fashion" sense, it was precisely this antifashion statement, however, that established credibility and appealed to the buying public. While "fashion" is elusive, what is fashionable is far easier to identify: it is what more and more people begin to accept and wear at any given time. The disdain with which the fashionistas looked down at the spectacular success of the Gap was proof positive of its credibility with the consumer.

In San Francisco, after all, those protesters could go from one Gap store, to the Banana Republic flagship store, continue to the locations-under-renovation for Baby Gap and Gap Kids and end their protest at Market and Fourth streets, where a flagship Old Navy store was then under construction. It would take no more than fifteen minutes—a standard coffee break— to stroll from one Gap subsidiary to the next, chanting the insidious slogans—"Everybody the *same!*" "Everybody *insane!*"—as interchangeable as the clothes they denounced.

In a Warholian twist, in the present everyone will be able to reach the Gap within fifteen minutes. The story of the Gap is the story of American retailing and merchandising in the last quarter of the twentieth century.

I interviewed several of the protesters to understand the passion that suffused their outrage. When I pointed out that the Gap was just an inconsequential store selling jeans and T-shirts, I was rebuffed. "It's wrong to underestimate the social violence this company inflicts on all of us," I was lectured by a civic-minded member of Generation Y. "It isn't as if we're talking about the Diet Coke of Evil: there's more than one calorie of malice here!"[14]

With the multitudes moving on, the police officers were disbursing, allowing unfettered access to the vilified store, taking down the blue barricades as the maintenance staff descended in moments to sweep and hose the sidewalks clean. I then turned my attention to confused shoppers who were trapped inside the Gap, who had been staring in disbelief at the spectacle before them and who watched the protesters as they marched off in the distance.

One disinterested shopper, a woman in her mid-thirties who worked as an associate for one of the law firms located in the office towers above this store, shook her head and said with simple exasperation, "Honestly, people in San Francisco will find a reason to protest anything."

Some people will protest anything, of course. They are called malcontents. But those protesters weren't young curmudgeons; they were young people, swept up in the idealism that comes with the exuberance of youth. Who, in fact, were *these* particular "people" who were bringing traffic to a halt in the streets of San Francisco?

These people were members of Generation Y. This is crucial to the telling of the story of the Gap for the Gap is the story of bridging the gaps between generations—and the economic consequences of failing to do so. There are four generations in the twentieth century and how they interact with each other has shaped the story of retailing and the evolution of merchandising. These generations are the Matures, baby boomers, Generation X and Generation Y.

A brief overview is in order. The Matures are people born in 1909 through the end of 1945. The baby boomers consist of people born after 1945 and through 1964. Generation X is defined as the 45 million people born between 1965 and 1978. And Generation Y is composed of the 70 million people born after 1978.[15]

The Matures generation, to which Donald Fisher belongs, looms large over the baby boomers and Generations X and Y. They are also the least understood, which is why it is necessary to understand how they see the world if the Gap's impact on American society is to be understood properly. The Matures generation grew up with a distinct worldview and singular sense of purpose. As heirs to the Victorian and Edwardian ages, theirs was a world in which dress expressed social status—and required a certain decorum. When it comes to dressing and one's appearance in public, there is an emphasis on what is tasteful, refined and proper. A sense of propriety suffuses their worldview. The Matures began to come of age in the twenties, but it was in the forties and fifties—when they began to become parents—that they came into their own on the stage of the civic and economic life of the nation.

Think of the films of the forties and the early sitcoms of the fifties. Dress was taken seriously. Thorstein Veblen, writing in 1899, set the standards that influenced the generation born almost half a century after he wrote down these words:

This spiritual need of dress is not wholly, or even chiefly, a naïve propensity for display of expenditure. The law of conspicuous waste guides consumption in apparel, as in other things, ... by shaping the canons of taste and decency. ... It is not only that one must be guided by the code of properties in dress in order to avoid the mortification that comes of unfavourable notice and comment; but besides that, the requirement of expensiveness is so ingrained into our habits of thought in matters of dress that any other than expensive apparel is instinctively odious to us.[16]

Consider how the Matures generation dressed. Writing in *The Language of Clothes*, Alison Lurie notes:

The childlike fashions of the twenties passed away far more rapidly than those of the previous century. ... The thirties idea of good looks, as portrayed in advertisements and on the screen was sophisticated and assured. Heroes had to be seen [to be] able to withstand the blows of adversity as well as to make love and perform daring deeds; they therefore needed to be larger and stronger. . . .

The standard of female beauty, too, had changed. The flapper was passé; the ideal woman of the thirties was in her thirties, and classically handsome rather than childishly pretty: Greta Garbo had replaced Clara Bow.[17]

The Matures came of age with the imperative of classical beauty, sophistication and maturity, traits that would help them as a generation—and a nation—overcome the challenges the Great Depression mandated first and the resolve World War II would demand a few years later.

This serious attitude about life carried through far beyond World War II and the Marshall Plan, well into the end of the Eishenhower years. Again, Alison Lurie points out that "[b]etween 1940 and 1955, though clothes went through many changes, they remained the clothes of grownups. The postwar New Look with its longer skirts added years and dignity to women, and the sober, well-tailored Man in the Gray Flannel Suit was their fit companion."[18]

This image was projected throughout the country with breathtaking speed as television united the nation as it had never been before. As the Internet now spreads across our lives with daunting speed,this generation is living through the same phenomenon that gripped the world of the fifties and was made possible by nationally broadcast television programs. Recall the men and women who populated television shows such as *Perry Mason*, *I Love Lucy* and *Father Knows Best*.

There was a certain elegance that members of the Matures generation strove to achieve and project unto the world, as much to define themselves individually as to dress appropriately for the emergence of the United States as the leader of the free world. This quintessential American optimism was reflected in a sense of dressing as leaders should dress. This very idea of propriety was delightfully challenged by the tail end of the Matures' reign and by the first members of the baby boomers, and was reflected in the inspired musical *Bye-Bye Birdie.*[19]

Social trends—and the stuff of musicals performed every year in thousands of American high schools—need a human face if they are to be understood more readily. Consider what happens when a man, a member of the Matures generation, firmly educated to distinguish between right and wrong, proper and improper, is forced to behold in confusion and bewilderment his son, a baby boomer, with certain Generation Y aspirations.[20]

This is how John Seabrook describes breakfast at his parents' home in the suburbs in 1999:

"What are you advertising today?" [my father] asked.
. . . My father thought it was in poor taste to wear logos or brand names or words of any kind on the outside of clothing. . . .
I said, "It's a Chemical Brothers T-shirt."

Silence. . . .

My father took this sort of thing seriously. You start wearing T-shirts with words on them at the breakfast table, and pretty soon you're amusing yourself by watching daytime TV, or smoking. When I was growing up, Seabrooks did not do such things. . . .

I could have tried to explain to my father that in my world, two hours up the New Jersey Turnpike, there was an important distinction between a T-shirt that says, say, BUDWEISER or MARLBORO and a Chemical Brothers T-shirt that says DANÜCHT. In a system of status that values authenticity over quality, a Chemical Brothers T-shirt will get me further in many places than my father's suit. . . . I said nothing and ended up feeling a little like a traitor for not trying harder to keep the commercialism of my city existence out of the quieter, genteeler spaces of life down here on the farm.[21]

Baby boomer John Seabrook, however, describes eloquently the fiction in lines drawn in the sands of generational conflict. While his father, a member of the Matures generation, may not understand the mundane and common dress the Gap pioneered, John Seabrook himself is drawn to a certain understanding and rapprochement that is only possible through the one thing so often overlooked by far too many social scientists and theorists: human relations are governed by that irrational emotion of love.

Despite his own aspirations to be the "flyest of the fly"—sauntering into MTV's studios in New York wearing a Chemical Brothers T-shirt to be one up on members of Generation Y half his age—John Seabrook is moved by the process of personal growth and the love he feels for his father. There is that bond between fathers and sons that transcend conflict.

John Seabrook notes:

When I was fully grown, and turned out to be more or less my father's shape and size, there was rejoicing in my parents' household. Naturally my father was pleased. He had never spent much time with me as a boy, being so busy providing all the advantages we enjoyed. . . . But in the art of dressing for success in the adult world he would gladly be my adviser and my friend. . . .

Not long after I moved to my first apartment in New York, my father took me to his New York tailor, Bernard Weatherhill, to have a couple of his old suits refitted on me. . . .

But all my father's efforts to clothe me in the style of the young gentleman he hoped I would become were almost entirely unsuccessful. Around the house I wore jeans and T-shirts with words of all kinds on them—TV shows, brand names, sports, *Star Wars*, MTV, Ralph Lauren, Calvin Klein, *Jesus Christ Superstar*. Insofar as I had a style it was bad '70s.[22]

And yet, as prisoners of our DNA, John Seabrook recounts, how twenty years after indulging his appalling taste, he finds himself looking at the world through his father's eyes, the ghost of that Victorian Thorstein Veblen looming close at hand. John Seabrook recounts a dinner at his parents' home in which:

to cheer my parents up, I dressed myself in an old gabardine suit of my father's. It was a surprise. I had found the suit in the attic the day before. . . .

My father was delighted by how well the suit fit me. My mother seemed genuinely pleased, too. . . .

"An old suit calls for an old bottle of wine!" my father declared, and, moving slowly but purposefully, went down to his cellar to fetch a '71 Palmer, an amazing bottle. The ritual of decanting was wisely denied to me as a boy—it was the kind of thing I would make a mockery of, or at least not care about enough to perform properly, but on this evening I was grateful for the opportunity to show I knew how to do it right. . . .

"To your new suit," he said, and then, smiling across the table at my mother, who lifted her water glass and smiled back, he let the wine run into his mouth without any drawing suction, sighing through his nose as he tasted it. He swallowed, replaced the glass noiselessly, reflectively, on the table, and said, with quiet, absolute certainty, "That's good wine."[23]

There comes a time when every son wants to demonstrate to his father that he can properly do something his father holds dear. And a man understands that a wine as good as a '71 Palmer, is, in fact, best enjoyed with his wife and the son who makes him proud. A generation gap is thus bridged in a way no retail anthropologist anywhere on earth could ever hope to engineer.

The story of the Gap is a story of fathers and sons, mothers and daughters, parents and their children. In this respect, the genius of the Gap cannot be underestimated. Founded in 1969 by Donald Fisher, the five brands that make up the Gap—Gap, Gap Kids, Baby Gap, Banana Republic and Old Navy—have pioneered the mass merchandising of clothes and the emergence of the antifashion explosion in America. It is the commoditization of clothes, where "back to basics," "simple chic," and "classics" have pioneered the antifashion notion that inexpensive clothes are egalitarian—and chic.

Gap-label clothing is found in virtually everyone's closet in the United States. The same khakis worn by the mail room clerk were likely to be worn by the chairman of the board, a notion made more poignant by the fact that, a few miles away from the Gap's headquarters, thirty-something billionaires in Silicon Valley were riding the Internet gold rush dressed in ripped jeans, pocket T-shirts, and unbuttoned bowling shirts. At the monolithic Bank of America building on California Street, an investment banker who had been interviewed for *Wired* magazine to discuss specialized financial services for the new Internet millionaires, dryly noted afterward that at this bastion of capitalism, the dress codes of customers whose net assets exceed a minimum of $10 million, have changed to reflect the casual demeanor of the wired-and-way-too-rich, noting that, "T-shirts are O.K.—provided they're not wet."

Dry T-shirts? Is this, then, the logical conclusion of the Gap's impact on American society?

Of course not.

The Gap is an American success story. One doesn't open a store that sells discounted LPs for one dollar and thirty years later have sales approaching the $14 billion mark worldwide without making enemies along the way. What is remarkable, however, is that the Gap emerges as the Gap's worst enemy. The story of the Gap is nonetheless one of drama and controversy as much as it is one of success and genius. But as those demonstrators in the streets and those young people on MTV suggest, beneath the soft-focus corporate image and the ubiquitous presence of the Gap brand in American society today, along with the story of success, there is also a parallel tale of naked greed and the struggle for democratic values.

1

GET INTO THE GROOVE

"Groovy, man."

It was the thing to say in 1968—in keeping with the spirit of the Summer of Love in San Francisco. Never mind that Doris Fisher wasn't, in the first place, a man. Never mind that what she had just said was audacious, an idea that had never been attempted before in American retailing. Never mind that there was no assurance that any of it would make sense to consumers who lived far from the multitudes of stoned-out youth protesting the Vietnam War between the blackouts that were *de rigueur* after the Janis Joplin or Jefferson Airplane or Grateful Dead concerts held throughout the one and only Haight Ashbury.

Never mind any of that: It was a *groovy* idea.

And what was so groovy about the power of that idea, in fact, is how, through serendipity, hard work and just plain luck, Doris's husband, Donald Fisher, would take his own concept of what a shopping experience should be and, in the process, transform American retailing in the last quarter of the twentieth century, reverberating throughout the economy with such force that it shifted the balance of power between consumers and retailers.

Through "the Gap" Donald Fisher would launch nothing less than an antifashion revolution and create one of the most recognizable and success-ful consumer brands in the United States while amassing a personal for-tune and becoming a multibillionaire—when becoming a multibillionaire meant achieving something more than adding "dot com" to the name of something and then launching an I.P.O. (initial public offering).

"The idea," as Doris Fisher explained it once and again at cocktail parties in San Francisco in the waning days of the Summer of Love, "is to bridge the generation gap between parents and their children. That's why the store's going to be called 'the Gap.' "

Groovy, man.

On August 22, 1969, the Gap first opened on Ocean Avenue in San Francisco. Located on a corner, the store beckoned passersby with the message that it sold "Levi's®, records and tapes." With concentric circles in bright yellows, oranges and reds, evoking LP records, the color scheme was in keeping with the times; 1969 was when Woodstock rocked America and when the Apollo astronauts brought back rocks from the moon. Donald Fisher swept the floor after the first day of business and folded the stacks of Levi® bell-bottom jeans that were the craze that year.

Donald Fisher was forty-one years old. His business career was in real estate development, not retail sales. Born a few years before the nation was plunged into the Great Depression, Donald Fisher represented the generation of Americans who fought in World War II and who, returning home victorious, would witness the birth of the baby boomers. It was the baby boomer generation of Americans that rebelled against their parents with unprecedented affirmation of their independence.

The baby boomers were not like the adolescents on *Leave It to Beaver* and *Father Knows Best* of the fifties. The entire generation was unfathomable to their parents. When Leonard Bernstein declared, "I dig absolutely," in response to a Black Panther field marshal's call for Marxist revolution in America at a proper and chic little fund-raiser Mr. Bernstein was hosting in his swank duplex on the Upper West Side for these radicals, nothing better epitomized the breakdown in communication between the generations.[1]

Across the continent America's youth were engaged in various kinds of protests. There were sit-ins (blocking traffic by sitting in the streets) to protest American foreign policy in Southeast Asia. There were love-ins (sex at concerts and parties in private homes) to protest the Puritanism of American society.

The anti-establishment sentiment extended to how one dressed as well. If Donald Fisher's generation was the last to dress properly and modestly, the baby boomers were the first to dress without rules or regard. The sixties had unleashed a rebellion against proper attire, with its strict rules for coordination and styling. Americans coming of age in the sixties were sweetly ignorant of what a proper fit was, or how to discern fine tailoring. The meticulous attention to personal appearance—the pearls for women, the tie clips for men, the hats for both—that dominated the fifties, when American political-economic hegemony in the world was established, were absent in the sixties. There was concern for fashion, of course, but it was a fashion that rebelled against everything that was perceived to be part of the establishment; the immaculate look of Gregory Peck had given way to the wrinkled attire of James Dean.

The Gap opened its doors, enticing customers to come in by selling discounted records and tapes, hoping then to sell them full-priced Levi® bell-bottom jeans. The splendid thing about the Gap was that it was devoid of intellectual pretentiousness and unburdened by ideological doctrines; it wanted to prove no market theory about consumer behavior. Rather, it wanted to offer a pragmatic solution in an ingenious way: if the distance between generations could be bridged through a common experience, why not create a retail environment in which young people (and their parents) could find something they all wanted?

"It wasn't what might be called a 'shop-in,' " one veteran San Franciscan who shopped at the first Gap store said, "but it was a happening place for the time."

It was a happening place because of what was happening inside—and outside—the Gap. In an accidental moment of inspiration, the fact that the store sold music brought together both entertainment and fashion. The Gap was not the only store to sell Levi's®, of course, but it was the first to sell Levi's® *exclusively*. The music section created an ambiance that reflected what was happening in pop culture, which was always foremost in the minds of youthful consumers.

That the store was run by a man over the age of forty only added a certain appeal to the store. " 'The Man's a cool cat,' the kids would say," one long-time associate remarked. "The Man" was Donald Fisher, who had successfully bridged the generation gap between his generation—the Matures, born between 1909 and 1945—and the baby boomers, who had come of age in the sixties.

The net result was a company that was as fluid as water: malleable, elusive, seeking the path of least resistance. It is true, however, that often times the path of least resistance sends one plunging into a torrent. The Gap would be marked by spectacular risk taking—which has led to a whirlpool of surprising failures, stunning defeats, remarkable turnarounds—but without the initial philosophy of no philosophy, it is doubtful it could have achieved as much as quickly as it has.

Unburdened by theories about consumer behavior and willing to assume risk—which meant "repositioning" in corporate speak years later— the Gap, from its inception, was an experience-in-evolution. There is no other way to describe what the Gap, born in those heady San Francisco days of "flower power," was. The sight of Donald Fisher fussing over how the Levi's® were folded, or looking carefully to see what items, by their stock-keeping-unit, or sku, number, had sold the previous week, while the psychedelic music played overhead and the stoned hippies shoplifted cassette tapes, was one to behold.

One of the first instances that illustrates how sharp Donald Fisher's focus was, in fact, occurred before the end of 1969. After only three months of opening its doors, Donald Fisher realized that, on a square-foot basis, the records and tapes did not merit either the floor space allotted to them, or the shoplifting and employee theft—nowadays euphemistically called "inventory shortage"—they were causing. The full-priced Levi's® were selling better than the discounted music, so more floor space was earmarked for the clothes, and the music was out the door.

We tried it. It didn't work. What can we learn from this experience?

The simplicity of this pragmatism was a refreshing approach to retailing, and a successful one. This was a time before there were such things as computers and bar codes and scanners. Today, the moment a shipment is delivered at the back door, it enters a store's inventory control system. As each item is sold, the time of sale, the price at which it sold, the style number, the size, the salesperson making the sale and the clerk manning the cash register are duly noted by computer. An analysis of what is moving, what is not, when sales are made, by which salespeople, and so on, is instantly prepared.

What Donald Fisher instituted—"Let's reposition"—was an innovative approach to merchandising, revealing a flexibility and willingness to evolve continuously that would become the hallmarks of Gap, Inc. Perhaps no other firm in the history of retailing has, over the course of its history, "repositioned" itself so many times, in so many ways, with as much candor as has the Gap. Indeed, after being open only three months, the first "repositioning" took place; over the next three decades, hundreds would follow throughout the entire company.

When the Gap first opened, however, retailing was a less sophisticated enterprise than it now is. If a store had, for instance, 2,000 square feet of floor space and it allotted 25 percent of its space to each of its four product lines, the analysis would be rudimentary. In this example, a store allotting a quarter of its floor space to jeans, records, tapes and shirts, for instance, would have to wait until the end of the week to review the register tape to see what was being sold. If it turned out that 40 percent of its sales were generated by blue jeans, then it made sense to increase the selection and space allotted to blue jeans. If it discovered that only 10 percent of its sales were generated by records, then perhaps the music division should be revamped, or reduced—or eliminated. By comparison, it is now possible to see what is selling by the *hour*—and to modify the merchandise mix, or floor displays, to see if sales are affected by different presentations, pricing structures or how salespersons present the product.

Donald Fisher instinctively realized that the key to success was to have what customers wanted on hand. It may have been Doris who dreamed up the name, but it was Donald who had the idea for the store in the first place. And his idea for selling jeans arose from his own frustration at not being able to find a pair of jeans that fit him exactly. In the sixties one didn't just walk into a store and see, for example, a display of size 32 waist jeans in every conceivable length. There were only the more "standard" sizes available. What if one's size was 32 waist, 38 length? Or 38 waist, 32 length? Or 28 waist, 36 length? Then one had to special order and wait.

The Gap on Ocean Avenue, however, was the first to stock Levi's® exclusively and to keep an inventory of all sizes. When anyone in San Francisco wanted a pair of the hottest fashion item in 1969—those groovy Levi® bell-bottoms—they knew that the Gap would have it in stock.

To make sure this was so, Donald Fisher instituted a novel idea: whenever a sale was made, part of the Levi's® tag was ripped off and put in a box. The portion told the model number and the sizes of the waist and length. These tags were then sent to a service bureau and analyzed and when the report arrived back, Donald Fisher knew exactly—by model, waist and length—what was moving out the door. To understand his customers' shopping patterns better, every hour on the hour he would note the time on the register tape, which would then be analyzed.[2]

It may seem strange to modern shoppers that any business could be profitable before technological innovations made retailing more scientific, but there was a crucial difference between then and now. Back then, discounts on many product lines were rare. Indeed, every pair of Levi® jeans the Gap sold, it sold at full retail price. It was not until the Federal Trade Commission issued a directive in 1978 ending "price maintenance" that retail discounting of Levi® jeans became possible.

"County Seat was the first to start discounting," Donald Fisher said. "Imagine taking a popular product that has never been discounted and suddenly reducing the price. Everyone and his brother wanted to buy them and business was tremendous for a while. But the little discounts kept getting bigger and bigger, and the price wars got worse and worse. Once Levi's began selling at Sears and Penney, in the late seventies, the bottom fell out on margins."

It is this kind of competition—and pressure on margins—that accelerated the technological revolution in retailing; the profits are too low not to know what is selling, when, where, at what price, in what size and color, to which customer and by which clerk.

Compare the relentless nature of retailing at the beginning of the new century with the last quarter of the twentieth century: when Gap officials wanted to know, for instance, if it was worthwhile to stay open an extra hour on Sundays at the first store in Florida, they called and asked if, for a couple of months, the store could stay open until six P.M. on Sundays. They also asked if, at five P.M., with a pen, someone could write "it's 5:00 P.M.," on the cash register tape, so they could "analyze" the sales made between five and six P.M. on Sundays at Midway Mall in Miami, Florida. This would determine if there were sufficient sales between five and six P.M. on Sundays to warrant a permanent change in store hours in Florida. They hoped, that

3,000 miles away, the manager on duty, or whoever, would actually remember to scribble the time on the cash register tape.

I know, because I took the call from corporate offices in California and conscientiously made sure at five P.M. sharp that we noted, in red ink, the time on the register tape every Sunday afternoon. This is what "state of the art" in retailing "know-how" entailed at the end of the seventies. If this all seems naive and backward by today's marketing practices and standards, it was nonetheless an enterprising and innovative approach back then. It was, in fact, nothing less than pioneering.

All, however, was not smooth sailing. The Gap failed to make a success out of selling records and tapes. In the end, it didn't matter; the profit margins on discounted music were very low and shoplifting was very high. But if the sale of music was done away with by Donald Fisher, music in the store itself wasn't. On the contrary, music was played continuously throughout the Gap, creating a singular shopping experience for its time. Donald Fisher brought a fresh eye, a crisp approach and an adventurous sense of play to retailing.

" 'Are you having fun?' he would ask his employees," a customer from the early days recalled. "When in corporate America did the boss ask anyone if work was fun?"

The sense of "fun" that permeated the Gap was, in essence, the sense of success. The unintended effects of bringing young people's music to the stores and the careful attention paid to stocking the right inventory contributed to the Gap's success. There were two other competitors on Ocean Avenue, but neither one had a cat as cool as Donald Fisher minding the store.

What Donald Fisher had stumbled upon was the fact that by marrying entertainment (hip music) with an exhaustive selection (inventory), the net result was higher sales—and a fatter bottom line.

"When we closed shop on that first day," Doris Fisher recalled in an interview in the early nineties, "Don and I wondered if we would ever see a return on our investment! Imagine thinking that back then!"

If there were any misgivings, they were short-lived. The winning formula, engineered by Donald Fisher through his innovative methods, proved irresistible. Within a year, a second Gap was opened and by the end of 1970, a third opened as well. What differentiated the Gap was the splendid way in which elements of pop culture were incorporated into the shopping experience. Far more than merely integrating music to create an ambiance—an inescapable strategy that would, in subsequent incarnations, backfire on occasion—it was the ability of the Gap to project to its customers the mood of the times that generated the buzz that, in turn, generated the traffic.

Think of it this way: at a time when young people were rebelling against the materialism of "the establishment," here was a balding forty-one-year-old Donald Fisher, in his Levi® bell-bottoms jeans, running a few stores in

San Francisco that embraced the spirit of youth. Whether or not the Gap actually bridged the "generation gap"—there were few examples of actual families, à la "the Partridge family," shopping at the Gap together for outfits—the simple fact that the proprietor was a man from the generation that preceded the baby boomers was enough. What was important was that the baby boomers trusted the judgment of Donald and Doris Fisher, who, although way over thirty, could be "trusted" for their integrity and taste.

When the original Gap enthusiasts complimented "the Man" for being a "cool cat," Donald and Doris Fisher had, *ipso facto*, achieved the spiritual essence of their "mission statement"—as articulated at cocktail parties by Doris Fisher.

"After the fifth store opened," a friend of the Fishers from the early seventies said, "then Don knew he was on to something." He also realized that the proper managing of a string of stores was a different matter altogether from a mom-and-pop operation where he and his wife folded and swept up after the kids at the end of the day. It cannot be overemphasized how, by concentrating on the popularity of full-priced Levi® jeans, the Gap was able to enjoy a vibrant cash flow that proved enticing.

"Back in the early seventies, credit and charge cards were not widely used. People used cash or wrote checks. So at the end of the day, you could see how much was sold in an undeniably concrete way: a wad of cash," one former associate said. "There was the kind of cash flow that instilled confidence in the entire enterprise."

It was the healthy bottom line that facilitated expansion. As the seventies began to unfold, the Gap began to expand its outlets. But if this growth was to be sustained, the Gap would have to build on its reputation of being the one-stop store for Levi®. There was more to clothing than blue jeans, and Donald Fisher realized that selling tops—T-shirts, shirts and blouses— would be a natural way to increase the amount of the sale made when the customer went to the check-out counter.

That the Gap, by virtue of its identification with youth, enjoyed a reputation of rebelling against the status quo gave it a power over young people's imagination. During a time when the idea that how one dressed should reflect "individuality"—a code word for less conformity and more casualness—the Gap was at the vanguard. Through the incorporation of the elements of pop culture, the Gap shopping experience was different from that at any other retailer, whether Sears or J.C. Penney or County Seat.

The stores themselves began to reflect the increasing acceptance of informality. The most popular television program, for instance, was the *Sonny & Cher Show*, with its hip stage in bright colors and iconic lights that bore the image of the two stars. The Gap stores, which incorporated the circular designs of the first store (an homage to the memory of the records and tapes), began to reflect the color and accents that resembled the *Sonny & Cher Show*.

The lighting fixtures, for example, were large glass globes that, when suspended in rows across the ceiling, gave the store the feeling of being a television stage. The hues of yellow and orange on the walls above the stacks of neatly folded blue jeans worked well visually. The white Formica floor stands complemented the dark gray carpets. The bright orange and red backgrounds behind the cash registers exuded a warmth and liveliness to the entire store. The drawstring plastic bags became a favorite among students, widely used to carry their books before backpacks became fashion statements.

Gap stores definitely captured the colors and feel of the seventies, echoing the visual immediacy of popular television entertainment shows. That the musical staples of the day—Fleetwood Mac and the Rolling Stones—were played throughout the stores was in keeping with the Gap's image of independence from parental authority.

The introduction of in-house labels—Gap as a brand of clothing, not just as a retail store—offered a new set of opportunities. Levi® jeans were sold at full retail price, and the Gap brand was sold at a discounted price. This permitted the consumers to mix and match brands depending on their budgets. It also allowed for the beginning of what would become a fundamental strategy in the success of the Gap two decades later: the introduction of a "basic" collection, one in which the staples of one's wardrobe were provided once each season, with subtle changes in colors or cuts.

The revolution in how clothes were displayed in the stores rejected the traditional notions of fashion being elitist. Consumers were seduced by the down-to-earth merchandising. The colors that reflected what Middle America saw on the *Sonny & Cher Show* made the Gap a familiar—and inviting—store. The rather ordinary goods offered by all the Gap brands require entertainment to work in conjunction with advertising in order to move merchandise out the door. That Donald Fisher understood how to manipulate the sensational idea of the allusiveness of fashion has resulted in nothing less than the transformation of merchandising in America. It is the successful bridging of entertainment and retailing that has transformed the Gap into the authoritative voice in American antifashion.

Paco Underhill, who has pioneered the field of retail anthropology, which is the study of how humans interact in shopping environments, explains the Gap's approach to retailing this way:

Right inside the door at the Gap and its younger, trendier sibling, Old Navy, there's what's known as a power display—a huge, horizontal bank of sweaters, for instance, or jeans that act as a barrier to slow shoppers down. Kind of like a speed bump. It also functions as a huge billboard. It doesn't necessarily say, "Shop me." It says, "Pause a second to look at what you're walking in on."[3]

Gap's innovative approach to merchandising became a harbinger for the revolution in American fashion in the seventies. If the sixties had witnessed political rebellions that were anti-establishment in their focus, the seventies now saw the proliferation of an antifashion sentiment among baby boomers. The popularity of *The Partridge Family*, after all, resided in the portrayal by Shirley Jones of a woman who was not only a single head-of-household (as the U.S. Census phrases it), but also a professional working woman.

In the seventies, American women entered the corporate workforce as they never had before, earning advanced degrees from colleges and universities and going into the professions. American women no longer had idle time to contemplate fashions; they were in the market for clothes that reflected their lives as they now lived them. The Gap offered a wide selection of affordable, comfortable and stylish clothes that could form the bulk of their wardrobes—and those of their families as well.

Teri Agins explains the phenomenon this way:

Beginning in the 70s, retailers had a reason to expand so rapidly: a new generation of baby-boomer career women who were filling their closets with clothes to wear to work. Thus began the explosion of women's brands like Liz Claiborne, Jones New York, Chaus, and J.H. Collectibles, which dominated the women's floors in department stores. Those mighty labels were joined by dozens of specialty chains like The Limited, its sister Express, and Casual Corner and Ann Taylor, all with their own private-label lines.[4]

If this was the beginning of the "antifashion" forces, then the Gap was in a position to lead the movement by offering professional women (and their families) no-nonsense staples that rounded off everyone's wardrobes. That it could do so with such ease was as much a result of Donald Fisher's dogged determination and persuasive optimism as it was the momentum of the force the baby boomers were exerting throughout the whole of the American economy. No one embodied the California laid-back attitude of the Gap better than Donald Fisher himself.

A short time after the first Gap in Florida opened, one could witness how easy it was to be taken aback by Donald Fisher's approachable and warm manner. Wearing Gap clothes—and canvas sneakers—he walked around the store, making sure things looked right, and was inquisitive about how receptive consumers in south Florida would be to the Gap. This was the first store, he said, in a primarily Hispanic market—most of the sales associates were Cuban-American teenagers and the managers were from the Midwest.

He was curious, particularly since, after this visit, he was on his way to San Juan, Puerto Rico, to check out the first Gap in the Caribbean. He presented himself with a quiet confidence, well centered and humble, eager to listen to the ideas and observations made by the staff present. He didn't offer to sweep up, but he did offer mints he had bought at the convenience store next door.[5]

The answer to all his questions, however, would be known soon enough: actual sales in Miami exceeded projected sales by a record-breaking percentage, making that particular store profitable in less than a year, which was nothing short of surprisingly remarkable. America loved the Gap because it offered selection and value. Teri Agins summarizes the retailing sensation the Gap became in the eighties this way:

> Gap's unpretentious, "real clothes" stance reflected the changing consumer attitudes across America starting in the late 1980s. . . . But just as important as Gap's easy-to-read clothes was its image. . . . With its ubiquitous, seductive advertising, Gap created its own fashion moment in 1984 with a $12.50 pocket T-shirt that continues to be a wardrobe staple for millions of Americans. . . . In the world according to Gap, fashion was beyond the clothes and all about the individual who wore them. As Gap's credibility climbed, the chain became retail's most formidable fashion authority, usurping the role department stores had owned for years. Gap didn't need designer pedigree, it didn't need snob appeal, it didn't need high prices. And, ignoring fashion's revolving door, Gap still managed to make money, even though its clothes didn't go out of style each year. Shoppers came back for more Gap basics, attracted by the new colors and other flourishes Gap created to keep its styles fresh—underscored with Gap's marketing magic.[6]

For Americans who came of age during the fifties, the images of Gregory Peck and Audrey Hepburn are the ones that defined the idea of American elegance. For the baby boomers, who came of age between 1965 and 1975, on the other hand, it was James Dean and Marilyn Monroe who embodied the new American ideal.

The fine tailoring and sumptuous clothing of Peck and Hepburn had given way to the motorcycle wear of Dean and Monroe. Americans, quite simply, had lost the ability to discern fine tailoring—when tailoring meant measuring a garment in quarter inches, and the elegance of the cut precluded unnecessary fussing. In the seventies, on the other hand, women no longer wore slips and men no longer wore undershirts and personal "tailoring" was reduced merely to knowing whether one's size was "small," "medium" or "large."

In other words, it was the *statement* that clothes made, not their *cut* that mattered; it was the *image* the clothes projected, not their *construction*, that was important. It was their *comfort*, not the formal *details*, that consumers sought. As long as the Gap introduced clothes that made a fashionably antifashion statement, that reflected the new ideology of comfort, ease-of-care and casualness, that was all that mattered.

Price mattered too. The Gap offered a good value; this was not lost on America in the seventies, when inflation, recession and an oil embargo had unleashed the most serious economic crisis in the second half of the twentieth century. "Stagflation" had entered the American vocabulary. Recession became not an economic theory but an economic fact of life.

A child of the Age of Aquarius, the Gap, through the first half of the seventies was moving along famously, adding store after store, reaching across the time zones, from West to East, with relentless speed, giving American families value for their money and a wardrobe that was both comfortable and immune to the whims of fashion. As for the stores themselves, the same formula that played well in one mall in one part of the country was as successful in another mall half a nation away; the visual immediacy of the clean lines and the entertaining atmosphere was inviting. In no time dozens of Gaps began to appear across the land.

When the United States celebrated its bicentennial in 1976, the Gap had grown to a total of 204 stores throughout the country, and had just acquired thirty You & You stores. It was a period of tumultuous developments, one that taxed the management skills of Gap executives; Gap stores were expanding ever faster, the in-house brands of shirts, tops, T-shirts and jeans were growing strongly in all key markets; the company was getting ready to launch an I.P.O. (initial public offering) and Donald Fisher's formula for the business end of an apparel company selling an antifashion look was proving to be more successful than anyone had anticipated.

The "look" of the store in the mid-seventies was a clean, crisp look that was unlike any other comparable retailer. A customer walking through any mall in America could easily identify the Gap without having seen the store's name over the door. The color schemes, presentation and "feel" were consistent with what was "cool" in pop culture at the time. County Seat, by comparison, had a certain cheesiness to it with its *faux* cowboy image and, worse still, it looked dirty.

The Gap had no other competition of which to speak other than Miller's Outpost. That retail chain of casual clothes and jeans was one step ahead of the Gap, and the two occupied parallel positions in the marketplace for much of the seventies. The rivalry—when one opened up in a mall the other was bound to follow—continued until Miller's Outpost made a strategic error. In a foreshadowing of the perils that exist when a company is too closely identified with a certain look, thereby alienating the majority of the consuming public, Miller's Outpost decided to restrict its product lines to denim clothing.

Inspired by the success of the "look" projected by John Travolta in the 1980 film, *Urban Cowboy,* Miller's Outpost went all out in its Western, cowboy and jeans look, at a time when the Gap was introducing its first line of khakis, and increasing the use of private labels to compensate for the razor-thin profit margins from the sales of Levi's®. "I never understood their reasoning," Donald Fisher said of Miller's Outpost. "Why were they emphasizing denim when there was so much competition already?"

Whatever the reasoning behind this campaign, Miller's Outpost did splendidly well for itself, successfully cashing in on Travolta's urban cowboy image. That Ronald Reagan, photographed with his Western boots up on his desk and wearing a cowboy hat indoors, had been elected in November 1980 meant that from the White House to your house, the cowboy motif was the look to end all looks. And the Eighties were dominated by the television program *Dynasty* with Larry Hagman wearing the cowboy hat of an

obscenely wealthy Texan. There were, of course, objections to having investment bankers *wear* their cowboy hats while riding up and down the elevators in financial centers around the country, but it was not uncommon to
visit someone's office and see cowboy hats, vintage photographs of West-
erners on horseback and, at times, a saddle prominently displayed to one side.

Despite the remarkable confluence of a blockbuster film, a hit television
show and the first Western president, "cowboy chic" was not a sustainable
dress style. "Miller's Outpost had their day in the sun," one executive from
Levi's said. "But that all ended when the cowboy fad was over." The influence of film on popular culture waxes intermittently, and is soon replaced
by the next runaway blockbuster. Americans were not about to dress up in
Western clothes for the rest of their lives. They, in fact, weren't interested in
wearing a regional costume for long. Indeed, what also undermined
Miller's Outpost was the simple fact that Nancy Reagan was adamant
about the president's propriety. What they wore when horseback riding at
their ranch in California was completely different from what they wore at
the White House. All the eager cowboy wannabes who paraded about the
nation's capital affecting the Western look as interpreted by John Travolta
or Larry Hagman—or to ingratiate themselves with Reagan's inner cir-
cle—were not suffered for long. Bill Blass and Mary McFadden were more
at home in the Reagan White House than were Roy Rogers and Dale Evans.

Miller's Outpost's fortunes reversed shortly after their explosion of success. While Miller's Outpost rode the urban cowboy success, the Gap's
quiet strategy to incorporate a more suburban look to its collections paid off
handsomely three years later when the coming-of-age film *Risky Business*
became such a runaway blockbuster; Tom Cruise's dress in that film became the *de rigueur* look for suburban youth. It was stunning to see how the
downfall of Miller's Outpost could be hastened by its blinding success. At
the end of the twentieth century, Miller's Outpost operated 215 stores in
only sixteen states, mostly in the West, Southwest and the Great Lakes.[7]
This was a lesson the Gap would forget when, in 2000, its successful strategy at Banana Republic translated into a catastrophe at the Gap's core business. As we shall see later on, when Gap made the same mistake as had
Miller's Outpost, J. Crew and Abercrombie & Fitch were then able to reach
out to the most desirable demographic segment of American consumers.

But in the eighties, the Gap worked hard to broaden its appeal. Khakis,
shirts and blouses expanded the appeal. Adolescent baby boomers and
Generation X-ers flocked to the Gap for one-stop shopping to meet their
needs for school and casual clothes. As the eighties unfolded the Gap was
able to foster loyalty, if not to Gap as a brand, then certainly to the Gap as a
store that offered value and comfortable clothes.

"The thing about the Gap is that I could always get the Levi's® in the size
I wanted and it was a fun place to shop in for other clothes. Its decor back
then had always been like something out of some television show or some-

thing," said a seasoned middle-aged customer interviewed while shopping at Gap Kids over the Christmas 1999 season in New York, while her three kids were running circles around her. "It was what was so cool back then. And do you know what? This is what my kids want to wear. The Gap's still cool as far as I can tell."

When asked to identify what a Limp Bizkit and a Blink 182 were, however, she was dumbfounded. When she was asked who had starred in *The Matrix*, she didn't know. She knew what MTV was, but not TRL. She could identify ELO but not LFO. When asked to agree or disagree, true or false, with the following statement, "The two hottest Latin artists today are Jennifer Martin and Ricky Lopez," she answered true.

When a suburban middle-aged working mother of two, who shops at the Gap at the turn of the new century, attempts to be hip and finds something cool, don't her kids roll their eyes and look away in, like, total embarrassment? These did. As any teenager anywhere in the world can tell you in no uncertain terms, parents are clueless when it comes to being hip.

"I worry that I am raising a philistine, or, that I myself am a philistine, or, at the very least, a far too indulgent parent," Constance Rosenblum reflects in the *New York Times*, writing about taking her daughter to Paris on vacation in the summer of 2000—and then going to shop at the Gap. "My husband thinks we're insane to spend a single moment of precious vacation time this way. 'You're going to a Gap?' he'll exclaim as we set off. 'You're crazy! You can do that at home!' "[8]

This may not be insane, per se, but it does offer a cautionary tale of how misguided American parents not only nurture philistines, but worse still, render their children unhip, subjecting them to ridicule from their peers. For example, that for Constance Rosenblum's daughter, her mother's exhibitionistic confession of cluelessness in the nation's newspaper of record is, without a doubt, the ultimate public humiliation. "Yet there is something oddly familiar about the sight before my eyes—perfectly folded stacks of stone-washed jeans, endless piles of rainbow-colored T-shirts, crisp arrangements of khaki pants and, most of all, the distinctive, no-frills navy and white logo," Constance Rosenblum delights, contemplating the merchandise she beholds in the Gap store on the Left Bank. Reason, however, makes a momentary appearance in this otherwise tiny tale of terror. "No, dear, no Gap today," she speculates a "proper" mother would say.

The entire tone of the article reminded me of listening to someone who was culturally insensitive speak about what she did while on vacation in Paris. The voice of reason in her private reflections are inexplicably ignored and mother and daughter are off to shop at the Gap. Constance Rosenblum apparently is incapable of telling the difference between the importance of her daughter becoming an accidental tourist in Paris and her daughter becoming accidentally ostracized by her peers back home for going to Paris to shop at the Gap.

2

Falling Into the Gap

In 1974 Gap launched its "Fall into the Gap" advertising campaign. It lasted only through 1979 but even now, more than two decades later, that slogan holds resonance with consumers. It was a stroke of marketing brilliance; when surveyed in 1999, almost as many respondents were able to identify "Fall into the Gap" as "I've Got You, Babe," the signature song of the *Sonny & Cher Show*.[1] This is proof positive of how much the Gap was in tune with the American public's mindset: it entered the realm of pop culture itself and has become a legendary cultural icon of the American experience in the last quarter of the twentieth century. This singular achievement constituted the triumph of "branding," much the same way that Coca-Cola today identifies American culture around the world.

The Gap's success was also a matter of "ambiance," of course, as well as Donald Fisher's courage to take risks, make mistakes, recognize errors early and correct them by trying something new in short order. The Gap had taken the rebellion against the formality of fashion and pioneered an antifashion look eagerly embraced by the tail end of the baby boomers. It had taken the idea of basic clothes and offered newly professional working women a solution to creating and maintaining casual wardrobes.

The simplicity of the campaign, particularly when it was "back to school" time and families were stocking up on clothes for school, proved electrifying; entire families shopped for most of their school clothes the moment they happened to fall into the Gap. The Gap, by the mid-seventies, had taken pop culture and made it an integral part of the contemporary shopping experience. These continuous processes of trial and error were instrumental in helping the Gap, during the first decade of its existence, successfully find its groove in the American psyche.

Throughout the first half of the seventies, the Gap expanded at an unprecedented clip. Since Donald Fisher did not have any formal training in merchandising, the rag trade or retail marketing he had to learn and innovate as he went along. Herein lies the secrets to the Gap's success: Donald Fisher revolutionized retailing in America by learning from his mistakes, improvising as necessity dictated and inventing a winning formula. The popularity of Levi's®, of course, was an immediate draw wherever the Gap opened a new store. But there was the irresistible appeal of the retail shopping experience that kept the kids—and their parents—coming back over and over again.

The Gap's "secret formula" evolved into a way of doing business that accelerated its own momentum. If, as Diana Vreeland pronounced, "the seventies were boring" compared to the sixties, the one experience that provided the exception to the rule was the Gap. In fact, the five-part approach to retailing developed by Donald Fisher proved to be an antidote to the boredom of that decade.

The Gap's success in the seventies can be broken down as follows:

RETAILING AS ENTERTAINMENT

The legacy of the sixties was one in which the consumer had more choices—and a shortened attention span. This acceleration of life has not gone unnoticed. Writing in *Faster*, James Gleick reports that "[s]ociologists in several countries have found that increasing wealth and increasing education bring a sense of tension about time. We believe that we possess too little of it: that is a myth we now live by."[2] Donald Fisher observed this phenomenon as well.

"These kids are so impatient," he said back in 1974. "If they don't find what they're looking for in less than a minute, they just walk away and leave."

It was no longer enough to have hip merchandise. A store needed to have all sizes in stock—these consumers were not about to come back for anything if it had to be special ordered—and it needed to entertain the impatient. For the Gap, which had soon discarded attempts to sell records alongside its clothes, that music played in the stores remained a part of the ambiance and was a strong selling point. A customer who, not immediately finding what she wanted, might impatiently walk out of store, but she might, on the other hand, slow down if a favorite song was playing, if for no other reason than to listen to the entire song. An average pop song is just under three minutes and that is the window of opportunity to entertain a shopper who scans a store quickly and looks away with indifference.

"Coming to the Gap can't be a *chore*, it has to be a *fun* thing that people look forward to," Donald Fisher explained to the employees of a new store in 1977 before it opened for the first time. "Coming here should be a bright spot in their day. It should be a place where shoppers can relax, find what they are looking to buy, and enjoy the entire process. We have to be courteous, helpful. We have to be pleasant with each other and project that."

The Gap also had to play music, innovate and pioneer the idea of shopping as entertainment. The Gap had to incorporate the anti-establishment attitudes of the sixties as its own in order to make its philosophy of casual clothes that defied traditional notions of fashion resonate with consumers. That Levi's® jeans had transcended the whims of fashion for a century offered credibility to Donald Fisher's position that a wardrobe of laid-back clothing offered the idea of *permanence* that transcended the whims of fashion.

YOUTH CULTURE

Entertainment is closely linked with pop culture. And pop culture is about youth for the simple reason that it is the current generation of humanity that is discovering itself, the world and their place in it. They are finding out that they can help shape what is happening. Being young at heart is an admirable and sweet sentiment, but it borders on the delusional, and it certainly is not happening. Being young at heart is an older person's attempt to embrace the vitality of youth when one's youth is relegated to memory. For Donald Fisher, the Gap's happy association with the sixties and San Francisco made these truths very clear. The Gap had to reflect, if not nurture, Youth Culture.

"From the streets and into the stores" is how one Gap executive reflected the attitude throughout the seventies. "This is one reason Don launched the private labels. He felt that Levi's wasn't reflecting popular culture as aggressively as they should. If Levi's was going to be caught playing catch-up on bell-bottoms and Western vests, there was no reason the Gap had to suffer for it."

Donald Fisher believed that Youth Culture, as idealized in fashion magazines and worn by celebrities, was the one way to remain on the cutting edge. Unlike other clothing retailers who could maximize on the current fashion sensation, the Gap, by offering everyday clothing, was unable to compete with either fads or fashion, and as such it had to reflect the thinking of young people. In the seventies the Gap attempted to reflect Youth Culture through private-label collections with such names as Foxtails and Fashion Pioneers. If Levi's was slow to introduce bell-bottom jeans, then the Gap's private labels would do so.

"Youth Culture," Donald Fisher said in 1980, "has always been the Gap's focus. It's what we want to reflect in our stores and our clothing. We have to be cool with the kids."

One could be cool without being a slave to fashion; the Brady Bunch look was hip on television perhaps, but it wasn't the kind of casual classics life in the real world demanded. Family economics encouraged a greater acceptance of the Gap's emerging antifashion philosophy: well-constructed, durable, comfortable clothes that defied fashion. The proliferation and the standardization of casual attire throughout American society accelerated this acceptance of the Gap's antifashion vision. The rising standards of living that transformed attitudes of American consumers gave a tremendous boost to the Gap. American families were delighted by the hassle-free classic basics the Gap offered. Well-made clothing that required little fussing was welcome. That the Gap offered a good, solid value was a delightful surprise.

After it went public, Gap was afforded the resources to embark on a national expansion program, one that would take its message of Youth Culture as pop culture to the four corners of the United States. Other retailers, however, were also cognizant of the rising power of Youth Culture. Whereas the Gap could outfit America for their school clothes, it was unable to translate its appeal into a broader market; fashion retailers were not threatened by Donald Fisher. They did, however, notice the speed with which the Gap's celebratory approach to Youth Culture—music first, then television monitors—altered in fundamental ways the relationship between merchants and young consumers.

RISK TAKING

Had Donald Fisher been formally trained in retailing, it is most probable he would not have been as successful as he has been. Retailing is a difficult industry, one in which there are many risks if for no other reason than the fickle natures of trends and consumers. Anyone who has seen racks and racks of clothes on sale at the end of the current season has an idea of the miscalculations buyers can make. The end-of-season sales, with dramatic discounts, are evidence of errors in judgment or overly ambitious estimates of demand. Veteran retailers understand only too well that what appears to be a hot item when ordered can very well end as the season's disappointment. Clothing retailers are notoriously risk averse, more comfortable following a trend than anticipating one.

Its willingness to take risks has set the Gap apart. To be sure a good many of its ideas have flopped with a thunderous thud, but the ones that succeeded have more than made up for them. It is here, too, where the vital role of advertising and self-promotion has paid off handsomely: by being willing to cut losses quickly, Donald Fisher has been able to relegate the failures to distant memories, long since banished from the collective memories of the consumers' minds.

Think, for a moment, and try to recall if Gap Shoes, Hemisphere, *Trips* or the "My chosen family" campaign bring any association with the Gap.

They don't, do they? That these monumental fiascoes are largely forgotten is testament to Donald Fisher's approach toward risk.

"We have not been afraid to try things," Donald Fisher explained once. "It's what has given us the experience that made our innovations successful. This risk taking and not being afraid to fail is part of our corporate culture."

As the seventies unfolded, then, Donald Fisher's approach to business was to embrace risk. The familiar mantra, *We tried it. It didn't work. What can we learn from this experience?* now expanded to include the following rhetorical corollary: *Let's move on to something else. Let's "reposition."*

Of equal importance, moreover, is the unsentimental manner in which Gap's unsuccessful experiments are ended. If something's not working, good money isn't thrown after bad. Whatever bad memories linger in the minds of consumers are then banished through advertising designed to distract and distance from the failed experiment. Quick, remember Gap Shoes? This deliberate amnesia has worked splendidly; consumers still remember the fiasco that Coca-Cola's "New Coke" turned out to be, for instance. But no one remembers the Gap's embarrassingly failed division, Hemisphere.

The extraordinary risks taken over its history are indeed remarkable in the annals of corporate America. Few other firms have implemented as many "respositionings" at its divisions as has the Gap. Few other executives have managed to survive the relentless pace of risk-and-failure and risk-and-success as has Donald Fisher. The constant re-invention of the Gap into, essentially, the same thing is without precedent in the history of American retailing.

"How many different ways can you offer a customer a glass of tepid water?" one fashion maven said, summing up the Gap's history of repositioning itself as purveyor of the casual clothes of antifashion.

But risk, however, has been an instrument to innovate, to fine-tune and to incorporate the Youth Culture that suffuses its merchandising of unexceptional clothes. It is precisely because it offers the fundamentals of a basic wardrobe that the Gap has to look for ways to make the experience of shopping at the Gap entertaining to consumers, who increasingly suffer from stunted attention spans. Risk, in essence, is what makes it possible to keep merchandising fresh and enticing. The constant need to take risks is the price the Gap has had to pay to compensate for its forfeiting of the currency fashion affords. If the wardrobes are basically the same season after season, then innovations in merchandising have to make up for the lack of innovation in the clothes offered.

REWARD TALENT

As Gap embarked on a nationwide expansion program after it went public, it was clear to Donald Fisher that to sustain the firm's growth and secure its presence as a force in retailing, it would need to attract outside talent. Indeed, if Gap was to identify talent, court talent and hire talent, it would have to offer enticing opportunities and compensation.

Whether it is enticing a senior executive from Ralph Lauren or Calvin Klein, Donald Fisher through the eighties recruited executives from his rivals—and in the process he acquired a reputation for the shameless raiding of competitors' management teams. Whether this characterization is fair or not, what is true, however, is that all the executives who joined Gap did so of their own choice.

Corporate America at the end of the twentieth century—as it now is at the beginning of the twenty-first century—was a far different place than it had once been. The days when, for instance, Barney Pressman of Barneys out of respect and ethical consideration would not even dream of making an offer that was not becoming of a gentleman are gone and such quaint notions of propriety no longer apply.

"In today's world," Diana Vreeland said, "a man will have an affair with his friend's wife and then defend himself by saying, 'Well, I didn't force her to have sex with me; she wanted to do it.' It isn't about any of that, is it?"

To someone of Mrs. Vreeland's generation, the points were first that a gentleman would never even contemplate doing such a thing to a friend, and second, even if a woman were to throw herself at his feet, by virtue of her being married, he would have to fend off her advances.

Whatever relevance that might have had once, it no longer applied to American business. Donald Fisher, with no apologies, identified talent, wherever it might be found, and then made offers that were too good to pass up. If the Gap needed these individuals to grow and prosper and reward shareholders, then so be it. In his defense, Donald Fisher has maintained that it wasn't so much that he was "stealing" talent from other companies, but that other companies were failing to keep their very talented.

"If they accepted an offer from the Gap, then they did so because they saw a better opportunity," Donald Fisher said, explaining his position on the matter.

To his credit—and to Gap's good fortunes—Donald Fisher was able to recruit executives with strong backgrounds who strengthened the executive teams at the various divisions. This was crucial because as the eighties unfolded the Gap was expanding as it never had before. Its success would depend on the skills, determination and hard work of its managers. As industry observers watched in breathless awe, a complaint spoken in whispers was that Donald Fisher, by offering such enticing compensation packages, was upsetting the industry. It was a complaint people in publishing voiced about Tina Brown, who, after taking over at *Vanity Fair*, began to pay writers princely sums that few other magazines could match. Gap, in turn, was accused of making it impossible for rivals to attract—or keep—talent unless they took out their checkbooks.

VALUE PEOPLE

Attracting talented people is only part of the challenge. Of equal importance is keeping them, and to do that money only goes so far. New recruits
become long-term employees if they are treated fairly and with respect.
Consider that accusations about how Gap's contractors overseas treat their
employees, made at the end of the nineties, were all the more devastating
because of the fine reputation Gap has regarding how it treats women, gays
and minorities. The reason Gap has been so sensitive and fair on a corporate level, without a doubt, stems from the experiences Donald Fisher has
lived through in his own lifetime.

For all its pretensions to sophistication, in its most fundamental ways
San Francisco remains a provincial city. The men who first thrived here
were men of action, men whose values and perceptions still reverberate
throughout San Francisco society. It makes no difference that Donald
Fisher's family has been in this city for over a century, or that he and his
wife are worth more than $7 billion, or that Gap, Inc. is the city's largest pri-
vate employer. None of that matters, other than the fact that the Fishers are
Jewish. They are thus excluded from the Protestant establishment that rules
over the clubs, society and events that punctuate the social life in the city.
This has been the way of American life throughout the twentieth century.

Consider similar realities across the country in south Florida. Writing in
Miami, Joan Didion states, "There were Cubans in the board rooms of the
major banks, Cubans in the clubs that did not admit Jews or blacks . . . the
entire tone of the city, the way people looked and talked and met one another, was Cuban."[3] In the adjacent suburban city of Coral Gables, the "blue
laws" that controlled, among other things, that properties could not be sold
to blacks or Jews were on the books through the sixties.[4] While neither
south Florida nor northern California is as famously anti-Semitic as is the
community of Palm Beach, the unspoken rules, however more subtly they
may be manifested, still prevail throughout the whole of the United States,
from East Coast to West coast, from southern cities to northern California
progressive enclaves.

These social attitudes and cultural practices, which were the norm
throughout American society, were revealed in Hollywood's *Gentlemen's
Agreement*. In that film Gregory Peck portrays an investigative reporter
who masquerades as a Jew in order to expose the virulent anti-Semitism in
the high society of the forties. This is the world in which Donald Fisher
lived in San Francisco, where exclusive clubs, such as the Pacific Union and
Bohemia, once banned members of certain faiths. Indeed, even when an individual of exceptional accomplishment, such as Henry Kissinger, is admitted to the Bohemia Club, there are rumblings among other members
about a "loss of traditions," and fear for decorum. This anti-Semitism is a
subtle thing, of course, but its sting is still felt deeply.

"This isn't something that's talked about openly, of course," Paul Rampell, an attorney in Palm Beach said, "but traditionally Jews have been forced to establish their own clubs and society events."

In Palm Beach, when the Bath & Tennis and the Everglades clubs uniformly excluded Jews, the Palm Beach Country Club was founded by wealthy Jewish businessmen for their own social events.[5] In San Francisco, a similar, parallel social structure had long been established from the time of the Gold Rush days. The proud men who, as stalwarts of the Protestant work ethic, created vast fortunes building the railroads, clearing the timber, extracting the gold and establishing commercial ports that reached the corners of the world were not about to let successful San Francisco Jews, such as Levi Strauss, into their private social clubs on equal footing. "Separate but equal," in fact, applies to more than segregation between blacks and whites in the Jim Crow South or the parallel lives between the 45 million Hispanics (Spanish speakers) and the Anglo-Americans (English speakers).[6] Donald Fisher was subjected to the segregation, enforced with equal rigor, that characterized the lives of, and suffused the relations between Jews and Christians in American society of the forties and fifties.[7]

If the Fishers suffered by being shunned, the net effect of this social exclusion and discrimination has been a commendable one: it has made Don Fisher, a self-described moderate Republican, head of one of the most progressive, inclusive and nonjudgmental companies in corporate America today. Gap, Inc. is heralded as conducting itself, as far as its treatment of corporate staff and employees throughout the United States, as a model company. As we shall see in chapter 7, the evolution of Gap Warehouse into Old Navy brought praise from advocates of diversity in the workplace. Donald Fisher lived through a seismic shift in power elites of American society. The White Anglo-Saxon Protestant ethic—and restrictiveness—crumbled as America became more diverse. Brains won out over bloodlines, and Gap, among corporate America, stood out as a firm that pioneered diversity in the workplace.

These, then, are the five principles that coalesced into a fluid process that became the pattern woven into the fabric of Gap's corporate culture. Throughout the seventies Gap's growth was shaped by the evolutionary processes that Donald Fisher did not consciously recognize at the time that are clearly discernible from the perspective of hindsight. Throughout the seventies, however, Gap's formula for success was one reminiscent of Hegel's dialectic, each successive business experience affected the model—and it thus became more and more refined.

When Gap went public in 1976, its corporate culture was afforded the opportunity to be tested on a grander scale, simply because it took on a more deliberate, if not more bureaucratic, character. Gap itself took off—expanding across the nation's landscape. The rapid expansion at the end of the seventies and the beginning of the eighties was an overwhelming development. Gap's antifashion stance was cheered on by consumers who delighted in the solid American values to be found at the Gap stores. A fabled store, which had been relegated to California, began to appear in shopping malls in Middle America. The clever use of Youth Culture as an integral part of the shopping experience was welcomed by the last members of the baby boomers and the emerging Generation X-ers.

The advertisements imploring Americans to "Fall into the Gap" had the same effect that Barney Pressman's "Calling all men" had had a generation before. Recall for a moment the America portrayed in *The Brady Bunch* television show; that is what the Gap was in the seventies. It was a hip place for the Gregs and Marcias to go to, hang out, meet up with friends, try on clothes and shop. While teenagers no longer pointed Donald Fisher out, praising him as a "cool cat," they nonetheless were grateful that there was a store that understood them—and one that had all the right clothes at the right prices.

It was, naturally, an easier process to fall into the Gap now that the publicly traded company was mushrooming everywhere. Thus as the eighties arrived, the Gap emerged as a household word. If the County Seat was identified with Wrangler® and Lee® jeans, the Gap was synonymous with Levi's®. This fast association spoke volumes of the symbiotic relationship that had developed between Levi's and the Gap. Donald Fisher came up with the idea of opening his jeans store, after all, because of his frustration in readily finding jeans in his size. It was his idea to stock Levi's® jeans in every waist and length size so that no one would walk out because his measurements weren't in stock.

To do this, of course, meant having more stock on hand than other stores; few retailers, for instance, had jeans in waist sizes 35 or 37 on hand. As the Gap stores grew in number, the amount of Levi's® in stock exploded.

It was Donald Fisher who pioneered the contemporary approach to self-service retailing, where an entire wall was outfitted with shelves, jeans stacked neatly by size, and customers could walk up, find their size, and proceed to the dressing rooms. The days when salesmen and saleswomen took the customer's measurements and then disappeared in the back to bring out the jeans were long gone.

It was faster to find the items one wanted, even if it meant that clerks were reduced to folding and re-shelving jeans by the dozens. What mattered to the Gap was that customers could find what they wanted. There was also a certain anonymity to the process. This was important to female customers who were insecure about their self-image and were loathe to disclose their waist size to clerks.

The Gap's self-service approach to merchandising made it possible for a young woman, who thought (or would have liked) her waist was 28, but was in fact 31, to be spared the embarrassment of having a tape measurer reveal the unflattering truth to the entire store. It was in the seventies that

American women began to acquire eating disorders with greater frequency. As much a result of the more sedentary lifestyles of suburban America and the proliferation of fast foods, as the images glamorizing the ideal female bodies dreamt up by Madison Avenue, the obsession with self-image of young women found a discreet accomplice in the Gap. For every self-confident Marcia Brady who would have several saleswomen bring her outfits to try out, there were four or five Jan Bradys.

Levi Strauss & Co. was only too happy to work closely with the Gap; the merchandising strategy of having all sizes available all the time had catapulted the Gap in a few short years to the remarkable position of being the world's leading retailer of Levi's® jeans in the world. The Gap sold more Levi's®, and in more styles and sizes, than did any other chain store. The entire Brady Bunch could show up with all their friends and everyone would find jeans in his or her size, as well as entire wardrobes for everyone. This made the Gap a shopping destination for teenagers, who were pulled into the lively stores by the droves.

And their parents didn't mind at all. For adults, in fact, a more compelling reason for their gratitude was that the Gap was a one-stop shopping destination for outfitting the entire family. As the summer ended, entire families were a common sight, shopping for their back-to-school staples. The Gap's antifashion stance—school wardrobes that would last for the entire school year—made parents loyal to the Gap. Three or four pair of jeans, six or seven shirts or tops, a couple of belts and that was it. Levi's® held more cachet than did Wranglers®, and the Gap was a more pleasant store in which to shop than either County Seat or Sears. Early into the eighties, the Gap had emerged as a welcome fixture in shopping malls throughout the United States.

"The stores have to be clean and attractive," Donald Fisher explained in 1981. "The clothes sell themselves because people want casual, comfortable clothes."

It was also Donald Fisher's penchant for analyzing the numbers that helped him identify what was working, what was not and how to go about making changes. The sales figures were examined over and over, as if some Delphic message would emerge from the numbers on a page. The Gap's explosive growth as the seventies ended coincided with Donald Fisher's growing obsession with making things work perfectly. The Hegelian evolution of Gap's corporate culture accelerated after Gap went public.

"We have to get things right," Donald Fisher told Gap managers in 1979. "We have to be willing to take risks. But we also have to be humble enough to recognize when something's not working out the way we had hoped."

What made Gap able to expand nationwide was the timing of its initial public offering (I.P.O.). Armed with sufficient market capitalization, Gap combined a winning retailing formula with Donald Fisher's knack for identifying great retail locations. Blessed with an astonishing gift for zeroing in on the location that proved to be a winner, Gap expanded with daunting speed. And everywhere the Gap opened its doors, it learned more about the American consumer.

What makes Americans American, Gap soon learned, was the confidence in their own skins. If Americans were seen as insecure adolescents when abroad, at home they exuded an unshakable confidence that what was American was best. That the Gap stores reflected the colors, feel and sounds of pop culture was a bold affirmation of national identity. The Gap was the right store in the right place at the right time. It would not be until decades later, when both Ralph Lauren and Tommy Hilfiger appropriated the American flag in their advertising and clothing, that a more quintessentially American image would be projected. The use of more patriotic hues in the seventies, however, would have been ill advised for the Gap because of the conflicts and dissensions both the Vietnam War and Watergate had inflicted upon the nation.

None of this mattered, however, for the Gap was performing splendidly as it was. That the Gap's leading competitor, Miller's Outpost, was in a period of retrenchment fueled the Gap's growth. If *Urban Cowboy* had proved to be a fad that did Miller's Outpost in, then *Risky Business* was proving to have the staying power of a film that resonates with mainstream culture. With each new Gap store that opened up somewhere, anywhere, everywhere in America, information flowed in that was analyzed and incorporated into the emerging fine art of merchandising Donald Fisher was masterminding. Its distribution system became fine-tuned. Its inventory control was better refined. Its antifashion philosophy could be summed up in three words: classic, comfort, casual. With the system and the people to support its growth, the Gap pressed forward through the seventies using Donald Fisher's strategic vision: *Take a risk. Analyze results. Reposition. Repeat as necessary.*

The result of this strategy proved to be a singular sensation. Retail anthropologist Paco Underhill describes how the Gap's pioneering approach of marrying retailing and entertainment revolutionized merchandising:

The trademark of the Gap . . . is that you can easily touch, stroke, fold and otherwise examine at close range everything on the selling floor. A lot of sweaters and shirts are sold thanks to the decision to foster intimate contact between shopper and goods. That merchandising policy dictates the display scheme (wide, flat tabletops, which are easier to shop than racks or shelves). It also determines how and where employees will spend their time; all that touching means that sweaters and shirts constantly need to be refolded and straightened and neatened. That translates into the need for lots of clerks roaming the floor rather than standing behind the counter ringing up sales. Which is a big expense, but for the Gap and others, it's a sound investment—the cost of doing business. The main thing here is that it was a conscious decision.[8]

The Gap established itself as a presence on the American landscape and in the lives of Americans. The congruence of the following three trends allowed Donald Fisher and Mickey Drexler to develop a strategy that revolutionized merchandising in America.

THE ADVENT OF ANTIFASHION

In the nineties fashion, as it had been understood since the conclusion of World War II, came to an abrupt halt. The doctrine of "real clothes" and "dress-down" was now a crucible in the balance of modernity of American life. The Gap was at the right place (everywhere) at the right time (when "casual Friday" is every day of the week) to position its unpretentious, casual clothes as the harbinger of antifashion philosophy. It was the preppie handbook of the eighties meets the boys' high school locker room, where everyone felt comfortable walking around in tube socks and over-sized pastel polo shirts.

Consumer attitudes had changed; that American youth embraced the laid-back dress and mannerisms of urban street culture in its music accelerated the trend. The Gap simply had to freshen the colors and patterns of its cookie-cutter basic designs to create multiple wardrobes based on the staples of blue jeans and beige khakis, with matching tops and socks. That the Gap only carried clothes designed in-house transformed it into an arbiter of taste for America's youth.

The Gap was a "rebel without a pause": undermining the traditional concept of fashion altogether, relentlessly offering nondescript everyday clothes as chic. The fashion of antifashion itself was as diabolical as it was disingenuous; it allowed the Gap's philosophy of subterfuge to emerge as the most authoritative voice in American fashion by the end of the nineties.

THE USE OF POPULAR CULTURE IN RETAILING

Gap refined the strategy of marrying popular culture as part of the shopping experience.[9] The combination of pop culture appealed to consumers from the entire spectrum of American life; whether they were urban kids or affluent middle-class women from the suburbs, proud to boast about the bargain they found at the Gap, it was chic to wear Gap clothes because it was so closely associated with the "hipness" and vitality of Youth Culture. As the eighties gave way to the nineties and MTV secured its hold on the medium around which youth culture orbited, the Gap was there, not only feeling the pulse of America's Youth Culture, but fanning a frenzy through its seductive advertising.

By the 1990s the Gap had in fact become so synonymous with youth culture that the classic pocket T-shirts were known as "X" shirts at some after-hours dance clubs, including The End Up in San Francisco, The Mix in Miami Beach and Splash in New York. That's "X" as in Ecstasy.[10] The youthful indiscretion of these teenage rave enthusiasts was to be expected, of course.[11] But in the antifashion craze, middle-aged indiscretions made front-page news as well.[12] In America, if everyone wore Gap, then the Gap would be associated with everyone, right?

In this manner, the Gap began to usurp the traditional role of department stores, appealing to youngsters as well as more sophisticated consumers. Its fast association with Youth Culture and MTV cemented the success the Gap had found by designing in-house its collection of jeans, sweaters and T-shirts as its antifashion statements. Teri Agins, the senior special writer at the *Wall Street Journal*, who has covered fashion for ten years, explains it this way:

As more women shopped for clothes that were affordable, comfortable, and casual, the retailer they now turned to was the Gap. With its combination of well-made classic clothes, the right price, and a hip, modern image, Gap had become the new fashion destination for millions of women and men.[13]

The emergence of the Gap as a "fashion destination" among the average consumer and the *cognoscenti* alike was not only ironic, but also nothing less than the recognition that it had succeeded in combining merchandising and entertainment like no other merchant had before.

THE REVOLUTION IN MERCHANDISING

To walk into a store and encounter television monitors playing music videos represented a gradual evolution of the seventies Sonny & Cher–inspired Gap stores into the mock MTV sound stages of today. It has broken down the elitist nature of what once was fashion. The Gap stores, sprawling luxuriously throughout the land, are as much mischievous takes on what once was fashion, as they are the buoyancy that keeps the antifashion philosophy alive.

It is not an overstatement to say that Donald Fisher's ubiquitous presence in American retailing for the past three decades has been revolutionary. While critics point to the Gap brand as testament to the dysfunctional domesticity of American life at the end of the twentieth century, it is wrong to remain fixated on mass consumerism. The savviest of shoppers watch the videos playing in the stores. They are not gimmicks, but rather, they have become an integral part of the shopping experience—a shopping experience the Gap has to work relentlessly to keep fresh.

There was an unmistakable sense of urgency to this mad desire to be on the cutting edge for one simple reason: other retail chains were copying the Gap's look and merchandising practices. This created a greater sense of urgency at the Gap to stay one step ahead. It was not uncommon, for instance, for Gap to send assistant managers to compare prices in rival stores in shopping malls around the country. All this information was pored over

over and over again, trying to spot trends and patterns reflected in the price figures. It wasn't that the Gap would match prices (though it sometimes did), but it wanted to see what the competition was doing, and how price differentials affected sales.

If an anchor store at the other end of the mall had a sale, how off were the Gap's sales for the duration of the sale? The inquiring mind of Donald Fisher most surely wanted to know. Who was selling what and at what price in every market across America? Where were the kids and their parents window shopping? What stores actually made the sales? Which radio station played the Top Forty in every major American city? Were those stations being played in the Gap stores? What could be done to keep customers entertained—and in the stores—for longer periods of time? What could the Gap do to *seduce* the American consumer?

Donald Fisher needed to know all of this and so much more if he was to compete effectively in the highly charged retailing environment that emerged after the Federal Trade Commission changed the rules of the game in 1978. But what is remarkable is that, for the phenomenal growth it experienced throughout the seventies, there were, from a management point of view, rather few problems associated with growing pains. The Gap was a solid operation and Donald Fisher was anything but naïve. In the early eighties, when Gap encountered its first reversal of fortune, it was more a matter of the accumulated impact of years of Levi's® being discounted by competitors than a question of the internal management structure put in place by Donald Fisher. Since 1978 the Gap had been forced to compete ever more aggressively; problems with stagnant same-store sales could be overlooked by the breakneck pace of new stores opening, but there had to be a limit to this strategy.

If the Gap was to succeed and thrive in the eighties, it had to compete. If it was to compete effectively, it needed information and the wherewithal to make rational business decisions. This, Donald Fisher knew instinctively, was the way of the world. This unpleasant reality had set the Gap on a collision course with Levi Strauss & Co., a collision course that would pit two San Francisco–based firms on a confrontation of seismic proportions.

3

THE RIFT WITH
LEVI STRAUSS & CO.

Donald Fisher needed to know the answer to all these questions and many more.

"After the FTC [Consent Order] came down," Donald Fisher said, "it was a whole new ball game. It changed the face of competition for us and for everyone else."

The Federal Trade Commission's 1978 Consent Order that Levi Strauss & Co. could not establish the retail price for its jeans sent shockwaves through the retailing business.[1] The government wanted to inject more rigorous competition into the economy in the hope that consumers would benefit from greater choices and lower prices. If manufacturers were prohibited from setting retail prices, the thinking among economists and policy makers went, then the American economy would be invigorated by healthy competition that would make the United States more competitive in the global economy. There were other structural changes unfolding in the nation's economic life during the seventies. The United States had abandoned the gold standard, freeing the exchange rate to the forces of supply and demand. The Arab oil embargo had unsettled the price of the one raw material upon which the industrial world depended.

Economic liberalization gave an impetus to policy makers advocating deregulation in many areas of the nation's economy, such as the airline industry. Before airline deregulation, for instance, the government—and not the marketplace—approved routes and fares. This mentality affected many other areas of economic life. The FTC's efforts, as well as those of other agencies and commissions, were intended to benefit American consumers while preparing corporate America for the challenges of the global economy. For businesses involved in retailing this meant, among other things, that products would have a "suggested retail price"—but not a *mandatory* price. Whereas competition had previously been confined to nonprice matters, such as the product selection, customer service and convenience of store locations, now the *cost* of the product entered into the equation as never before among the major retailers. The "price wars" common today were unseemly back then. It is difficult for us today to remember that once there was a time when, for instance, a pair of Levi's® 501™ jeans cost the same just about everywhere—simply because Levi Strauss & Co. established the strongly suggested retail price that was almost universally accepted by retailers. While in practice stores were free to discount, few chose to do so; discounting was in fact a rare occurrence.

Allegations were made that Levi Strauss & Co. was engaged in behavior that undermined competition. "It is important to remember that the specific allegations against our company were not proven," Albert Moreno, senior vice president and general counsel for Levi Strauss & Co., said. "The Consent Decree was the product of a settlement. It is wholly inaccurate to suggest that the FTC turned a faucet that unleashed price competition for the first time when it reached agreement with Levi Strauss & Co. in 1978."[2]

If few retailers had discounted before, after the FTC issued the Consent Order, the world of retailing began to change. Retailers were now in a position where they competed more vigorously by exercising their right to discount all kinds of consumer products, including, for instance, Levi's® jeans. For of most the first decade of its existence the Gap had only competed by differentiating itself from other stores by embracing Youth Culture, now the arena of vigorous competition shifted suddenly to price. What had previously been a contest in *merchandising* now became a contest on *prices*. This raised the following question: If the same pair of Levi's® jeans were sold at a lower price by another store, would customers still shop at the Gap—or at any other retailer that refused to match price cuts?

No one knew in 1978. What was known, however, was that Levi Strauss & Co. had been a steadfast partner in the Gap's success throughout the seventies. The Gap profited handsomely from the army of baby boomer women who had joined the workforce and teenagers who shopped where their mothers told them to shop. American families had many demands on their time and they welcomed the Gap's antifashion approach—that is to say, clothes that did not go out of fashion after one season, because Gap clothes were not *about* fashion. The Gap also offered value in the sense that it purveyed quality clothes at fair prices—and had the best selection of Levi's® clothing of any retailer. While working mothers picked their dress-for-success ensembles at the Limited or Jones New York or J.H. Collectibles, their children selected clothes for school and to hang out with their friends at the Gap.

It was a familiar pattern at the Gap during the late seventies: the Marcias and Jans picking out wardrobes for each other while the Gregs and Peters disagreed over certain looks or whatever. The Gap was thus reduced to an extension of the Brady Bunch, one in which the insecurities and aspirations of teenagers and young adults were allayed with a mix-and-match approach to clothes. It was all very convenient, very modern and very successful.

The FTC's Consent Order changed all that. In short order, mothers rushing off to shop for their own working clothes passed stores that were selling Levi's® products at a better price than the Gap. And when they returned to pick up their kids, they would put back the Levi's® products, telling their children they could get exactly the same pair of Levi's® jeans at a discount store on the way home.

The Gap's explosive growth had transformed it into the largest retailer of Levi's® jeans in the world. In the two years following its I.P.O., Gap had launched an ambitious program, buying chains of troubled retailers and opening stores far beyond California. That it was able to charge full price for Levi's® products made for a very healthy cash flow, fueling further growth. After 1978, however, the Gap saw its margins on jeans begin to fall. Its profits from selling Levi's® products plunged as the Gap was forced to match price cuts and discount the quintessential American jeans.

"At least once a week we walked throughout the mall checking out the prices on Levi's® at every store that sold Levi's®," someone who managed a Gap store in New York at the end of the seventies explained. "Then we'd report back to the district manager all the prices. We didn't always match prices, but it helped corporate offices assess how price differences affected the store's sales."

It was not without irony that within two years of having gone public with tremendous investor enthusiasm, Gap confronted its first major crisis in its existence. To outsiders, this was not obvious. If Donald Fisher was worried about the fact that discounts would now be a fact of business life, he hid it well. Whatever concerns the highly competitive market may have produced were masterfully eclipsed by an ambitious expansion program. In a bold marketing campaign that accelerated linking pop culture with retail merchandising the Gap sought to embrace the cult of celebrity among the young. The marriage of music and retailing across the United States had enabled Donald Fisher to build a vibrant franchise. If the Gap was to remain a fun place to shop, one that validated Youth Culture, the thinking went, then the kids would hit their old man up for an extra couple of bucks to buy a pair of Levi's® jeans at the Gap.

The Gap–Levi Strauss & Co. relationship benefited both companies, to be sure. Despite eroding margins and the Gap's introducing more private-label clothing, both companies complemented each other. The Gap diversified its selection by introducing tops; Levi Strauss & Co. had never been very successful at designing and manufacturing shirts. Through diversification the Gap was fast becoming the youth-oriented destination for young people everywhere in the United States. Wrangler® and Lee® jeans were not as cool as Levi's® jeans. County Seat was not a hip store. As the Gap expanded across the United States, it relegated its competitors to forgotten or regional chain stores.

For Levi Strauss & Co. the relationship was splendid: the Gap was a single account that was building a larger and larger network of retail outlets. For Donald Fisher, on the other hand, there was a dilemma. Whenever the Gap opened a new store, competitors would cut the price on Levi's® jeans. If every other store was prepared to discount Levi's® jeans, the Gap would not be able to make enough money on Levi's® jeans to be as profitable as he wanted the Gap to be.

As far as Levi Strauss & Co. was concerned, it was selling more jeans than ever before. Competition had resulted in steady growth rates. For the Gap the FTC Consent Order meant thinner profit margins on the sale of Levi's® jeans. It also made Donald Fisher realize that the only way his business could grow was to manufacture his own jeans. The Gap had proven that it could have private label shirts and tops manufactured for its stores. Why couldn't it do the same with jeans?

Then came the rift. "Betrayal" has been used to characterize this rift. It is perhaps too harsh a word to describe what Gap did to Levi Strauss & Co. "Rift" or "calculated callousness" are more precise characterizations of what happened. The problem is that, even twenty-five years later, there is no agreement or consensus on who did what to whom. Many at Levi Strauss & Co. felt betrayed. Gap maintains it was the harsh realities of a fierce marketplace that forced changes in their working relationship. What is clear is that Levi Strauss & Co. found itself in a more highly competitive environment, one that would culminate in the mid-nineties when it faced an unprecedented crisis.

In interviews with executives and former employees of both firms, there is a serious discrepancy in their versions of what went wrong. Basic facts, however, are not disputed. The Gap introduced its own less expensive lines of jeans and casual shirts. Sales of Gap-brand jeans cannibalized the more expensive Levi's® jeans. Donald Fisher pushed for lower production costs by shifting manufacturing to developing countries with lower labor costs. It was not until Donald Fisher hired Mickey Drexler that the Gap was able to commence integrating its operations vertically. Levi Strauss & Co., because it manufactured almost exclusively within the United States, was at a further disadvantage as its sales to the Gap chain deteriorated.

"We had to do what was best for the Gap," Donald Fisher explained. "We had an obligation to our shareholders."

Donald Fisher was making shareholders happy without a doubt. With his extensive background in real estate development, Donald Fisher had a gift for scooping up prime real estate locations for stores that subsequently

enjoyed tremendous pedestrian traffic. The Gap stores were located in excellent spaces, where shoppers "discovered" the store, or where seasoned
veterans found them convenient to their daily lives. The Gap was not simply growing: it was *flourishing*. Donald Fisher's vision found resonance
with the American consumer, resonance made manifest at the cash register. Success instilled confidence and confidence nurtured ambition. *Take a
risk. Analyze results. Reposition. Repeat as necessary.*

"We *had* to compete," Donald Fisher recalled, with no apologies to offer.
"The margins on selling Levi's weren't there. If it hadn't been for our private labels, I don't know what we would have done."

Levi Strauss & Co. executives were surprised as they watched the Gap
order fewer and fewer jeans on a per-store basis. The impact of economic
liberalization was being seen as the effects of competition reverberated
throughout the U.S. economy. One unexpected effect was the way in which
competition affected both personal friendships and business relationships.
Competition, in essence, disrupted familiar ways of doing business. For the
Gap, there were new entrants, both in terms of manufacturers and retailers.

The very idea of "denim" changed through seductive advertising that
made blue jeans sexy. Where once kids wore "dungarees" while growing
up and men wore them while working on the farms, suddenly they were
presented to consumers as *fashion*. Exciting, suggestive and aggressive
marketing campaigns by companies like Sergio Valente and Jordache
turned the image of denim inside down. When Calvin Klein pushed the envelope by presenting Brooke Shields in the photo spreads that scandalized
the public, jeans became hotter still.[3] Suddenly, denim jeans were hot—and
Americans began to wear them to social functions. The sight of young men
and women wearing starched white shirts and blouses, patent leather
shoes and blue jeans to cocktail parties turned heads.

"What happened in the airlines, was happening everywhere," Donald
Fisher reportedly stated in 1982. "Pan Am might have been America's flagship carrier, but [after airline deregulation] it didn't matter. Pan Am had to
compete on price—and so did we."

The lessons of competition sunk in. Competition was foremost about
control. The Gap and Levi Strauss & Co. both realized that, however splendid their business relationship may have been in the past, things were now
different. Robert Haas, the great-great-grandnephew of the Levi Strauss
founder, who ran Levi Strauss & Co., saw his relationship with Donald
Fisher change in disturbing ways. There was a time in American history, after all, when anti-Semitism was rampant and Jewish businessmen had to
support one another if they were to survive. In the clothing business in
New York, Jews depended on a close-knit fraternity that was marked by integrity and loyalty.

California is not New York, however. And the business world of the seventies was not like the twenties and thirties. Those were decades when Jews

confronted fierce discrimination. Consider the story of Barney Pressman, founder of Barneys. When Barneys first opened, the retail business was dominated by white Anglo-Saxon Protestants. Many established retailers in New York were enraged that a Jew had the audacity to compete with them. While Jews were common in the *manufacturing* of clothes, they were not in the business of *retailing*. Jews could stitch the garments, in other words, but they couldn't be up front dealing with customers.

In the early years of its existence, in fact, many established stores attempted to ruin Barneys by pressuring manufacturers not to do business with him at all. Barney Pressman evaded being blacklisted by being discreet and circumspect. He pleaded with Jewish manufacturers to make clothes for him. A few consented and the relationships that followed blossomed into strong friendships. When the United States was subsequently engulfed in the Great Depression years later, the strength of Barney Pressman's gratitude became evident. Barneys, for instance, made advance payments to suppliers in dire circumstances just to make sure they could meet their payrolls.

One business associate with whom Barney Pressman did business was William Kessler. Consider this account of the terms under which their business relationship ended:

Over the course of the fifty-odd years the Kesslers and the Pressmans did business together, various discrepancies crept into the books. Kessler always charged for the hangers their suits came on; Barneys made it a practice never to pay for hangers. Barneys would send back a suit because the seam was manufactured improperly, and charge the suit back to Kessler; Kessler wouldn't accept the charge and [would] fix the seam and send it back to Barneys, but Kessler never rebilled the store, so Barneys kept the credit for the suit on its books.

These were just the stray threads from a lifetime of doing business together. When Chester Kessler closed his books for good, he simply wanted to tie them up so this chapter of his life could be finished neatly. He presented Barneys with a bill for close to forty thousand dollars, although, he admitted, he no longer had any idea how to verify each individual transaction, or indeed whether the mistakes were Barneys' or his own. Barneys' accountants spent many months hunting through its records. Almost a year later, Barneys mailed Kessler a check for $26,809.16. "Now that's what I call integrity," says Kessler, shaking his head ruefully.[4]

The sense of morality and personal commitment on a human level, consistent with the values instilled in Jewish religious upbringing, were brushed aside in the decades that followed. That internal cohesion within the Jewish community that characterized a Jew's dealings with suppliers began to waver in future generations. In a newly competitive business world, business was business; Donald Fisher was not about to treat Robert Haas in the manner that the Pressmans conducted themselves with the Kesslers.

What Donald Fisher realized above all was that the Gap and Levi Strauss & Co. were, in a peculiar way, mirror images of each other: The Gap controlled the merchandising of clothes, but not their design or manufacture, and Levi Strauss & Co. controlled their design and manufacture but not their merchandising. Donald Fisher believed that the Gap's future success depended on greater control over both aspects of the clothing business.

The solution would be to accelerate the process of vertical integration, which meant manufacturing and merchandising clothes to consumers. This is how the Gap would enjoy full control. Of course the introduction of private labels had afforded Donald Fisher some experience in dealing with manufacturers and deciding what to order, but it also made him realize his own limitations. Innovating better ways to market Levi's® jeans—the ultimate *brand* name in denim jeans—had been made easier by the decades of marketing that made the buying public very aware of the product. Levi Strauss & Co. had been around for well over a century and its marketing savvy was second to none. The Gap had benefited tremendously from this brand recognition. But Donald Fisher wanted more.

If Gap were to aspire to develop its own brand, it would need phenomenal amounts of money to launch an advertising blitz. After all, despite the monied glamour of her family name, Gloria Vanderbilt needed the backing of wealthy investors before shopping bags filled with her line of jeans moved out the doors of department stores around the country. It would also be a monumental undertaking to compete in the increasingly crowded field of denim jeans when Jordache, Sergio Valente, Calvin Klein and—that new entrant in casual jeans—Ralph Lauren were all jockeying for position. Traditional denim jeans makers, like Wrangler, Lee and Levi Strauss & Co., were facing unprecedented competition, particularly at a time when actual production was shifting to the developing world where labor costs were down.

"In the seventies, Jordache and Gloria Vanderbilt jeans were made in factories in the developing world far from the regulatory eye of the American government," one industry observer in New York explained. "That's when paying workers next to nothing for making a pair of blue jeans became 'the thing to Do!' "

Perhaps, but it was beyond Gap's reach. There was only so much money and Donald Fisher had embarked on an expansion program. First, the Gap would need to secure its network of retail stores by setting up shops everywhere. Then it would hire the management talent that could implement Donald Fisher's vision of vertical integration that would ultimately *replace* Levi Strauss & Co.

"No one in top management saw it coming," a former Levi Strauss & Co. executive explained. "We were arrogant! We never thought the Gap was working to phase us out. We were *Levi's*, after all! We invented *blue jeans!* The Gap would *always* need us!"

If Levi Strauss & Co., when it became apparent that it had been replaced by the Gap, felt betrayed, it was because it had been blinded by its own complacency. The Gap's private labels kept selling more and more and in the mid-seventies Donald Fisher introduced with little fanfare, but prominent store display, something extraordinary: Gap's own line of denim jeans.

Gap wanted to control its future by selling only what it manufactured. Levi Strauss & Co. was undeniably complacent about both its brand and its relationship to the Gap. As the eighties began, however, Gap was looking for someone to carry out Donald Fisher's grand vision. Until he could find the right executives, Donald Fisher concentrated on refining his secret formula for killer merchandising: taking a risk, analyzing the results and changing as required.

The risks that paid off famously were the expansion of the private-label clothes and the introduction of Gap's eponymous jeans. "Gap"-labeled jeans, in fact, began to sell briskly, to the detriment of the Gap's sales of Levi's® jeans. A quick summary of the figures speak for themselves: in 1969 Levi's® jeans accounted for 90 percent of the Gap's sales; by 1984 this had been reduced to 25 percent, and in 1991 the Gap stopped selling Levi's® jeans altogether. It was clear to see what had happened: whereas in 1969 Donald Fisher saw Levi's® jeans as the brand-name product he could sell at full-retail price and delight in the terrific profits, after the FTC Consent Order, Levi Strauss & Co. was solely the middleman making a product the Gap sold. But with Levi's® being discounted by so many retailers, Levi's® jeans fast became a product that offered little profit margin for the Gap.

"It wasn't fun for us either," a former Levi Strauss & Co. executive said.

Before the FTC [Consent Order], we set the price of our blue jeans. Period. After that, we were at the mercy of retailers. A pair of Levi's® was as likely to be sold for suggested retail price at an upscale department store as it was to end up on a discount table. But whatever problems there were, we could have worked them out with Don. He didn't have to turn his back and double-cross us! Our jeans made the Gap successful! No matter what the problems were, we could have worked them out *together*. At Levi's we thought Gap was more than a business relationship. We thought it was a personal friendship as well. We were wrong about knowing who our friends were.

The turmoil wrought on retailers by slashed prices cannot be underestimated. Yet, it was inevitable, given the intellectual thinking of the time. The writings of influential economists in the sixties, such as Alfred Kahn, began to change how government saw its role in the economy.[5] As academics argued that Adam Smith's "invisible hand" could best determine the winners and losers, the idea of deregulation gained currency. The FTC's Consent Order was a vote of confidence for the ability of the marketplace and competition to determine the outcome in economic contests. Consider the situation with booksellers at the end of the nineties. When a store has to compete with Amazon.com and offer a 40 percent discount on the bestsellers, there is no profit in that sale: the bookstore is depending on customers buying *other* books, not just the discounted ones. If the only books sold, how-ever, are the ones priced virtually at cost, it seems hardly worth the effort. The Gap approached this similar business climate without sentimentality.

Business was business, Donald Fisher had a company to run and he made up his mind. Levi Strauss & Co. was a *vendor*, Donald Fisher con-cluded. It was therefore *superfluous* to his vision of the Gap's future as a ver-tically integrated company. He never looked back. A former Gap employee familiar with the growing tensions between Gap and Levi Strauss & Co. de-scribed acrimonious relations between officers from both companies in the early eighties. Phone calls were sent from one firm to the other. Orders were delayed. When Levi Strauss & Co. voiced concern that its products now ac-counted for less than half of the Gap's sales, the response was akin to "Can't they see we've moved *beyond* them?"

This scene would play itself out again at the end of the eighties when Donald Fisher unceremoniously disposed of the founders of Banana Re-public. In his mind, the Gap may have "moved past" Levi Strauss & Co., but however unhealthy a symbiotic relationship they enjoyed, they needed each other. Donald Fisher, after all, still did not have the managerial where-withal to carry out his lofty vision of being a completely vertically inte-grated company. Donald Fisher's frustration, indeed, was a result of his inability to free himself from Levi Strauss & Co. completely. His personal aversion to these kinds of confrontations and shouting matches only con-vinced him that these problems would be eliminated once the middlemen were eliminated. Gap, Inc. had to be in control of its own production. It was that simple. Donald Fisher, then, knew where he wanted to go, but he didn't know how to get there.

When Ann Taylor died, speculation was that her label would close. There are few designers whose labels last beyond their own mortality. Coco Chanel in France and Perry Ellis in the United States are rare exceptions. Halston disappeared altogether, save for licensing agreements for a few accessories and perfumes. It is difficult for another person to step in and carry forward something as personal as a sense of style, a way of looking at fashion, the approach to energy of the moment—and then translate all that into a viable business that is based on changing taste. People will always drink soft drinks and drive cars, which is why Coca-Cola and Ford are companies whose brand-name products enjoy stability, but a pair of jeans is a pair of jeans.

Consumers invest far less capital (financial, status or emotional) in a pair of denim jeans, which is why they are a much less differentiated product. The Jordaches of yesteryear became the Calvins of yesterday, which then became the Tommys and the Abercrombie & Fitches at the end of the nine-ties. It was Mickey Drexler, however, who was able to translate Ann Tay-lor's vision—and business—beyond the founder's death.

The Gap, as the eighties began, was flush with cash. It had grown from one store in 1969 to almost 500 in 1980. This was an opportune moment for

Donald Fisher to step back and implement the future as he envisioned it. What Levi Strauss & Co. executives subsequently called a "stab in the back" was, in essence, Donald Fisher's recognition that the business world was fundamentally altered after the FTC Consent Order. Before the FTC Consent Order, the Gap and Levi Strauss & Co. worked in a complementary fashion, effortlessly transforming the Gap into the world's premier retailer of Levi's® jeans. After the FTC Consent Order only a vertical business model made sense in the long term.

Once any store could undercut the "suggested retail price" set by Levi Strauss & Co., the Gap and Levi Strauss & Co. were no longer a team, but two independent companies. Because the Gap did manufacture its clothes and Levi Strauss & Co. was a manufacturer with only a handful of owned -and-operated retail stores scattered around, they could not "cooperate." That would have amounted to collusion—an illegal business practice.

As the eighties began, Donald Fisher grew anxious. Heightened competition meant stagnant sales and falling profits. Donald Fisher realized he was in over his head. Whatever was required to turn the Gap around, he had to call on outside expertise. There was no question in his mind that it would have to be done by someone else, since this brutal competition was far afield from Donald Fisher's expertise. "For years I was looking for someone to implement vertical integration," Donald Fisher repeated in interviews granted over the years. "I needed to find someone who could carry this out."[6]

To his credit—and the Gap's saving grace—Donald Fisher was possessed with a clear idea of who he was, where his strengths and weaknesses lay, and the wisdom not to let personal pride or arrogance stand in the way of the Gap's success. "Don's a sensible and down-to-earth man," one industry observer said, echoing a sentiment heard often. "Some of the people in this industry have enormous egos. I think that the fact that Don was always an outsider gave him a very clear perspective about the entire thing. When he called on Mickey Drexler, he did it without reservation."[7]

Unlike other designers who mistakenly believe their sense for fashion will translate into business sense—Donna Karan specifically comes to mind, given the very well publicized turmoil at her company—Donald Fisher was a merchandiser advocating an antifashion philosophy. When Mickey Drexler was hired in 1983, there were no "fashion philosophies" to reconcile.

Mickey Drexler was there to solve two specific problems: first, turning the Gap around now that the full impact of deregulation was affecting the bottom line; and second, bringing together a program that would allow the Gap to manufacture everything it sold. "This is the end of the middleman as far as this company is concerned," Donald Fisher said in 1983, shortly after Mickey Drexler came aboard.

The first order of business was to clean up the more than a dozen private labels the Gap was selling. Simplicity was key to helping consumers develop an image of and loyalty to the Gap. "If the store is the Gap, then the exclusive private label will be the Gap," Mickey Drexler concluded. All the other private labels were discontinued. And if the Gap was to compete effectively, it would have to shift production to overseas factories that were churning out the Gloria Vanderbilts and Sergio Valentes and Jordaches that were making their way onto the bodies of the American consumer.

For Mickey Drexler the Gap's reference to the generational "gap" meant working to bring parents and teenagers together into the one store upon which both could agree. "All these kids who want Jordache are a problem for their parents who resist paying $40 for a pair of jeans," Mickey Drexler said in 1984. "We have to make the Gap hip enough for the kids to want our products, and provide the kind of price point parents can live with."

Price point refers to the entire *price range* consumers anticipate paying for a product or service. As we shall see later on, when Gap Warehouse became Old Navy Clothing Co., the Old Navy's brand clothes were approximately 40 percent less than those at the Gap. An outfit that cost $100 at the Gap would set one back only $60 at the discounter Old Navy, a consideration for families with several children.

But before the Gap could apply these lessons in the nineties, when it was building the Old Navy brand, it had to secure its future in the eighties. With Mickey Drexler firmly in charge, the Gap thus embarked on a program to become a differentiated label in the minds of young consumers while not breaking the family budget. The challenge was to bridge the antifashion philosophy across generations—between baby boomers and their Generation X offspring.

It worked. With strong campaigns for school-age youngsters and college students, the Gap was on the threshold of consolidating its hold on youth. It took almost four years before Mickey Drexler secured the Gap's position as America's preeminent retailer. He was rewarded by being named president of Gap, Inc. in 1987, the same year that Levi's® jeans accounted for a mere 10 percent of sales.

Nothing could go wrong because everything was going right. Production continued to shift overseas, Generation X music filled the stores, the price point was just right. Sales of the Gap-brand products fared very well. The sale of Levi's® jeans, the only product sold at the Gap but not manufactured by the Gap, continued to plummet. By 1990, Levi's® jeans accounted for less than 5 percent of the Gap's sales. Donald Fisher and Mickey Drexler faced the question that was now inevitable: should they discontinue selling Levi's® jeans once and for all?

The answer, as the falling sales figures proved, was obvious to everyone. In 1991 the Gap stopped selling Levi's® jeans altogether. The last vendor, or "middleman," was history. Officials at Levi Strauss & Co. were not entirely displeased about this turn of events. They, too, had become frustrated in their dealings with the Gap. From Levi Strauss & Co.'s perspective, the Gap had become a troubling account as the eighties ended. While the Gap was responsible for selling millions of Levi's® jeans, dealing with the Gap had become a headache.

To understand the level of conflict that came between these two San Francisco companies, consider that by the time the Gap stopped carrying Levi's® products altogether each company claimed that it was the one to sever relations with the other. Gap claimed it no longer needed Levi Strauss & Co. at all. Levi Strauss & Co., on the other hand, replied that the Gap was no longer worth servicing as an account. Levi Strauss & Co. points to its sustained growth overall from the mid-eighties through the mid-nineties as evidence that, even as its sales to the Gap were in a free fall, it was enjoying overall growth.[8]

Regardless of who cut whom loose, the end result was the same. The Gap was now the only clothing retailer that had hundreds of stores throughout the nation selling exclusively what it manufactured. Donald Fisher's vision of a completely vertically integrated company was now a reality. That this rift was seen as betrayal by many executives at Levi Strauss & Co. suggests which party was more surprised by this turn of events. With offices a few miles from each other, and as small a city as San Francisco is, executives from both the Gap and Levi Strauss & Co. moved in the same circles, and this resulted in many awkward encounters.

What Gap saw as a business decision, however, was seen by many in the San Francisco business community as a calculated affront masterminded by Donald Fisher himself. "The Gap undermined us," one exasperated Levi Strauss & Co. executive, in a moment of despairing exaggeration, was quoted as saying in 1991. "When he had only half a dozen stores, we helped him stock his shelves. And this is how he repays us."

Stories took on lives of their own. San Francisco businessmen whispered gossipy tales of how the Gap, when it was starting out, would have a new store stocked fully by Levi Strauss & Co. and the Gap would pay as the merchandise sold. This was presented as evidence of the friendship that transcended business between Donald Fisher and Robert Haas. Theirs was the kind of business relationship that was also a personal friendship. "Jews have always looked [out] for each other in this industry," a veteran clothing executive said. "The same way that Barney Pressman worked with Chester Kessler, Donald Fisher and Robert Haas should have looked out for each other."

Neither Donald Fisher nor Mickey Drexler had any apologies for dropping Levi Strauss & Co. The world had, indeed, changed: merchandising in the nineties was as much a business as it was an *art* form. Under Mickey Drexler's brilliant management, the Gap had emerged triumphant, winning over the members of Generation X and positioning the Gap not as a store but as a *brand*.

The successful introduction of Gap Kids in 1986 and Baby Gap shortly thereafter only worked to reinforce further the idea that the Gap was, in fact, a brand. It also bridged the generations of American consumers, seducing them with familiarity and success. What made Mickey Drexler different from Donald Fisher was his willingness to cut losses and move on. While Donald Fisher agonized for almost fifteen years before dumping Levi Strauss & Co., Mickey Drexler was always prepared to cut loose and move on. Within a year of his arriving at Gap, for instance, when Donald Fisher insisted on Gap, Inc. purchasing Pottery Barn, he told him that that was a "distraction"—and therefore a mistake. Within thirty-six months, Gap, Inc. had sold Pottery Barn. This proved instructive, for it indicated that Donald Fisher wanted to have his business grow through diversification. The problem with the purchase of Pottery Barn was that housewares proved to be too different a business from clothing for it to work, particularly given the management resources upon which Gap, Inc. counted.

Donald Fisher was undeniably demanding with himself. Pottery Barn was his call, it had been wrong, and Gap quickly divested. It was clear that going too far afield from clothing was not a natural complement to Gap's expertise. Expansion itself was not abandoned as a growth strategy. Rather, whatever expansion that would take place would center on clothing retailing. This was clear enough when Donald Fisher decided to launch an upscale chain, Hemisphere, in 1987. He waited less than twenty-four months before pulling the plug and bailing out of that misguided foray as well.

Both Fisher and Drexler approved of opening Gap Shoes in 1992, eighteen months later, but if it didn't work out, it didn't last. This was Mickey Drexler's take on Donald Fisher's risk-assess-evaluate-then-reposition approach of their business model. The speed with which it all unfolded was daunting. Consumers were led toward the successes, while Gap, Inc. distanced itself from its mistakes. Few shoppers at the Gap have any idea about the dismal failures. They only remember what has worked. This is brilliant spin control, a control that speaks volumes of Donald Fisher's and Mickey Drexler's ability to push the right button and make everything seem logical, correct and inevitable, even what Gap, Inc. did to Levi Strauss & Co.[9]

By the time Robert Haas recruited Philip Marineau in the summer of 1999 to take the helm of Levi Strauss & Co. later that fall, the firm was in disarray. For Levi Strauss & Co. Gap's dream of vertical integration became its nightmare. When the Gap stopped selling Levi's® jeans, the loss of retail outlets to Levi Strauss & Co. unleashed a series of challenges for the venerable jeans manufacturer. Despite the fact that the Gap–Levi Strauss & Co. relationship had eroded, the Gap was still the largest clothing retailer in the United States. Though Levi Strauss & Co. achieved record sales in the years that followed, the full impact would contribute to their problems in the medium term. From being the worldwide leader in denim clothing, Levi

Strauss & Co. was now relegated to diminished status, struggling to regain lost market share. The bitterness between Levi Strauss & Co. and the Gap proved to be of legendary proportions. While Levi Strauss & Co., cut loose from the store that had been its largest retail outlet, fared well in the short term, it encountered significant difficulties as the nineties unfolded. Indeed, Levi Strauss & Co., around the world, stumbled.

Things were far different as the nineties ended. The company's future profitability was threatened.[10] Levi Strauss, the world's largest manufacturer of a clothing brand, was in a crisis. At the end of 1999 Levi Strauss & Co. had eliminated 18,500 jobs, closed twenty-nine plants and its revenue fell to $5.1 billion from $6 billion just the year before.[11] The survival of the 147-year-old company hung on its ability to reintroduce itself—and win over—Generation Y in the first decade of the new century.

A troubled Levi Strauss & Co. worked hard, first to arrest its decline and then to embark on a marketing strategy to leverage its brand. In the fall of 2000 its "Make them your own" campaign was accompanied by a 52-page insert titled, "Women to Watch," in *Vogue*. Its success was not taken for granted. While Levi Strauss & Co. held its own among women, in the crucial market for men's jeans, it continued to decline. "Levi's® is an icon brand," Philip Marineau argued, promising to make the Levi's® retail brand strong again.[12]

"[V]irtually every aspect of Levi's is broken," Carol Emert reported in the *San Francisco Chronicle*. "[Marineau's] strategy [is] to repair the company's operations side, its relationships with retailers, its fashions, its marketing and its corporate culture."[13]

Levi Strauss & Co. was struggling to make its owned-and-operated, Original Levi's Stores® (Levi's retail shops) profitable. It also had to improve its working relationships with major retailers, including Sears, Macy's and J.C. Penney.

Levi Strauss & Co., looking to the future, has also embarked on innovative products. In the fall of 2000, Levi Strauss & Co. and Philips introduced to the European market jackets that have electronics gadgetry built into them. The $900 water-resistant jacket, sold exclusively in Levi Strauss & Co.'s high-end fashion boutique in London and at other upscale retailers in major European cities, is equipped with an MP3 player for playing music downloaded directly from the Internet, a headset, a cellular telephone and a remote control. The ICD+ brand—which stands for Industrial Clothing Division Plus—is expected to help revive Levi Strauss & Co., which is presently working on a second-generation line of electronics one can wear. This new line consists of conductive fibers that are controlled with infrared technology and transmit signals without wires.

If successful among Europeans, technologically compatible state-of-the-art garments might very well be introduced in the United States. "It is important to integrate the new technologies that are a part of consumers' lives into their clothes," Santiago Baluducci, an industry observer, said in Milan. "Levi's has a global brand that lends itself nicely among Generation Y. While one garment won't revive a multi-billion dollar company, the ICD+ can cast a very splendid halo effect."

The rift with the Gap had been a blow, one whose impact was felt years later. Coupled with other challenges, Levi Strauss & Co. confronted a monumental task as the 2000s began. It is a long road without guarantees and one that requires years of hard work before it will see success. Donald Fisher, whom many considered to be responsible for much of Levi Strauss & Co.'s recent hardships, was unconcerned.

It had all been just business. One man's business decision, however, is another man's betrayal. The Gap and Levi Strauss & Co. were now less than strangers.

4

THE COUP AGAINST THE BANANA-REPUBLICANS

There was always something unsettling about the Hemisphere store a few doors down from the Banana Republic on Grant Avenue in downtown San Francisco. Hemisphere was the Gap's first venture into the upscale retail market. Few people remember anything about this Gap division, however, because it was such a short-lived venture. Hemisphere was the kind of store that was reminiscent of the Armani Exchange with a little of Dolce & Gabbana thrown in for good measure. The stores had wide, open spaces with white walls. Clothes were stacked on grand shelves made of sumptuous woods, or hung on expensive chrome fixtures. The lighting was recessed and discreet. The floors were polished sandalwood. White noise in the background muffled footsteps. Hemisphere, in essence, had the familiar look of a museum: the clothes were on display. This minimalist, almost Japanese, look emphasized horizontal lines. Hemisphere gave the impression that it was a place where one could go either to meditate about clothes, or simply to admire the reality of the beauty of their simplicity. Consumers, however, were intimidated and cool to the "look-but-don't-touch" haughtiness about the place—and to the idea of buying rather expensive European-style sportswear from the Gap.

The price point and the minimalist decor were not the only things that kept customers away. That Hemisphere was too clean, clean in an antiseptic sense, was something that could be dismissed. But its location proved problematic. The downtown San Francisco store, like the others in this franchise, looked like it was on the wrong street, that it belonged on Union

Square, snuggled somewhere between Saks, I. Magnin, Chanel and Neiman- Marcus.

Then there were problems with the apparel itself. Hemisphere was Donald Fisher's idea of what upscale looked like. There was a problem with where the stores were located physically. The clothes were too luxurious to be located one block from the entrance to Chinatown, where tourists shopped for bargains and snapped photographs. The downtown San Francisco Hemisphere was surrounded by the stores and restaurants that catered primarily to harried office workers. This was a world away from the haughty boutiques that flanked Union Square and catered to the "ladies who lunch."

Hemisphere represented the Gap's attempt to expand by going upscale. If the foray into housewares via Pottery Barn taught Donald Fisher that he had to remain in a familiar industry, then Hemisphere indicated how he was approaching this challenge. At the same time a remarkable little company continued to make news. Banana Republic, founded by the husband-and-wife team of Mel and Patricia Ziegler, projected an image of fun—and profit. Their delightful catalog and eclectic collection of safari-themed clothes created a buzz in San Francisco.

It was the brief news stories—"What's Hot"–style columns—that first brought Banana Republic to the attention of Gap, Inc. Donald Fisher followed the adventures of this small, local enterprise; Banana Republic's spirit was reminiscent of the energy and hopefulness the Gap itself embodied in its early years. Mel and Patricia Ziegler respected how Donald Fisher had expanded the Gap into a national brand. They also were familiar with the less successful ventures—Pottery Barn and Hemisphere.

What struck Patricia Ziegler was that Hemisphere was so empty of what retailers need most: customers. This was not lost on Donald Fisher. Of course the clothes were luxurious—leather and suede and cashmere creations that spoke of opulence—but there was something wrong, something the merchandising wizards at the Gap were unable to identify, let alone correct. This stood in stark contrast with the fortunes of Banana Republic. While the antiseptic Hemisphere languished, a few doors down, customers piled into anything-but-sterile Banana Republic.

Founded in 1987, with a store a few doors from the Banana Republic on Grant Avenue in downtown San Francisco, Hemisphere grew to a total of nine stores before it was unceremoniously shut down two years later in 1989. Its lingering operations were absorbed by the then-struggling Banana Republic. It never made a profit and Donald Fisher had lost patience, particularly when, as the eighties ended, the Gap itself was in tremendous turmoil. Thus, the Gap's first venture into the world of upscale retailing was nothing but an absolute embarrassment.

The Banana Republic of the late nineties owes the post-modern sleek look of the current stores to what Hemisphere aspired in the mid-eighties.

Banana Republic's contemporary look is a world apart from the original look of the store. With its cluttered decor, evoking both a Moroccan bazaar and an African safari, it was a wonder that the staff knew where things were displayed. A former employee from those early years recalls there were times when " 'displayed' meant 'stacked in a corner over there.' "

The disorganization didn't matter to customers, however. To many, on the contrary, that was part of the adventure: "discovering" a pith helmet here, or an exquisite little book on the rivers of Southeast Asia over there. For the multitudes of customers who never set foot in the store, moreover, the catalog offered an opportunity to indulge in the fantasy of the adventure of exploring the world in the Victorian style of the nineteenth century. The imagery so masterfully evoked by Ralph Lauren's "Safari" line of clothing and accessories for the wealthy, Mel and Patricia Ziegler offered for everyone else whose romantic imaginations were titillated.

Founded by Mel and Patricia Ziegler, two free spirits, the word most often used to describe the original Banana Republic, which was located in Mill Valley in Marin County, was "funky." Mel Ziegler was a reporter for the *San Francisco Chronicle* and his wife Patricia was an illustrator for the same paper. Together they pooled their $1,500 in savings and opened Banana Republic Safari & Travel Co., with the goal of being able to sell enough of whatever they bought on their world travels to make a decent living—and finance additional travels to the farthest corners of the globe.

In 1983, when Gap purchased Banana Republic, there were two stores. Then an ambitious expansion program was launched: a Banana Republic opened somewhere in the United States about every other week, so that there were a hundred stores nationwide by the time the Zieglers were ousted in April 1988. This stunning growth was fueled to a large degree by the popularity of the films *Out of Africa* and *Indiana Jones*. Customers appropriated that romantic ideal with tremendous enthusiasm.

For younger consumers, who were unable to afford Ralph Lauren's "Safari" line, Banana Republic was an undoubtedly hip alternative, one that was seen as socially responsible in an age when deforestation and the fate of the world's indigenous people were fashionable causes. Patricia Ziegler excelled at cultivating what one fashionista characterized as "a flamboyant, anti-establishment image," one that fit in splendidly with the Gap's antifashion look.

Imagination is what the early Banana Republic catalog offered. What the Zieglers did was ingenious. They would travel the world in search of surplus clothing, often from European or Commonwealth military and police forces, which they would then purchase for next to nothing. They would invent a fanciful story about each garment to accompany the illustration in their catalog, and then they would watch the orders come in, selling out item after item. Mel, as a former reporter, had a gift for writing up something that engaged the reader. Patricia, as an artist, drew the most seductive illustrations in the coveted catalog. Enthusiasts awaited each issue with anticipation, vicariously traveling to wherever the Zieglers had journeyed.

When they managed to find surplus shirts from the Spanish military that were rejected because the sleeves were too short, for instance, the Zieglers bought out the entire stock, then concocted a ridiculous story. They wrote in their catalog that, in the fanatical demands of a true Fascist, General Francisco Franco rejected everyone whose limbs were out of proportion to his vision of what the perfect human ideal was. Thus Spaniards with longer-length arms were denied admission into the Spanish armed forces. With that, the irregular shirts the Spanish military authorities were about to discard—and were only too happy to get rid of at any price—became one of that catalog's hottest-selling items, with thousands of young men throughout America repeating the Zieglers' fictional nonsense as if it were fact.

It was difficult to read through the catalog, of course, without realizing that these were inspired descriptions of what were well-constructed, surplus military and adventure clothing. What the Banana Republic customer wanted was not truth in advertising, but a connection to a romantic past. Whatever the length on those Spanish military shirts, what really mattered was that, without having to travel to Madrid, the hipness of that shirt was available through this small store based somewhere in silly San Francisco.

The success of what otherwise would have been a mere mom-and-pop operation was apparent in how masterfully it nurtured an exuberant loyalty among shoppers; Banana Republic shoppers were devoted customers. In this affiliation lay the foundation for what the Zieglers hoped would develop into a larger enterprise: travel services. This began by selling travel books, maps and accessories. If customers were delighted by the pith helmets on the wall, they could easily pick up a book about a safari to Africa as well as a map of the dark continent. Those who were fascinated by, say, a bird-watching adventure to Costa Rica could also select a pair of binoculars or compass from those offered at the store.

The synergies envisioned were a clever marketing approach. This was not lost on Donald Fisher, who could only stand on Grant Avenue and watch pedestrians stroll up and down the sidewalk carrying shopping bags from Banana Republic—with hardly one from Hemisphere in sight. It was the dynamic and playful enterprise the Zieglers had created that led Gap to make the initial overtures. With Hemisphere and Banana Republic on the same block, was there, perhaps, some way that the Zieglers' magic could rescue Hemisphere, or at least offer the kind of innovation that would allow the Gap to enter that desired, but elusive, upscale market?

Donald Fisher was impressed by Banana Republic. It was obvious that this was the kind of energy and creativity that the Gap needed if it was to diversify and expand its business. The solution was obvious enough: Gap would simply make Mel and Patricia Ziegler an offer they could not refuse. When the acquisition of Banana Republic was announced by Gap, Patricia

Ziegler remarked that she "would have never believed that the same corporation that was capable of opening Hemisphere would be interested in our little shop! Oh, we are delighted!"

Gap, too, was pleased. In conversations with members of the press at one of the many receptions and conferences held, words and phrases like "exciting," "brilliant future" and "a natural combination" were spread around like the hors d'oeuvres from the first-class caterers hired for the affair. All one had to do was select which public relations take to put on this story, a far easier task than selecting which morsel to select from the trays.

The press thereby became an accomplice in spreading the myth that the Gap's acquisition of Banana Republic was a perfect union of two dynamic San Francisco retailers that promised to raise the city's profile in the fashion industry on a national level. The union was almost universally heralded as a coup for San Francisco. For a city where the world headquarters of Levi Strauss & Co. and Gap, Inc. were located, San Francisco was a marginal player in the world of fashion and retailing. Local retailers, from the Emporium to I. Magnin were under siege from new entrants, whether Saks, or Macy's or Neiman-Marcus. And as far as Seventh Avenue was concerned, there was nothing of interest in San Francisco for devoted fashion mavens. This was a city, after all, where young people mutilated their bodies with tattoos and piercings and "fashion" was little more than a Dead Head T-shirt with a psychedelic pattern in neon colors.

"We are delighted," Donald Fisher stated to the press. "This is a natural acquisition for the Gap."

While San Franciscans delighted in the great buzz surrounding the Gap–Banana Republic coup against the fashionistas in New York, little notice was given to the continuing losses at the now-forgotten Hemisphere. The stunning failure of Hemisphere, however, proved legendary in New York, assured that as far as fashion and style were concerned, San Francisco was lost in the fog. The Gap dismissed the Hemisphere as a fluke—not as a harbinger of more to come. In fact, the acquisition of Banana Republic by Gap promised to change whatever disappointment Hemisphere had proven to be. "We are delighted and we are looking to the future," Patricia Ziegler told reporters a month after the acquisition by Gap had been completed.

Delight would prove to be short-lived. This was as much a result of the inevitable consequences when people of strong wills clash with each other as it was due to the fundamental lack of realism in the expectations of Fisher and the Zieglers. That the Zieglers and Fisher may not have been completely honest with each other, or perhaps with themselves, was instrumental in the complete collapse of their merger.[1] For the Zieglers, they publicly welcomed the opportunities Gap's deep pockets offered. By selling their company to Donald Fisher, the possibilities for growth—and the financial backing required—were limitless. What otherwise would have been a decades-long process of arduous work could instantly be circumvented now with the stroke of a signature on one large check. For the Gap, a hip brand name was theirs now, and the marketing ingenuity of the Zieglers promised to help the Gap succeed where Hemisphere had proved to be a dismal failure.

These were the complementary interests of both parties that were discernible to the press. What was not evident were the obstacles that would prove insurmountable, however. With the perspective of a decade, it is clear that it was more than a question of chemistry that interfered in the ability of Zieglers and Fisher to work together.

Consider, for instance, that the Zieglers came out with *Banana Republic Guide to Travel & Safari Clothing* in 1986. That book, published by Ballantine Books, was nothing if not a manifesto of their vision for Banana Republic, a vision which they believed would be underwritten by the Gap. The ambiguities for Donald Fisher, on the other hand, were subtle, and operated on an unconscious level. The naive enthusiasm of Mel and Patricia Ziegler stood in sharp contrast to the misgivings and self-doubt of Donald Fisher.

The Zieglers, who did not see themselves as participants in the rag trade, were oblivious to the slings and arrows of the fashionistas on Seventh Avenue. Donald Fisher, on the other hand, not unlike other Jews who had been traditionally shunned by the industry in New York, including the legendary Barney Pressman of Barneys, was an outsider, one who had been discriminated against by Seventh Avenue despite the spectacular success of the Gap over two decades.[2]

This is not to say that there was overt anti-Semitism by the fashion industry, but merely that Donald Fisher was, by virtue of being a Jew, an outsider made it all the easier for industry insiders to roll their eyes and dismiss the Gap's antifashion revolution as a ghastly stunt by an unwelcome parvenu. "Hemisphere was always ignored by Seventh Avenue," an insider stated, echoing a sentiment expressed by others, a sentiment that the passive hostility against Hemisphere was, in part, payback for the Gap's audacity to challenge the very idea of fashion itself.

The Zieglers, on the other hand, were clueless about how the slights of Seventh Avenue affected their interactions with the Gap. Where they saw unlimited resources to make their own vision a reality, the Gap was counting on this radical approach to making a fashion statement as a way of receiving, finally, accolades from the industry observers. This, then, was arguably the hidden agenda behind the acquisition of Banana Republic. It was a way for Donald Fisher to overcome the failure that Hemisphere represented and to follow in the steps of Fred Pressman and reaffirm the presence of Jews in upscale retailing.

It cannot be underestimated how Hemisphere's demise—right there in the city where Gap had its worldwide headquarters—struck a blow to Donald Fisher's confidence. Banana Republic, as a brand name, and Mel and Patricia Ziegler, as its creative forces, would then allow Donald Fisher to re-engineer the concept of Hemisphere with a fresh brand, a fresh look and a fresh approach. The only thing that would be unchanged would be its location on the same block of Grant Avenue, as if, by not moving its geographic location, Hemisphere's failure could be denied.

This was all news to the Zieglers, news they would not learn of until long after they had been shown the door, of course. And they were shown the door soon enough.

How and why this happened remains surrounded in controversy. The Zieglers arrived at the corporate offices of the Gap like bright and eager schoolchildren on the first day of class. The only thing they failed to bring was an apple for Donald Fisher, but their gushing praise more than made up for it. But the Gap was not an operation that relied on inspired fiction about surplus garments found in some warehouse on the outskirts of Madrid or Madras or wherever. It was a massive corporate operation with worldwide stores that required not military surplus shirts but rather the discipline of a military bureaucracy.

A clash of corporate culture was not the only difference that surprised the Zieglers, however. It was the calculating style and personal aloofness of Donald Fisher that surprised Patricia Ziegler especially.

"We had to call and make an appointment to even speak to him," she stated once. "How could we work together when we couldn't even get a meeting with Don. We were completely out of the loop."

As outsiders within the Gap bureaucracy, the Zieglers soon realized how limited their clout was in a corporate context. But that was easily forgotten; they were in complete control of Banana Republic and whatever else they had to offer to Gap's other operations was deemed superfluous. A big check goes far in ameliorating wounded pride. This was no exception, and soon enough, regardless of what the stern officers from Gap, Inc. thought of the Zieglers, they were off and running.

And did they run!

The days of the giraffes were numbered, however, and so were the rhinos, the jeeps, the bush planes and everything else that looked like it properly belonged on the set of *Indiana Jones*. When one walked into the Grant Avenue Banana Republic—the one closest to the corporate headquarters of Gap, Inc.—by far the more interesting merchandise was in the basement. To reach the basement, one took a staircase that was flanked by a life-size giraffe, which, standing in the basement, had its head visible on the first floor. Other Banana Republic stores featured life-size rhinos, or jungle jeeps, or bush planes or other paraphernalia that had, as one critic noted, "a theatrical air that distracted from the clothing."

"Some of the Gap's executives were aghast at that decor," one Banana Republic employee said of one of the first visits by Gap officers to check out Donald Fisher's acquisition. "One remarked how the store looked like something from Disneyland's Adventure Land."

In memos circulated back and forth between the Gap and Banana Republic, comments were made about the daunting challenge in attempting to duplicate the stark idiosyncrasies of Banana Republic's bizarre style into a chain of stores that could mushroom across the American landscape. There were also concerns expressed about, what one official termed, the safari "nonsense" that stood in stark contrast to the evolving minimalist approach of the Gap's current stores. Finally, there were Gap officials who were stunned at the cluttered mess of plastic jungle animal fixtures that dominated the tortured interior of the Banana Republic on Grant Avenue. Whether or not it was cheesy didn't matter. It was the formula that worked within the context of what was possible at Banana Republic prior to a significant capital infusion from Gap, Inc.

In fact, whatever misgivings about the rate of expansion the sedate accountants at Gap had about Banana Republic were glossed over and an ample budget was authorized, allowing the Zieglers to render what they imagined into bricks and mortar across the nation. Indeed, in no time the vision proclaimed to the world in their 1986 book was becoming a reality. "We will re-invent the idea of travel," Mel Ziegler declared when they announced to the press that Banana Republic would publish *Trips*, a magazine devoted exclusively to adventure travel. A quarterly that would spend lavishly to offer true accounts of "authentic" adventure travel, this magazine would give a voice to the Zieglers' evolving vision of what Banana Republic offered its customers—which was the world. The selection of travel books was expanded significantly. Accessories—from maps to binoculars to backpacks—exploded throughout the store. The clothes began to resemble something out of a Ralph Lauren "Safari" advertising spread in a glossy magazine.

It is important to bear in mind that in corporate America what the Zieglers proposed to do—transform Banana Republic into a "travel/adventure" destination—had its parallels on a larger scale. Consider alone the failed experiment of United Airlines (UAL), which in 1987 changed its name to "Allegis." In an attempt to create unique "synergies" UAL believed it could become a one-stop business/travel destination that, through Allegis, would provide air travel (United Airlines), accommodations (Westin Hotels) and car rentals (Hertz). The brainchild of Frank Olson, Allegis, as the holding company for all three firms, would coordinate and streamline reservations and services through United Airlines, Westin Hotels and Hertz. This kind of vertical integration of services was believed to offer a set of unique opportunities that would foster loyalty and market efficiencies. Vertical integration is difficult to carry off, and Allegis's attempts turned out to be better as an idea than as a reality: Allegis lasted only two years before it reverted back to United Airlines and its interests in Westin and Hertz were sold off in divestiture.

The Gap reacted coolly to the Zieglers' interpretation of a vertical integration strategy. Donald Fisher was more comfortable with a more traditional vertical strategy—if you sell jeans, then design the jeans, manufacture the jeans and market the jeans, but don't lose sight of the jeans. Then again, the Zieglers had managed to create a splendid little company following their own vision, and Donald Fisher generously gave them all the freedom they needed.

For Mel and Patricia Ziegler, however, it was not clear whether the freedom afforded them was a vote of confidence in their ability, or benign neglect from Donald Fisher, who never seemed to have much interest in meeting with them to discuss the future of Banana Republic.

"We were reduced to dealing with middle-level managers from the Gap's organization," Patricia Ziegler recalled shortly after her departure from Banana Republic. "It was as if, once the 'development budget' had been approved, [Donald] Fisher lost interest."

Whether Donald Fisher did lose interest or not, what matters is that the Zieglers were afforded tremendous freedom in carrying out their plans. *Trips* was creating a buzz in the publishing world. The Zieglers indulged lavishly, paying top dollar for writers they recruited for assignments from *Rolling Stone*, *Esquire* and *New Yorker* magazines among other prestigious publications. It was the kind of excitement that was only rivaled by Tina Brown's arrival at *Vanity Fair*. The expectations that *Trips*, which claimed a pre-publication circulation of 300,000 when it was launched, promised to revolutionize travel literature and adventure writing were great.

Articles about riding bicycles with the king of Togo, or searching for cannibals or having literary writers ponder "untranslatable words" in a journal that showcased Banana Republic's products and services was a grand experiment, one that tantalized the advertising and media industry. *Trips* captured the imagination of the publishing world for it evoked the kind of adventure writing and reporting not seen since Ernest Hemingway reported on his adventures from the far reaches of the globe. Patricia Ziegler, especially, realized that these kinds of comparisons were in keeping with the spirit of her "safari and travel" company. As important, she was having tremendous fun.

"It was clear that Patricia Ziegler was more interested in travel and publishing than in fashion and clothing," one former Gap executive who was familiar with the acquisition of Banana Republic said. "This raised concerns at the corporate offices for the simple reason that we are in the business of designing, manufacturing and selling clothes."

That conclusion was not inaccurate, but it was unfair. The Gap knew very well, after all, that the Zieglers were in the business of merchandising military surplus clothing—not in the business of fashion, or clothing manufacturing or creating an integrated (antifashion) statement. Patricia Ziegler did not understand why Gap executives were surprised by either her management style or her business priorities.

"Designers would meet with Patricia to show her preliminary designs of collections," an executive familiar with these meetings said, "and her eyes would glaze over the drawings. It was, 'Whatever. I can't be bothered.' All she was concerned about was Banana Republic as a travel services business with clothing occupying a secondary, perhaps even a peripheral, role. Neither Mel nor Patricia understood that the primary focus of the store was, after all, to sell *clothes*. Well, this did not play well with Don."

For the Gap, there was an ambivalence that betrayed tremendous insecurities. Patricia Ziegler was reluctant to introduce a line of women's clothing, which angered Donald Fisher. With the continuing failure of Hemisphere weighing heavily on everyone's mind, Gap executives were now confronted with both the nonchalant approach favored by the Zieglers and the lack of direction, or vision, of what the Banana Republic "look" should become after the *Out of Africa* phenomenon had run its course. Few were prepared to criticize the Banana Republic founders, who were overwhelmed by their division's explosive growth.

Donald Fisher's experience in retailing had convinced him of the prudence in creating basic wardrobes that were updated continuously. The word from Gap was for the designers to work diligently and quietly to create Banana Republic "basics" and to build a style around it. There was also a directive to let the Zieglers move forward with their magazine and related product lines without interference.

Officials at Gap point to this generous patience as evidence of Donald Fisher's benevolence and faith in the Zieglers. Perhaps, but it is also true that during the mid-eighties, Gap was experiencing the fastest growth in its history. If the Hemisphere fiasco represented an important psychological blow, financially it was of no consequence, but it convinced Donald Fisher that to grow successfully the Gap needed to recruit outside talent. The demands on Donald Fisher's time and energies were spectacular, which contributed to the Zieglers' free rein; not only did he not have the time to manage Banana Republic himself, but also there were no Gap executives to assign to such a task, particularly now that another hit formula had been struck with the launching of Gap Kids.

It was a curious phenomenon. The Gap was in an impressive expansion program, but sales at its core business were suffering. Gap Kids was enthusiastically received, but sales at Banana Republic were disappointing and sales at the Gap's core business were falling. Throughout 1987 sales were falling for all divisions of Gap, with the exception of Gap Kids. Profits plummeted. Investors sent its stock downward as the year progressed. On the first trading day of the new year, January 2, 1987, Gap's stock closed at $36\frac{7}{8}$ and on the last trading day, December 31, 1987, it closed at $20\frac{1}{4}$. Donald Fisher expressed concern about the expenses at Banana Republic. In order to scrutinize more closely the operations, Banana Republic relocated its headquarters to downtown San Francisco. Alan Zimtbaum, the CFO at Banana Republic, began to report more frequently to Gap officers. Donald Fisher may have been loathe to criticize either the Zieglers or Banana Republic's performance for one reason that was not immediately clear to most outsiders: he had placed his sons Robert and William in key positions at Banana Republic.

To be fair to Mel and Patricia Ziegler, they were not trained in proper business management. In a generous assessment of their tenure at Banana Republic, the Zieglers were described as "in business but not of business." Laurie Itow, a business reporter for the *San Francisco Chronicle*, summarized the Zieglers' failure as a classic example of an "entrepreneurial start-up that explodes in phenomenal growth and is forced to make a jarring leap from free-wheeling alliance into big business."

Then again, it was Robert and William Fisher who were charged with managing that explosive growth—from a couple of stores to a hundred five years later—and the Zieglers had never represented themselves as capable of managing a nationwide business in the highly competitive world of fashion retailing.

The profits at the end of the day spoke for themselves, however. While the Gap does not break down revenues and profits by division, analysts estimated that Banana Republic made profits of $25 million in 1986 and $20 million in 1987. Then *Out of Africa* and *Indiana Jones* had run their course. In 1988, Banana Republic lost $12 million and the following year it lost $8 million. Donald Fisher's sons were at Banana Republic throughout this entire period, and both emerged without being closely scrutinized in the press.

"How could anyone criticize Robert or William in front of their father?" one former executive at Gap, Inc. said. "It would have been very awkward."

Gap, Inc. is a publicly traded company on the New York Stock Exchange and Donald Fisher accepted his responsibility to shareholders as a sacred trust. Whatever accusations of nepotism the local press speculated about after the Zieglers were removed, reasonable voices questioned the ability of Robert and William Fisher to manage a national chain and to handle the undisciplined and exuberant Zieglers.

While concerns about Banana Republic continued to swirl through the corridors of Gap in 1987 and 1988, on occasion, Donald Fisher would show up at a store to see for himself what the Zieglers and his sons were doing. Once his driver took him to the Grant Avenue store. There was that life-size giraffe. There were stacks of books piled on tables. A map on the wall had pushpins marking Katmandu—a city in Nepal or Tibet or wherever—and the clothes were strewn about on hangars or in haphazard piles everywhere. Without saying a word, or being recognized by any of the staff, he got back in his car and was driven back to his understated offices, the walls of which were decorated with modern masterpieces from his private collection.

"If I wanted to own Rand McNally, I would have bought Rand McNally!" Donald Fisher reportedly fumed, venting his frustration.

Something had to give. Sales were falling. As will be shown later, the Banana Republic "look" was losing currency with consumers fast. The entire romantic ideal was neither cultivated properly nor was it sustainable—and it was fizzling fast by the end of 1987. A good number of copycat stores were mass-producing knockoffs of the safari style to no end. Without a staple of basics in khakis, a sustainable style could not be created. This was all news to Mel and Patricia Ziegler, who were thinking about expeditions to the Australian Outback and floating down the Brazilian Amazon River. Endless meetings were held, personalities clashed, but no happy compromise between Fisher's proven horizontal strategy and the Zieglers' trendy vertical vision was found.

Trips, which represented a $2 million investment, was launched to tremendous accolades on schedule in March 1988. With that single issue, Banana Republic was on top of the magazine world. Condé Nast took notice in New York; the exceptional writing was nothing less than literature. The monopoly New York coveted was challenged in one swoop. In San Francisco, the media buzz was on the sensation Banana Republic had created so effortlessly. It was an incredible thing to see: people were buying up copies of *Trips* by the dozen—to keep, to share, *to hoard!*

Patricia Ziegler announced projections of a worldwide circulation of a million by the end of the first year. *Trips* was an undeniable hit. The buzz it generated was fast and furious; Banana Republic was news once more and people were flocking into the stores nationwide. This is not to say that they were shopping for clothes, but they certainly came in to pick up copies of the magazine.

For Donald Fisher that was it. Mel and Patricia Ziegler had catapulted to become the darlings of New York's publishing world—and they were only getting started. Banana Republic was heading in a direction he could no longer control. "How would you feel? I mean, how would a teacher feel if he was eclipsed by a couple of apprentices?" a former employee familiar with Donald Fisher's reactions stated.

Envious? Resentful? Angered? In April 1988, one month after *Trips* had been launched to unprecedented accolades, Donald Fisher initiated a coup against the Zieglers. Gap announced that the second issue of *Trips*, which had become so hot after a single issue, would not be released and that the magazine itself was discontinued in order "to allow the company to concentrate on the new repositioning of the clothing business."

Mel and Patricia Ziegler resigned, noting "fundamental creative and cultural differences." Mel Ziegler elaborated by stating that "our marriage to the Gap allowed us to take our concept further and faster than we ever imagined. We never expected to stay with this forever. It's time for us to get on to something new."

Donald Fisher reiterated that they were not in the business of selling "ambiance" and that Banana Republic had to grow in a manageable way. Mickey Drexler was named president of Banana Republic, which henceforth dropped "Safari & Travel" from its name.

The employees at both the Gap and Banana Republic were ordered to remain silent and not make any comment to the press. There were internal accusations of virulent intensity thrown about by all sides. Banana Republic employees loyal to the Zieglers grumbled that the Zieglers had been made scapegoats. Donald Fisher, however, had always been one to reward talent, regardless of where it came from. Unlike Fred Pressman of Barneys who relinquished control of that remarkable store to his sons Gene and Bob, only to live long enough to see that elite retailer land in (and come out of) bankruptcy court, Donald Fisher looked upon Barneys as a cautionary tale—and never forgot the dramatic consequences of unchecked hubris.

There were other complaints, complaints of more absolute relevance to the circumstances of Banana Republic. The most urgent among these was the observation that the "cultural" differences—a code word for the inherent conflict in the "radical" vertical versus "traditional" vertical business models—made it impossible for the Zieglers to ever satisfy Donald Fisher and Mickey Drexler. Then again, if Allegis had failed to get United Airlines, Westin Hotels and Hertz to make it work, who could find fault with the Zieglers' failure to make "safari and travel" work out within the corporate structure of Gap, Inc.

"The key to the business is apparel," Donald Fisher explained, by way of asserting the vertical vision of the Gap that would now be implemented at Banana Republic. "We're not selling ambiance."

With the resignations of the Zieglers, Mickey Drexler assumed the top posts of both Gap and Banana Republic, leading industry analysts to conclude that the situation was "worse than anyone expected." In fact, it was "dismal." The surgery at Banana Republic in 1988 may have been both radical and clumsily executed, but it was effective. There was a major consolidation of administrative functions at a management level and hundreds of jobs were slashed from the payrolls as redundant tasks were consolidated.

At the end of the first quarter of 1989, Gap experienced record sales. Not that Banana Republic had much to do with that turnaround. At best, Banana Republic was no longer hemorrhaging money, but it was not out of the woods yet. To create a sustainable look—one that defied Hollywood-inspired fads—Mickey Drexler recruited Tasha Polizzi from Ralph Lauren to head creative design for Banana Republic. Later that year, Hemisphere's remaining operations and staff were absorbed by Banana Republic, further consolidating operations at the troubled divisions.

The *Wall Street Journal* summed up the changes by noting that Banana Republic had to trade "jungle-flavored khakis for genteel Lauren." In the months that followed the bloodless coup against the Zieglers, executives at Gap, Inc., in a perverse twist, walked down the corridors with dark humor: *Want to buy a bush plane? I know where you can get a great deal on a giraffe!*

"Meaningful improvements" is the phrase used by Donald Fisher to characterize that tumultuous year in interviews granted in August 1988. Noting that Banana Republic's "expenses were being brought more in line with sales," he expressed cautious optimism. But when the reaction to the first post-Ziegler collection came in, there was no comment from anyone.

In fairness to Tasha Polizzi, she arrived too late in 1988 at Banana Republic to impact the bottom line. Her first line was introduced too late for the Christmas season of that year. It bombed with a spectacular thud, the press remarked. Of greater concern to Gap officials was the spectacular misfire that occurred when Banana Republic was "reintroduced" to the American public.

In full-page advertisements in fashion and fashionable magazines, Banana Republic introduced the tag line, "My chosen family," featuring same-sex young people in provocative embraces and poses of such overt homoerotic sensuality that it caused alarm. The provocative use of pure eros and the celebration of deviant sexual longings may have played well in San Francisco and the gay ghettos of New York and Los Angeles, but it scandalized—and was repudiated by—mainstream America. From a playful look that evoked Meryl Streep and Harrison Ford and an inspired association with championing concern for the earth and its indigenous peoples, Banana Republic suddenly presented itself not as something out of Africa, but as something out of the closet.

The "repositioned" Banana Republic clothes aspired to be "urban" and "cosmopolitan." The shoulders were cut narrower, the shirt lengths were shortened—making men's shirts resemble women's blouses—and the over-fussed detailing gave them a slightly effeminate look. What doomed them, however, was the tagline, "My chosen family." The *perceived* homosexuality turned consumers off. It is astounding how much about the art of merchandising has to do with that ephemeral quality of perceived status and value. Humans are emotional beings and Tasha Polizzi's Banana Republic collections struck the average consumer as being something designed by and for gays.[3]

"Rags for fags" is how one fashionista in New York disparaged and dismissed the entire collection of clothing that seemed to aspire to an androgynous—but undeniably effeminate—look. Despite the enormous contributions that homosexuals have traditionally, and openly, made to the fashion industry, there is still a stigma attached to what is perceived as effeminate. "They *dress* the women so well," one socially prominent New Yorker explained, "because they are *themselves* women." Gay aesthetics, in other words, do not threaten heterosexual men, provided homosexuals design clothes to dress their wives, but when openly gay clothing is targeted to straight men, that is another story.

In San Francisco, the reaction to the new collection was bemused at the frivolous nonsense of it all. " 'Heterosexuality to Tasha! Heterosexuality to Tasha! Come in Tasha!' is what the telepathic messages around the office were like," a former Gap executive familiar with the scandal characterized the corporate reaction to the first post-Ziegler collection. "Tasha's mission was to develop a line of women's clothing for American women pretending to be Meryl Streep pretending to be Isak Dinesen [the Danish woman who's life in colonial Africa was the basis of the hit film]. Instead, we got—in the middle of an AIDS epidemic—all this 'gay' advertising for Banana Republic clothing. What the hell was the matter with her? Didn't she know how to design clothing for the other 90 percent of the people who also live on this planet?"

It is important to remember that as late as the eighties it was rare to find openly gay salesmen at respectable stores in the United States. The idea of having salesmen who sashayed to and fro in all their "fabulosity" throughout the stores only took hold in the nineties when flaming queens were suddenly everywhere. The offensively homoerotic advertising campaign was immediately pulled by infuriated Gap officials who were horrified.[4]

Still reeling from the closure of Hemisphere in early 1989 and by an almost 75 percent drop in profits throughout that year, the last thing Gap executives had was time to figure out what to do with the Banana Republic division. The decision to close down Hemisphere—mocked as "hemorrhage-sphere"—was an unsentimental one, which spoke volumes of Donald Fisher's no-nonsense approach to failed ideas or schemes.

There were, in fact, more pressing issues to which his energies should be devoted. Mickey Drexler was still working to engineer a turnaround at Gap, too busy to be concerned about the fortunes of that embarrassing misfire by Banana Republic. Despite those within Gap who stood up to defend Tasha Polizzi—blithely pointing out she inherited designers from Hemisphere—what remained clear to all, however, was that she had disappointed Donald Fisher tremendously.

This disappointment, however, was perhaps premature. If the "My chosen family" campaign was offensive in its public embrace of private sexual lives, it nevertheless foreshadowed one apparent future direction of how Banana Republic's men's clothing would be viewed by some consumers. As the collections were once again redesigned, what became evident was that, in the nineties, gay culture was becoming increasingly visible in mainstream American culture. The emergence of important writers like Andrew Sullivan and the accepted homosexuality of celebrities, from Gianni Versace to Elton John, from Melissa Etheridge to k. d. lang, changed the parameters and visibility of gays and lesbians within the greater mainstream American culture.

From Banana Republic, with headquarters at the epicenter of American homosexuality, the gay aesthetic emerged. If Tasha Polizzi's first collection had been ridiculed as "rags for fags," subsequent collections throughout the nineties included classic "twinkie wear." In American homosexual culture, a "twinkie" refers to an effeminate, shallow and frivolous homosexual man, usually in his mid-twenties. Imagine a grown man whose worldview is that of a six-year-old girl. While the term is not a compliment, it is not necessarily derogatory. It is a simple description of one kind of gay man. What that phrase conveyed, however, was the perception among some consumers that anyone walking into a Banana Republic would find clothes that appealed to the aesthetics of gay men.

That so many members of Generation Y recognized this and subsequently dismissed Banana Republic is probably as much a part of a political backlash against gay activism at the end of the nineties as it is based on the heterosexual perception that no self-respecting American male who watches *Monday Night Football* and has sex with women would wear anything sold at Banana Republic. Once a point is made by gays and lesbians, it seems, Americans want to move on; it was only after Ellen DeGeneres finally came out on her television show, *Ellen*, that America stopped tuning in and it was canceled. Members of Generation Y, likewise, seem to say of Banana Republic, "OK, so it's clothing for fags. Big deal? But I'm not gonna wear it." Whether because of homophobia, or by simply rejecting gay aesthetics, many Generation Y-ers *dissed* the entire Banana Republic brand as "too queer for words."

It has to be pointed out in all fairness that there are no empirical scientific studies showing that a disproportionate number of the men who shop at Banana Republic in 2001 are gay. It is, on the other hand, fair to say that if homosexuality is randomly distributed among 10 percent of the general population, it only takes the most casual observer to realize that more than one of every ten shoppers at Banana Republic is gay. There is nothing wrong with this, of course, but this goes a long way in explaining why heterosexual males between the ages of eighteen and twenty-five, who are most concerned with perceptions about what is masculine, have been successfully courted by other brands, such as Abercrombie & Fitch, J. Crew, Structure (Express Men's), Ralph Lauren and Tommy Hilfiger—in addition to a number of other, smaller brands, such as Mark Ecko and Phat Farm.

In the course of conducting research for this book, I have been struck by how many gays and lesbians are employed at Banana Republic stores. I know this simply because I have asked them.

The Banana Republics in Miami Beach, Rockefeller Center and Chelsea in New York City, and the San Francisco store at Sutter and Grant streets, in fact, resemble social clubs for the gay/lesbian/bisexual/transgender communities in those cities, much the same way that the cafes in the Barnes & Noble stores have become de facto public squares where people gather, socialize and meet one another. As we shall see later on, since 1997, intentionally or not, Banana Republic has boldly affirmed an urban look that can best be described as "gay aesthetics."

"The role brands play in [teenagers'] lives is an important one. It's how they define their sense of self," reported a researcher at a marketing company that specializes in assessing consumer trends among teenagers. "They often articulate this idea in terms of defining what is 'cool' and what isn't. What's cool is what they want to be, and what's cool is what's masculine. In this sense, the Gap has continued to fall [in its] . . . 'coolness' factor."

In American teenagers' perceptions of "coolness" there is a pronounced gender gap, one that has been quantified by independent marketing companies dedicated to understanding the consumer behavior of teenagers. One explanation for the widening gap in how teenage girls and boys appear to perceive the Gap as a brand is an indication of the failure of the Gap to convey the image of masculinity to heterosexual members of Generation Y. According to an authority on teenage consumers

Generation Y-ers have a need for "newness." The teenagers who become the "early adopters" of a given style set the trend for their entire peer group. It's really a question of, "Is this clothing for me?" For a brand like Banana Republic, the answer is clearly no. Banana Republic is "out of its cool" as far as young people are concerned. It may not be an articulate way of explaining it, but what Generation Y-ers mean to say is that Banana Republic is for "older" people—those who are in the workforce. It's impossible for one brand to be all things to all people. Young men, in particular, do not feel comfortable in their judgment about what is fashionable and what is not. The great thing for them is being able to step into a store and buy anything from Abercrombie & Fitch or Tommy Hilfiger—and know that when they step out, they'll look masculine.

That's not possible with Banana Republic, and it's not guaranteed anymore with the Gap. For teenage members of Generation Y, who are in the midst of puberty and the physical and emotional changes inherent in this, clothes are badge items that allow them to differentiate themselves and to fit in. They want to fit in and look like men—which is what they are physically becoming. This is what makes a brand "cool"—it's a matter of defining what "masculine" means as the twenty-first century begins.

Gap as a brand, since 1997, appears to speak to the aspirations of fewer and fewer young men. "Consumer companies of all kinds are having a more and more difficult time in reaching young men," an authority on teenager preferences stated. Indeed, the gender gap widened as the nineties ended, with the number of teenage boys ranking the Gap as "cool" in the low single digits. In 1998, for instance, three times as many girls thought the Gap was cool as did boys, reported Teenage Research Unlimited.[5] In 1999 and 2000, a survey by another firm indicated the gender gap had widened: for every four teenage girls who thought the Gap *was* cool, only one teenage boy agreed.

Tasha Polizzi's initial collection was clearly ahead of its time by an entire decade. It was too much for America in 1989. The "My chosen family" campaign was cancelled and the collection of clothes was discontinued, as executives from the Gap closed their eyes in despair and quietly massaged the throbbing veins in their temples. This Banana Republic "mess of a collection" had to be completely reworked. A style that appealed only to urban gay men would not be able to sustain a national chain of over 100 stores or meet with the approval of shareholders. An entire year after the Zieglers were out of the picture, sales were horrible, Banana Republic stores around the country were closing and Wall Street was neither amused nor forgiving.

"It may have been Tasha's 'chosen family,' but it certainly wasn't Donald Fisher's 'chosen consumer,'" one insider said. "Banana Republic had to become a store for everyone in America, not just dizzy homosexual men—and the desperately lonely straight women who hung out with them."

Gap's stock plunged in the first quarter of 1989 after the final figures for the previous Christmas season came in. Sales at Banana Republic were now in a free fall. In the spring of 1989 Banana Republic discontinued its fabled catalog, and the entire collection was repositioned yet once more, but no one knew from where the inspiration would come.

It was not without irony that Banana Republic, whose look had been ripped off by competitors, now found itself in a situation in which it would have to appropriate Ralph Lauren. It was decided that Banana Republic would be placed in a holding pattern—while sales per square foot continued to plummet from an estimated high of $650 under the Zieglers to less than an estimated $350 in the first year after Mickey Drexler was in charge—until Donald Fisher decided what to do to rescue this wayward division from itself.[6]

The coup against the Banana-Republicans had been a messy, dismal affair that left all parties bruised and diminished. What no one articulated at any point was the obvious challenge confronting Gap. Whereas Gap had built an entire store on the staple of blues—blue hues of denim clothing—Banana Republic struggled to duplicate this strategy with khakis—the beige hues of safari and adventure clothing. The fundamental psychology of the human mind, and how this translates into consumer purchasing choices, is the fundamental obstacle that stood in the way of the Zieglers' success. It was also the obstacle that crushed Tasha Polizzi's first collection.

Whatever it is about the human mind, building a sustainable collection around beige or khaki is a far greater challenge than designing wardrobes around hues of blue. Mickey Drexler understood this on an unconscious level, to be sure. Donald Fisher, too, understood the importance of using a tried-and-true formula that had led to spectacular success in the past. Human psychology is such that the eye wanders away from beiges, but is drawn to blues.

While Banana Republic remained aloft in a holding pattern circling over Gap, Inc., the company's executives and designers began to design distinctive lines, one for men and the other for women. The idea was to create a line of basic clothing that could be accented by different fabrics, materials and colors. It would take years to incorporate the safari heritage of the original Banana Republic with modern realities of the commoditization of clothes that took hold of fashion in the eighties.

The gay sensibilities embraced and celebrated by Tasha Polizzi had to be toned down, in other words, but not completely abandoned. The introduction of fabrics and materials—leather in 1997, suede in 1998 and cashmere in 1999—completed the introduction of industrial hues—steel blues, metallic grays, chrome greens. Together a postindustrial look evocative of modernity was nurtured. The expansion of the men's and women's lines to include shoes, accessories and body products strengthened the high-end appeal in a splendid little way, one that made the most of the minimalist look of Banana Republic, a look that was light years away from the its safari heyday.

As we shall see when we return to Banana Republic, after a frustrating period of treading water, under new leadership this division got its act together and became hot once more. But this would be only after the tortuous and drawn-out "repositioning" of Banana Republic resulted in one poetic twist of fate no one could have foreseen. For the millions of consumers who never once set foot inside the failed Hemisphere, there is this one consolation: step into any Banana Republic, and behold, what any fashion maven on Seventh Avenue would be proud to call "fabulous" is everything Banana Republic has become because Banana Republic is now everything Hemisphere aspired to be.

5

THE FABULOSITY OF SIMPLICITY

Gap, Inc. was able to absorb continuing losses at Banana Republic as the eighties came to an end precisely because the Gap, Gap Kids and Baby Gap were doing so well. Donald Fisher and Mickey Drexler had the cash flow to be patient. This, however, changed in the nineties. The confluence of three trends in the early nineties culminated in an unprecedented crisis for Gap in 1995. The first trend, the unprecedented proliferation of similar "basic" lines, a reflection of the consumer uncertainty about the economy, created pressures on the Gap stores. Not since 1978 when the Federal Trade Commission entered into an agreement that Levi Strauss & Co. could not set retail prices had such a competitive frenzy been unleashed. Gap reacted by slashing prices drastically in 1992 in an effort to revive sagging sales. This was not enough and a year later it was forced to open forty-five Gap Warehouses, which would soon be renamed Old Navy, throughout the United States in order to compete against discounters and to sustain sales.

Whereas in the Reagan eighties, consumers flaunted their money and paid too much for their clothes, in the nineties, there was an abrupt about-face. "In the eighties people would pay $50 for a blouse and say they paid $100," said a woman interviewed at the Gap on Fifth Avenue. "Then in the nineties, they would pay $30 and brag that they got it for $15. That's what made it possible for K-Mart—think of it! K-Mart!—to open on Astor Place in Manhattan and there was a line out the door and around the corner. Everybody in New York wanted to shop K-Mart! Can you imagine the low-brow horror of that?"

In the early nineties, suddenly, Americans wanted to shop at K-Mart. And Wal-Mart and Target, and Marshall's and Ross. The first trend was consumers' embrace of discounters as chic. It wreaked havoc on Gap's bottom line and it presented Donald Fisher and Mickey Drexler with an unprecedented challenge. As the nineties unfolded, clothes of comparable quality to the Gap's now were found at discounters. Gap was now competing with Wal-Mart, Target and J.C. Penney. That Gap was losing market share to these discounters is what prompted the opening of "warehouses" to sell a lower-priced collection. This represented nothing less than a seismic shift in how consumers shopped for their "casual" clothes. Indeed, when consumers found that the Gap's classic pocket T-shirt was available for about half the price at discount superstores and ordinary department stores, there was no incentive to purchase it, or anything else, full-price from the Gap any more.

It became painfully clear that the "Gap"—as a brand—held little intrinsic status among consumers insofar as they were responding to price above all else. The "Gap" was merely a collection of everyday clothes that were ordinary at best. At worst, moreover, value-minded consumers, regardless of income level, soon realized that "bargain" was a relative term: why pay full retail for Gap when everyone else had similar quality at lower prices?

The emergence of "discount chic" proved to be a terrifying development. While consumers turned away from the Gap in droves for the first time since its founding, to further complicate matters Mickey Drexler made the stunning misstep in 1993 of experimenting with "fashion" items. The Gap's success resided in its antifashion approach to clothes—casual, everyday clothes that one could wear year in and year out. When Mickey Drexler launched a fashion collection in 1993, it was not well received by consumers. Perhaps the pressure from falling sales prompted this decision, or it came from the realization that consumer attitudes had changed, or it rose out of desperation of losing market shares to discounters with a lower price point on identical merchandise. Whatever the reason, the Gap abandoned its antifashion stance with dismal results.

In direct defiance of the antifashion philosophy that had fueled unprecedented growth and success, the Gap launched a misguided line of so-called fashion items. The Gap, which had depended on jeans and casual clothes that were appropriate for denim and khaki pants, now embarked on a strategy of refurbishing its image by making the Gap "hip." This was an anathema to what had made Donald Fisher's approach so successful. By trying to be "hip," the Gap was now anything but hip. This second trend—Gap's misguided and disastrous foray into fashion—undoubtedly stunned Gap design teams throughout all divisions, which would sow self-doubt among individual designers and bitter internal recriminations among executives.

"The clothes were horrible," said a man in his thirties shopping at Abercrombie & Fitch. "I stopped shopping at the Gap around the time Bill Clinton became president. Gap clothes all of a sudden looked stupid." The "fashion" line of "stupid" clothes included things like *faux*-Western leather vests, leg warmers and other accessories that languished in the stores unsold.

If risk taking had proved to be a component instrumental to the Gap strategy pioneered by Donald Fisher, the excursion into "fashion," however, was nothing less than reckless. To be sure, Gap was overwhelmed with exciting new projects in 1994 and 1995, specifically the launching of Old Navy and Gap Scents in 1994, the third "repositioning" of Banana Republic, and the introduction of Gap Body Care.

With so many projects unfolding with daunting speed, it was not immediately obvious that almost all the "fashion" lines were largely unsold. What proved ironic, of course, was that most of the "fashion" items that bombed at the Gap were quickly shipped to Gap Warehouse where they were discounted as much as necessary just to get rid of them. Gap executives were worried, however. If the purpose of introducing a line of full-priced fashion clothes had been to shore up the profit margins that had been decimated by the unprecedented price cutting of Gap's line of basics and to "reposition" the Gap in the mind of consumers, then neither objective had been met to anyone's satisfaction. Consumers were still deserting the Gap and all other full-price retailers to the discounters, and few were interested in "fashion" from the Gap.

The grim reality was now clear for all to see: Mickey Drexler's failed experiment in "fashion" was costing Gap huge sums of lost profits by having to discount the unsold merchandise. It was money Gap Warehouses could very well use to expand further, but there was always that caveat: If one sells at a loss or reduced profit, what's the point of selling at all?

The third and final trend in the first half of the nineties was the consolidation of Generation Y's indifference to the Gap. Americans who became teenage consumers in the nineties dismissed the Gap as both "uncool" and too closely linked with the respectability of the establishment, meaning their parents, the middle-aged baby boomers. In fact, the Gap was what their parents—and grandparents—wore and embraced, enough reason for any self-respecting teenager to opt out of what members of Generation Y dismissively mocked as "Gap World" altogether.

"Gap World" had become a complicated universe by the end of 1993, however. Gap Body Care was underperforming. Gap Shoes had been a terrible disappointment. Radical surgery was still underway at Banana Republic, where it seemed as if the "under-repositioning" shingle had been hung out forever-and-a-day. Gap Kids and Baby Gap were both on course, to everyone's relief, generating money and causing little troubles for top executives. It was Gap and Gap Warehouse, however, which were on a collision course.

"It's like Dr. Jekyll and Mr. Hyde," one Gap manager said. "The Gap is spinning its wheels, digging itself deeper in the sand. On the other hand,

Gap Warehouse is unstoppable. The last time I saw anything like this was when Aca Joe almost went out of business and they got rid of their entire inventory at the Civic Center [in San Francisco during the eighties]."

This was one way of looking at things: Gap could only sell the Gap if it was discounted and in a warehouse setting. The dilemma confronting Donald Fisher and Mickey Drexler could be summed up with one question: Is discount retailing the logical conclusion of the antifashion revolution?

Gap was about to find out.

In the wake of the Mickey Drexler's fiasco selling fashion at the Gap, in 1994 three Gap Warehouse–style stores opened up but under the name "Old Navy Clothing Co." The small cities of San Leandro and Pittsburgh were working-class suburbs of San Francisco. Colma was a retirement community best known for its strip of car dealerships—and cemeteries. All were within a few miles of Gap, Inc.'s headquarters, where managers could monitor and fine-tune this experiment with the lower-end retailing market. All three are, in essence, bedroom communities near San Francisco whose residents are similar to consumers found in suburbs and rural communities around the country. Old Navy would help Gap make inroads by competing directly against Wal-Mart, Target, Ross and the other discounters on their own turf.

Old Navy Clothing Co., which was the new name of Gap Warehouse once it was set up as a separate division, was an unprecedented hit with young people. The only downside was that if youngsters flocked to the Old Navy, then they weren't flocking to the Gap. It was with unintended irony, therefore, that the entire crisis confronting the Gap in the mid-nineties could best be summed up in the slogan embraced by Old Navy as its own: "Shopping is fun again."[1] That is to say, shopping is no longer fun at the Gap.

Gap was no longer fun for Donald Fisher either. The relentless "repositioning" of the Gap and the explosive growth through expansion programs at existing divisions and the launching of new ones demanded more and more work and responsibility at a time in his life when Donald Fisher wanted to enjoy the fruits of his labor and pursue more philanthropic and leisurely interests.

The spectacular growth of the Gap in the mid-nineties—growth that generated impressive increases in revenue through expansion of new divisions and market lines but that only masked the disappointing flat same-store sales at Gap and faltering sales at Banana Republic—required dedicated executives who could oversee the expanding retailing empire. Mickey Drexler, who had been named president of Gap, Inc. in 1987, now replaced Donald Fisher as CEO of Gap, Inc. in 1995 as well. Donald Fisher remained the chairman of the board, affording him the freedom to focus on the grand vision of the Gap and the direction of its brand, while allowing him to pursue other activities outside the firm.

Mickey Drexler's ascendance to the top post, however, required some-one to take the fall for the undeniable fact that fewer consumers were fall-ing into the Gap. It would be unthinkable for Mickey Drexler to be promoted for having blundered into the fashion mishap at Gap and for fail-ing to revive sales at Gap's core division.

The calculated "callousness" for which Donald Fisher was notorious among New York industry observers came into play in a heavy-handed manner. Within a few months of Mickey Drexler becoming the CEO of Gap, Inc., Magdalene "Maggie" Gross, who headed Gap, Inc.'s in-house adver-tising teams, resigned. Her duties were taken over by Michael McCadden, who was recruited from Calvin Klein where he had been responsible for global advertising of Calvin Klein cologne, transforming that brand into a success. It was an unfortunate turn of events, one that left industry observ-ers stunned at how shabbily the woman who had transformed the various Gap divisions into one cohesive brand identity was treated.

Maggie Gross joined Gap when her boss at Ann Taylor, Mickey Drexler himself, was hired by Donald Fisher to head the Gap division. This was in 1983, the same year Gap bought Banana Republic and the year before Pot-tery Barn was acquired. Maggie Gross ran Gap's in-house advertising divi-sion, which had won accolades and praise from the entire industry. She was responsible for creating a single and singular image for a company that sold blue jeans and pith helmets—and whatever housewares it was that Pottery Barn struggled to move out the door. To manage such a monumental un-dertaking, Maggie Gross was known as a demanding, but fair, boss.

"It was wonderful working with her," a Gap executive reminisced. "She had the discipline necessary to remain focused on how an image should be projected to consumers. She set high standards for everyone and what she managed to pull off in those tumultuous eighties was astounding. She had to listen to what Donald Fisher said, what Mickey Drexler wanted, what Mel and Patricia Ziegler dreamed up, then articulate a coherent advertising campaign for Gap and Banana Republic. Of course there were some com-plaints about her being 'tough.' But then again, when a man is 'tough,' that's a compliment. When a woman is 'tough,' that's another way of call-ing her a 'bitch.' Sexism in corporate America is what it is, I suppose."

Maggie Gross was also breaking ground for women, showing that a female executive could be as effective as her male counterparts. What made her achievements more commendable was that on top of the disparate vi-sions and demands the emerging Gap family of brands demanded, she was largely credited for creating a unifying vision and brand identity. Consider, for instance, the successful advertising campaign that helped launch Baby Gap and Gap Kids, making both new divisions seem like natural and effort-less offshoots of what consumers thought of when they thought of the Gap. If this wasn't enough of a challenge, she also had to distance the company from the failed acquisition of Pottery Barn, the disastrous experiment with

Hemisphere, and the misstep with Gap Shoes. What helped make everything come together, however, was the simplicity of her approach to the tasks before her.

If the only intellectual achievement of Gap had been the introduction of the pocket T-shirt in 1984, then it was in the simplicity of this garment upon which the image of the Gap would be built. As an article of clothing, it required an article of faith to make it work. It was the simplicity of a T-shirt, however, that spoke of a creative genius. Whereas throughout the seventies, Gap focused on its success at merchandising blue jeans, the expansion of the line into khakis—beige and tan workday twill and cloth trousers—made the task of creating a cohesive image more difficult.

"Everything goes with blue jeans," a source at Levi Strauss & Co. said. "But when you get into khakis, it's a different ball game altogether. We learned that when we launched our Dockers® pants."

The lessons learned from developing an advertising campaign for Gap Kids in 1986 lent themselves nicely to incorporating the vision of a simple and spare identity for the Gap. Maggie Gross was smitten with the idea of showcasing the pocket T-shirt into a central theme from which other campaigns would be built. In 1986 Gap introduced a new logo. The new logo was clean and crisp.

"The advertising was great," a fashion writer in New York remarked of the Gap in the mid-nineties. "But the clothes were awful. That's why no one shopped at the Gap anymore back then; the same stuff was off-price elsewhere."

That was the problem then: Maggie Gross's advertising brought people into the stores, but they didn't like the Mickey Drexler clothes they saw when they got there. No amount of advertising could convince consumers to buy clothes that were unattractive and collections that they didn't understand. In the same way that Levi's stumbled its way through a learning curve when it introduced Dockers®, Gap was finding out for itself that its success with blue jeans was not transferable to khakis. This was the problem Maggie Gross confronted when she first arrived at Gap.

"The design teams at the Gap were clearly influenced by the turmoil at Banana Republic," one observer noted of the Gap clothes in the mid-eighties. "But the truth is that the *Out of Africa* and *Indiana Jones* [themes] were completely off the radar screens of consumers. And the Gap was left without an idea about where to go from there."

Matters had been further complicated back then by how consumer rejection of the fanciful European-style sportswear at Hemisphere, a failed division that closed in 1989, impacted Gap's designers. All this turmoil made Maggie Gross's job that much more difficult as the eighties drew to a close. The Gap's then-current lines reflected the struggles retailers encounter when merchandising khakis in a vacuum.

Maggie Gross was gripped by a sense of *déjà vu* in 1995 and she moved on. Hemisphere was a memory quickly fading into history. Gap Shoes followed suit three years later and was brushed aside. Gap Body Scents was a great unknown with its own set of challenges as the nineties progressed. And the transformation of Gap Warehouse into Old Navy was an experiment that would lead into the great retailing unknown. What was clear to everyone, however, was that in 1995 the Gap was once more in crisis.

"Individuals of style" was a campaign Maggie Gross launched in 1988 in response to the panic engulfing Gap. She was determined to rise above the corporate fray and concentrate on advertising. The campaign featured a stunning series of black-and-white photographs of the famous and noteworthy wearing Gap clothes. Whether it was Dizzy Gillespie wearing a Gap mock turtleneck with the tag line, "Full blown," or Kim Basinger in a white Gap men's shirt falling off her shoulder adorned with the single word, "Power," the campaign was a such a hit that it was covered as *news*.

Kudos for the Gap, was the resounding and overwhelming consensus within the advertising industry. When a series of simple and crisp ads for the pocket T-shirt was developed, it became the quintessential antifashion statement to the excesses of the "Go-Go" eighties. The conspicuous consumption best exemplified by Nancy Reagan's White House china crisis and the vulgar excesses of Donald and Ivana Trump had been answered in the simple garment introduced by the Gap.

"The advertising for the Gap at the end of the eighties was brilliant," Teri Agins, the reporter who covers fashion for the *Wall Street Journal*, remarked at the time. "It was the right campaign at the right moment."

No one could have been happier with this praise than Maggie Gross. Her success was not only a personal victory, but she became also a role model for other women executives. In short order, Maggie Gross broke through the stubborn salary barrier when she became one of the first female executives to receive a salary of one million dollars.

It was money well spent. Maggie Gross's monumental achievement was nothing less than building a uniform and consistent identity upon which a global "brand" could be built. She had inherited, in essence, a pocket T-shirt and with the new logo had pulled off a marketing coup.

The pocket T-shirt would become a hip response to the conspicuous consumption that characterized America as the Reagan White House replaced the frugality of the Carter administration. The Gap logo, too, reflected these changes. The original logo of 1969 was in lower-case type and curvilinear. The new design, for which Maggie Gross is largely credited, reflected the impact of several "repositionings" at Gap: it featured white lettering in an upper-case serif typeface suspended within a navy blue square.

Together the pocket T-shirt and the new Gap logo created a "visual identity" that could be used effectively to bring the disparate entities of Gap, Inc. under one brand. Despite the constant state of flux throughout the Gap, the constancy of the logo and the simplicity of the advertising master-minded by Maggie Gross made Gap a corporate "brand" in the minds of consumers. Both the logo and how consumers reacted to Gap as a brand became the envy of the retailing world.

The Gap's clothes, however, did not live up to the award-winning advertising. Detractors rolled their eyes and remarked that it was as if the same designers who had come out with the line for Baby Gap had been put in charge of the Gap as well. The complaint, loud and often sounded, in fact, was over the "infantalization" of casual clothes. This was, of course, consistent with Alison Lurie's observation of the impact of the Youth Culture of the sixties on how men and women dressed. If American society, in its embrace of "casual" clothes, was conducting itself in an aberrant manner, then the successive collections Gap now offered reflected the creeping influence of infants and children.

Gap was in yet another "reposition" mode as the nineties arrived. The Gap stopped selling Levi's® altogether in 1991 and there were structural problems once the market became saturated with similar "basic" lines of no-nonsense clothes: every retailer now had its own version of the pocket T-shirt.

The challenges, from an advertising perspective, were to differentiate the Gap from other retailers with similar product lines and create a visual identity for the brand on a company-wide level. If consumers could find no-nonsense clothes everywhere, then it became a no-profit proposition for retailers who had to compete on price. That is precisely what Gap had been forced to do in 1992.

Maggie Gross responded to the crisis of 1992 as she had to the crisis of 1988: with a terrific advertising campaign. The "Who wore khakis?" campaign in 1993, in an effort to boost sagging sales at the Gap stores, further defined the brand recognition for the Gap and created a consistent visual identity for the Gap brand. Once more, she had managed to make an advertising campaign into *news*, generating the kind of press coverage that won media attention from critics within the advertising industry and consumers alike, who were seduced by the visual immediacy of the entire campaign.

"We are in the business of selling clothes, not selling advertising," one source at Gap said at the time, a paraphrase of Donald Fisher's infamous remark when Mel and Patricia Ziegler were ousted from Banana Republic in 1988. "Maggie is a genius. Unfortunately for us she's not running the design teams coming up with the collections!"

Humphrey Bogart and Pablo Picasso wore khakis, true enough, but neither wore khakis from the Gap. That was precisely the problem: the clothes did not turn on consumers. Consider the sad commentary that Generation X-ers were more inclined to tear the "Who wore khakis?" ads from glossy magazine (and frame them) than they were to run over to the nearest Gap store and stock up.

If Gap had won the notorious reputation of co-opting aesthetics, raiding designers and talent from other companies and appropriating pop culture as its own, then something was terribly wrong for several reasons—and fashion seasons—since it seemed Gap could not find the right kind of talent to get the chemistry working right for the design teams.[2] Indeed, one collection after another faltered with a resounding thud and executives panicked at the sheer volume of merchandise that only left the stores after it either had been marked down or found its way to the Gap Warehouse.

"Isn't anyone willing to pay retail anymore?" one analyst at Merrill Lynch wondered in 1995. Wall Street was asking itself the same question. Gap Warehouse's reincarnation as Old Navy delighted investors, but the fact could not be ignored: discounting is discounting and discounting is a low-profit proposition. The comfort level began to evaporate rather quickly and many wondered if, as had occurred in 1992, the price of Gap shares would lose half their value.

It wasn't only Wall Street that was curious about what was happening at Gap. Americans on Main Street were scrutinizing the retailing, advertising and media industries as well. They didn't like what they were seeing. An unexpected complication in social and political terms emerged in the mid-nineties, as retailers came under criticism from consumer advocates and elected officials for what was seen as the shocking and irresponsible spread of advertising campaigns found in glossy magazines, television commercials and billboards across the United States that glamorized, what the pundits christened, "heroin chic."

Calvin Klein was the lightning rod for this criticism. The billboard with an emaciated waif-like Kate Moss seemed to celebrate—and promote among pubescent girls—eating disorders including anorexia and bulimia. Worse still were the stunning spreads in fashion magazines that portrayed young men and women, their clothes wrinkled and disheveled, lying prostrate on the floors of bathroom stalls, in trashed alleys and in proximity to objects that evoked drug paraphernalia. The advertising "look" of the mid-nineties, critics argued, embraced malnourishment, drug abuse and alluded to pedophilia.

It was a "look," as they say. However insidious and infuriating it might have been, it was a "look" that flashed in momentary brilliance across the landscape of the fashion world and afterward seemed regrettably stupid. It all outraged the American public. While Calvin Klein ads offered young women in Lolita-style sexual fantasies and presented young men as heroin users slumped against squalid toilets, Maggie Gross went no further (or controversial) than to present some rather androgynous-looking models wearing the new lines Gap was introducing.

This social and political controversy provided a perfect excuse to find a scapegoat, however. Maggie Gross was one way male arrogance in the executive suite protected itself. In an astounding display of the callousness with which the faltering sales at Gap were handled—and not without a definite sexism—Maggie Gross's advertising was blamed for the shortcomings of the Gap.

There was an undeniable element of misogyny when Maggie Gross was made the sacrificial lamb for Mickey Drexler's folly. When Gap, Inc. announced in April 1996 that Maggie Gross had taken a leave of absence for personal reasons, the only public comments from Gap officials at the time stated that this decision had been made ostensibly in response to the outcry from the "heroin chic" image of the previous season. No one believed it. Gap's woes weren't due to shooting heroin; they were due more to an overdose of Old Navy.

"Fisher and Drexler are sexists who cannot admit that they are responsible for Gap's misfortunes," fumed a top woman executive at a telecommunications company in San Francisco in the Crocker Galleria. "It's the same story everywhere: the good old boys taking care of their own—by blaming a woman."

The consensus within the retailing and advertising industries was that the only remotely valid criticism of Maggie Gross's management style, which most observers agreed was valid, was her iron hand in how she ran the advertising group. Executives throughout the advertising industry also often voiced the complaint that Maggie Gross would routinely ask advertising agencies to submit ideas for a campaign, not hire them, and then they would see some of these same ideas emerge in some fashion in Gap's advertising. These were minor flaws in an otherwise brilliant career at Gap. Three months after her leave took effect Maggie Gross resigned. (It seems hardly credible that an executive who had guided the development of Gap's brand for over a dozen years was so unceremoniously shown the door.) Michael McCadden, who was responsible for the global branding of Calvin Klein perfume, announced that Gap would spearhead a campaign directed at getting teenagers into the stores.

For many female executives throughout the fashion and advertising industries, Donald Fisher's and Mickey Drexler's treatment of Maggie Gross became a male chauvinist assault on all women. Women executives in northern California gasped in horror—and then were furious.

"Mickey Drexler and Donald Fisher were just looking for someone to blame for their collection of ugly clothes," a female executive who was at Levi Strauss & Co. at the time said. "They were so unfair and ungrateful. Maggie [Gross] did a *first*-class advertising job for a *second*-class line of clothes. They give her a stupid pocket T-shirt and a new logo, she makes miracles happen, and that's not enough! This is what men in business do all the time to us: they blame women for their own shortcomings and failure. It's testosterone and it's male pride and it's an injustice!"

Gap, Inc.'s credibility suffered a severe blow. If it was true that Donald Fisher and Mickey Drexler were taking a stand against irresponsible advertising and the "heroin chic" trend by firing Maggie Gross, then why was she replaced by Michael McCadden, who was an integral part of Calvin Klein's executives who glamorized these kinds of images? Many observers were convinced that the ongoing problems at Gap were the result of a maturing retailer that had lost resonance with young consumers.

It was 1997 and Gap was once again in a crisis. The fallout from the dismissal of Maggie Gross reverberated throughout the entire company. It also affected Donald Fisher deeply in a business sense and in unexpected personal ways. There were times when business and personal concerns collided. Indeed, tensions filled the boardroom, where Donald's wife, Doris, held a seat.

"I had never before seen her [Doris Fisher] so furious," confided a San Francisco hostess who had known Donald and Doris Fisher for many years. "Who can blame her for being angry? What Donald Fisher let Mickey Drexler do is an insult to all women! Men! All I can say is that Don's very, very lucky that Doris didn't smack him across the face for what he did to Maggie!"

Potential domestic violence notwithstanding, the controversy surrounding the resignation of Maggie Gross (and the refusal of Gap's press office to comment on the tensions among the Fishers that it is alleged to have caused) could not have come at a worse moment. Donald Fisher had expressed his desire to relinquish his day-to-day responsibilities in the increasingly far-flung (and perhaps over-extended) enterprise that Gap, Inc. had become.

With Maggie Gross taking the fall, a few months after being named CEO of Gap, Inc., Mickey Drexler announced that the Gap would "reposition" itself once more. Gap would go back to its roots by returning to its anti-fashion tradition that had served it so well in the past. The announcement that Gap would adopt a "back to basics" look represented a setback, and it raised the obvious question: Why had it strayed from a successful strategy in the first place?

When Mickey Drexler announced that the Gap would embark on a program to "reposition" itself and "refocus" on "basics," this was an admission that, from 1991 through the end of 1995, the Gap had been set adrift under his leadership. A year later there would be an attempt to rewrite this history. *Fortune* magazine reporter Nina Munk described these events in a more benign and sanitized manner:

One day in the summer of 1996, Drexler wandered slowly through a Gap store and was shocked. The clothes were ugly, the carpet was frayed, the fixtures looked cheap. Simplicity and cleanliness had been forgotten. But what he really hated that summer was a series of new Gap print ads that included a young, androgynous-looking man with long blond hair (unclean?), a pierced lip, and an attitude.[3]

This was his complaint? Potentially unclean hair? This in a summer in which Calvin Klein was criticized for advertisements that showed young men and women sprawled out in the stalls of public toilets, their clothes filthy, as if they had been shooting drugs or had been losers in a brawl or had just been raped? No one in the retail industry believed this official version of things.

"Mickey Drexler just 'wandered' through a store and 'discovered' what the Gap was selling? Give me a break! No one does anything at the Gap without that control-freak knowing about it!" a senior woman executive at Nordstrom stated, shaking her head in disbelief. "It was horrible the way they treated Maggie Gross. An absolute disgrace!"

Lisa Schultz, who had been responsible for the collections, was now charged with the overhaul of all the Gap's lines and given a much higher profile within the company. This was as much to atone for the inexcusable injustice against women as it was to arrest the state of suspended animation in which Gap found itself. Her instructions were: Take the Gap back to the future, which is to say, forward to the past.

Simplicity was the *word*. Fabulous was the *way*. The saving grace would be the *fabulosity* of *simplicity*.

Thus Lisa Schultz, who had worked for Ralph Lauren and Calvin Klein before joining Gap in the late eighties, now embarked on a radical program to get rid of anything that did not fit in with the Gap's traditional antifashion approach to casual clothes.

"We have to focus on simplicity. We have to find clear and crisp statements," she said to her top designers at the end of 1996.

And nice clothes, too. This was the word and the way.

There was an extraordinary amount of realignment at Gap in 1997 in response to the crisis. As Donald Fisher stepped aside as CEO of Gap, Inc., his sons, who were still resented by those who believed the Zieglers paid for their alleged mistakes at Banana Republic, also took center stage. William Fisher was put in charge of Gap, Inc.'s international operations and Robert Fisher became CEO of the Gap division.

With the new management players in place and with Lisa Schultz given her antifashion orders, off the design teams went! It is not without irony, therefore, that the same principles Maggie Gross had applied to the Gap's advertising were now being re-applied to the Gap's clothing business: the clear, crisp and simple.

"In a country where people are slobs, how difficult can it really be to 'design' sweats and T-shirts?" a contributing editor at W magazine rhetorically posed, amused at the unending string of "crises."

Back to basics meant doing away with any pretense to fashion. Introducing new "collections" every other month or so, Lisa Schultz thrust herself in an aggressive program to give consumers an explosion of choice.

"We need to see what works, to use colors in an easy way," Lisa Schultz explained. "This summer it is an explosion of blue and lots of white. It is white, white, white."

The year was 1997 when all of New York was still dressed in black, black, black, and the Gap stores were empty, empty, empty. No explosion of sales matched the explosion of color as the Gap pondered the metaphysical question: If one opens a store and no one enters, does the cash register make a sound?

Changing the clothes *alone* was not enough. What the Gap needed was exciting advertising to entice people to come back into the stores and check out all the new antifashion clothes everywhere. If only Maggie Gross had been around, it would have been easier.

After a five-year hiatus, the Gap returned to television commercials with the rapper LL Cool J. The television commercials, in fact, were inspired by Maggie Gross's print ads that had proved so successful.

With clean white backgrounds and the prominent logo, the ads attempted to seduce young people once more. In 1998, in fact, the "Khakis swing," "Khakis groove" and "Khakis rock" commercials were cited as among the best. The post-Gross Gap advertising didn't win much *public* praise, however, which itself constituted a powerful testament to the visual identify fostered for the Gap brand under her guidance. But having spectacular advertising meant nothing if the product did not impress customers.

Through this massive advertising campaign in magazines and on billboards, by the end of the summer of that year, things were coming together and sales were rising—sharply throughout the nation. The television commercials caused excitement and people began to visit the Gap in greater numbers. When they walked through the doors, moreover, all of Mickey Drexler's fashion was nowhere to be seen and stacked on the tables and folded in cabinets that lined the walls were simple, comfortable, casual clothes that were absent of all pretense. Same-store sales shot up almost 6 percent, something that had not happened in over a decade (same-store sales are sales at stores opened at least one year). These figures are an important indicator of a retailer's actual business because they exclude results at closed locations or stores recently opened. The Gap, analysts declared uniformly, was back where it had been: leading the antifashion revolution.

The media blitz further worked to showcase the positive changes at the Gap. *Time* magazine was taken by such surprise that it named Lisa Schultz as one of the twenty-five most influential Americans in 1997. It was ironic, however, that she was described as a "fashion arbiter," when in fact she was the opposite: an "antifashion arbiter." That the editors of *Time* magazine didn't understand the dynamics of the Gap's successful business philosophy only underscored the subtlety of the changes in American retailing since the seventies, and how these changes had affected the terms of retailing. *Time* magazine, however, was right on target in stating that "the Gap is an illusion."

Insofar as sustained success proved elusive and the cyclical pattern of "crises" was evidence of little brand loyalty to "Gap," what progress was made proved momentary. The television commercials and the simpler clothes resulted in a fleeting boost to Gap sales. Generation Y remained unconvinced that this was any longer the happening label or style or place in which to be seen. Gap sales became sluggish again by the end of 1998. Wall Street continued to punish the stock in 1998 the way it had during the "repositioning" of 1992.

There were problems with the core business on all fronts. Lisa Schultz's clothes were not as exciting as Gap's advertising. The explosive expansion of Old Navy served to highlight further the dismal performance of the Gap; and the Gap stores overseas were stagnant. The situation continued to deteriorate quarter after quarter in 1998. By the time 1999 rolled around, it was no longer a question of a simple "repositioning," but rather one of re-animating: Gap was stuck in a frustrating state of suspended animation, with its reputation faltering a little bit more with each passing day.

A perspective is in order. While there were consistent problems at the Gap's core business, Old Navy was moving full-steam ahead. As we shall see in the chapter that addresses the Old Navy division, up until mid-2000, Old Navy could do no wrong. This was the assessment on Wall Street, which is why investors rewarded the Gap's stock. Old Navy was such a cash cow that whatever problems may have been detracting from the Gap's core business, investors were not concerned for the most part. Consider how Gap stock fared in the wake of Old Navy's success. On July 1, 1997, Gap stock closed at 39⅛. It rose steadily, closing at 62¹⁵⁄₁₆ exactly one year later.

The problems of that summer—the white, white, white summer when everyone was still wearing black, black, black—caused great concern as sales at the Gap failed to pick up. "Sluggish sales" became a common refrain as the stock began to weaken and by October 1, 1998, Gap stock closed at 48³⁄₁₆. Investors were assured that the Gap's core business would be successfully "repositioned" and, more importantly, Banana Republic had finally gotten its act together. Old Navy and Banana Republic continued to perform exceptionally well, so much so that investors' concerns were assuaged. Gap stock resumed its ascent in the final quarter of 1998 after a disappointing fall.

As 1999 unfolded, however, despite the success the dynamic duo of Banana Republic and Old Navy continued to be, it could no longer be denied that the problems at the Gap's core business persisted to the bafflement of observers. The Gap, a store that Teri Agins at the *Wall Street Journal* had praised as a retailing "sensation," appeared to have lost its magic touch. Sales continued to be stubbornly, inexplicably, exasperatingly sluggish—and no one knew why. There were theories galore: collections failed to connect with the public, prices at Old Navy were pulling from the Gap's traditional customer base, fashion forays were off the mark, and Generation Y had grown up on MTV and connected to clothing in a different way.

No one could say for sure. Wall Street analysts, however, began to question what they, for lack of a better characterization, began to call the "troubling trend" at the Gap stores. The undeniable weakening of same-store sales impacted negatively on the Gap as investors grew uneasy. By July 1, 1999, the stock began its retreat from its all-time high, attained with the euphoria surrounding the success of Old Navy. The stock closed that day at 50. The Gap entered a downward spiral and continued to slip through the summer. The results were disappointing for the crucial "back to school" month of August as well.

Rumors circulated that a management shake-up was necessary. Gap stock drifted lower and lower throughout the fall and hovered around the mid-30s amid fears, gossip and speculation. With no convincing explanation to account for the Gap's sluggish sales during a time of robust growth for Old Navy and Banana Republic, Robert Fisher announced his resignation as president of the Gap division. Consider the collective sigh of relief expressed by Wall Street at this piece of news. Gap stock had closed at 34⅛ on October 28, 1999. Robert Fisher announced his resignation the next day. Gap stock immediately jumped almost 10 percent in a frenzy of trading that very day to close at 37⅛.

It was a confusing situation, to be sure. Old Navy continued to be praised as the *new* retailing sensation. Analysts showered accolades on Jeanne Jackson and her splendid turnaround at Banana Republic. So why was the stock price so volatile throughout 1999? If things were so terrific, investors wondered, what was going on at the Gap's core business. "The stock had lost almost half its value by the fall of 1999 compared with the fall of 1998," a retired investor who checked his portfolio at the offices of Charles Schwab on Montgomery Street in downtown San Francisco complained. "What's going on with that company? How can they be opening more and more stores every day and their stock is just getting clobbered by the market? It doesn't make any sense. I should have sold a year ago!"

This sentiment was echoed by institutional investors throughout Wall Street and in San Francisco. There had to be significant management changes to try to arrest the faltering investor confidence in Gap's ability to pull things off. Success at Old Navy and Banana Republic was not enough: the Gap had to contribute to the bottom line. As Gap, Inc. grew, the question of succession emerged as a consideration. What would become of the Fishers? With the resignation of Robert Fisher, no one from the Fisher family was now involved in the day-to-day operations of Gap, Inc.

Perhaps mindful of the failure of Fred Pressman to replace his sons before they drove the once-fabled Barneys store into bankruptcy, Donald Fisher was not about to make the same mistakes. If outside talent was needed to run Gap, Inc. properly, then outside talent he would recruit. (William Fisher was first to go. In 1998 he resigned from Gap, Inc. and is no longer connected with the company.)

Robert Fisher used to brag to anyone within hearing distance that the difference between Levi Strauss & Co. and Gap, Inc. was that the Gap was fully in control of the distribution of its entire line. Whereas a pair of Levi's® could very well end up in the discount bin of some unknown store somewhere, a pair of Gap jeans would never suffer such a humiliating fate. But he was mistaken about that, as we shall see, for to Generation Y consumers Old Navy was nothing but an enormous walk-in discount bin for the Gap. In fact, as will be shown in chapter 7, the failure of the Gap to arrest its decline between 1997 and 2000 was indicative of how completely it had not grasped the imagination of Generation Y. This generation of American consumers realized the Gap was a full-price version of Old Navy.

When asked to comment about these observations, Maggie Gross replied, "No comment."

She didn't have to say anything.

6

THE TRIUMPH OF THE PLANET OF THE BANANA-REPUBLICANS

Banana Republic itself remained adrift, lost on a sea of confusion and consumed by an identity crisis, a crisis that stretched from the ouster of Mel and Patricia Ziegler through a series of failed attempts to "reposition" itself through 1995. The famous safari look of Patricia and Mel Ziegler had been unceremoniously dropped in 1988, of course, and Tasha Polizzi's line had bombed with an unfabulous thud, sending shockwaves through the corridors of Gap, Inc. For the next six long years of anemic growth, Banana Republic meandered about, not so much treading water as losing ground. The clothes were uninspired and the designers charged with coming up with the collection suffered from low morale.

"Banana Republic had no vision of itself," said an executive who left at the end of the eighties. "No matter how talented the members of the design team were, without some sense of what they were supposed to do, whatever they did was only an improvisation."

"Improvising" is not the most effective manner of building either an identity or a brand. But the fundamental question remained unanswered: What was the *purpose* of Banana Republic?

Was it simply a horrible and mistaken approach to diversification, as purchasing Pottery Barn had been? Was it Donald Fisher's stubborn insistence on building a brand that would win respect from the industry observers on Seventh Avenue? Or was it the means through which an upscale version of the Gap could be developed in order to establish a presence in a high-end—and high mark-up—market?

The answer was a combination of classic stubbornness, desire and greed. Donald Fisher was determined to make it in the high-end market, to gain the respectability of the arbiters of taste who had dismissed the Gap for two decades, and to reach into the disposable incomes of young urban dwellers. The economic expansion of the second half of the nineties meant fat wallets—and it proved to be too irresistible of a temptation from which to walk away.

The "purpose" for Banana Republic to exist, which had proved elusive for so many years, now materialized with breathtaking clarity: the deadly sin of greed. How the quest for riches through upscale rags came to pass, however, is a story of accidental brilliance, encapsulated in one word: "banana." It was in those six letters that the wayward division found a coherent focus. If Patricia and Mel Ziegler presented a romantic view of the adventure of travel through their safari clothing, and if Tasha Polizzi was prescient in identifying homosexual aesthetics as the fashion look that would dominate American fashion as it entered the twenty-first century, then there had to be a vision that reconciled Banana Republic's past and the undeniable inevitability of the future. The accidental brilliance was in nurturing an *evolution* between these competing looks.

But going from a "safari travel" to a "metro" and "urban" wardrobe is one enormous leap on the evolutionary scale. One does not walk out of some savanna of the Serengeti and fit right in among the skyscrapers surrounding the ice rink at Rockefeller Center just like that, or does one?

Of course not. Not unlike human biological evolution, giant leaps forward are rare. Smaller steps along the way are far more common. Stepping out of a bush plane among the likes of Ernest Hemingway is a different world from stepping out of a taxi with Audrey Hepburn. For Banana Republic's own tortured and aimless evolution since its acquisition by Gap, Inc., where's the missing link?

"When we were filming *Planet of the Apes*," Kim Hunter is quoted as saying, "Roddy [McDowall] took a keen interest in the wardrobes that the chimpanzees wore. He had definite ideas about how the chimpanzees should dress and look in that distant future."

Roddy McDowall portrayed Cornelius, and Kim Hunter interpreted Dr. Zira in the *Planet of the Apes* series of films, the first of which was directed by Franklin J. Schaffner, and was released in 1968 by 20th Century-Fox. Recall for a moment those campy sci-fi films. In *Planet of the Apes* the gorillas wore drab militaristic uniforms and the orangutans wore unimaginative over-sized casual outfits in garish colors. It was the chimpanzees alone who had any sense of style, taste or fashion on that hairy planet of some dismal future.

"I didn't care what the gorillas wore or what the dress of the orangutans looked like," Roddy McDowall himself once said. "But I wanted to make sure that it was the chimpanzees who were at the forefront of making an appropriate fashion statement on the set, regardless of what anything else in the 'future' looked like. The chimpanzees had to be fabulous."

Roddy McDowall's discerning eye influenced how the most chic inhabitants of the safari-like landscape and mindscape of *Planet of the Apes* dressed, and he carried it off with a true gay's panache. In that sci-fi film series, the gorillas wore militaristic outfits and the orangutans wore "nutty professor" clothes. The chimpanzees, on the other hand, wore smart, close-fitting minimalist clothes that were simian versions of the style favored by Giorgio Armani. The initial Banana Republic collection designed by Tasha Polizzi, in retrospect, in fact resembled, to an uncanny and creepy degree, the outfits the chimpanzees wore in *Planet of the Apes*.

The other force simultaneously unfolding at Banana Republic was the realization that gay aesthetics were very much an urban phenomenon. The overwhelming majority of gays and lesbians lived in cities. Whatever "look" Banana Republic would present to the world, it had to reflect the demographics of an urban reality, coupled with the ironic campiness of a vision of what the future would be like, as interpreted by Hollywood primates, right?

That future was not one in which the real world was ruled by apes, of course. America in the nineties was a world in which urban dwellers led fast-paced lives and workplace dress rules embraced—and encouraged—a dressed-down look. The antifashion revolution celebrated and promoted by Gap had taken deep root; even the sanctuaries of propriety at private clubs throughout New York were forced to relax their rules about members' attire. The only reason the rules were modified at places like the Harvard, Yale, Cornell and Princeton clubs, after all, was economics: the clubs needed to have the current generation of Ivy Leaguers use the facilities and it was clear that they would only do so if they were not forced to dress in a certain way.

It is therefore more poetic than facetious to argue that the evolving aesthetics of Banana Republic, as articulated by the visionary Roddy McDowall, captured the sensibilities of that very conflicted brand at the dawn of the twenty-first century. The evolving look of Banana Republic collections since the mid-nineties is consistent with gay campiness and sci-fi aesthetics of the sixties.[1]

Primates may not be edifying role models, but they are better than improvising. To spearhead this third overhaul of Banana Republic, Gap turned to Jeanne Jackson, who was then president of Victoria's Secret. When she was named president of Banana Republic in 1995, that division had annual sales approaching $650 million, making her one of the most important female corporate executives in northern California. She was active on the social scene in San Francisco, whether attending fashion shows with New York socialites such as Nan Kempner or cavorting with local luminaries like Harry de Wildt.

It was Jeanne Jackson who was likely to attend fundraisers for the San Francisco Museum of Modern Art as well as a fashion show by Oscar de la Renta. Always, everywhere, it was Jeanne Jackson, the "ambassador from Banana Republic" to the "republic of ladies wearing Agnès B and Chanel," who cut a high profile among arbiters of taste in San Francisco social circles. This exposure and social visibility was crucial. Banana Republic needed the right kind of attention, attention from those who mattered, to be—finally—taken seriously. This was a prerequisite if Jeanne Jackson was to engineer a successful "repositioning."

A San Francisco society hostess expressed it this way: "Jeanne is a lovely woman, but let's face it: she used to sell dirty underwear to loose girls! There is a certain thrill in having her attend any of these parties and soirées and things, I mean, selling underwear is semi-pornographic, isn't it? That's what made it such fun, because it was such a naughty thing to do! Whatever she was doing at that Banana store, well, that sounds even *more* scandalous than selling dirty underwear! A 'Banana' store is outright pornographic! Oh, if it were! Pornography is still naughty, isn't it?"

Whether Victoria's Secret is semi-pornographic or merely titillating is beside the point. Donald Fisher was convinced that Jeanne Jackson's business acumen and marketing skills would prove invaluable as Banana Republic sought to reposition itself, revolutionize upscale merchandising and take the retailing world by storm. Donald Fisher, quite simply, wanted to cause a sensation that translated to sales, sales, sales.

"It was made very clear to Jeanne," one source at Banana Republic confided, "that she was given tremendous discretion to turn around [Banana Republic] however she thought best, but the litmus test would be sales at the cash register. Don Fisher made it very clear that at the end of the day, it was the day's sales that would make or break her tenure at Banana Republic."

In other words, Donald Fisher didn't care how many parties and benefits with social "x-rays" and prissy closet cases she attended provided that sales were sustained and profitable growth was recorded at the repositioned Banana Republic division. Jeanne Jackson took charge with tremendous enthusiasm and hit the floor running. The distraught and demoralized designers were now given a focused mission: create an urban line of clothing that professional men and women could wear in a corporate setting.

The inspiration of Roddy McDowall as Cornelius loomed large over the Banana-Republicans. "We had this mental block: no matter what Jeanne said, we still kept reverting to the images of the safari look that Banana Republic had once been," a designer on staff when Jeanne Jackson came aboard told me. "That was always our spiritual starting point, and it impacted how we saw the 'Manhattanization' of where we wanted our customers' environment to be."

The "starting point" remained *Out of Africa* romance, and it impacted the urbanization of the Banana Republic look. It was, as one source confided, not always an unconscious association: "Behind her back, a few of the catty queens mocked Jeanne Jackson as 'Dr. Zira'!" To understand how Jeanne Jackson's objective of urbanizing Banana Republic might very well be interpreted, consider the insights offered by Alison Lurie:

Clothes worn on the job, for instance, are supposed to downplay rather than flaunt sexuality, and to conceal any specialized erotic tastes completely. . . . Antisexual clothes may also be imposed by an external authority. . . . As [Robert] Herrick points out, looseness and disorder in dress are erotically appealing. Soft, flowing, warm-hued clothes traditionally suggest a warm, informal, affectionate personality, and the garment that is partially unfastened not only reveals more flesh but implies that total nakedness will be easily achieved. Excessive neatness, on the other hand, suggests an excessively well-controlled, possibly repressed personality.[2]

At first it might appear that these observations stand in contrast to what one normally associates with homosexual preferences in clothing as they have evolved in American mainstream society since the Stonewall riots. What Alison Lurie characterized as "antisexual" clothing is, in fact, gender-neutral. When one considers the androgynous look in the primal ape future as conceived by Roddy McDowall three decades before the arrival of Jeanne Jackson, then one can make sense of the fashion look driving the evolution of the clothes one finds at Banana Republic at the dawn of the twenty-first century.

The cuts were close fitting, the colors mimicked industrial hues, the tailoring was unadorned and the aesthetics resembled those associated with space travel, almost as if the crew of the *Starship Enterprise* shopped at Banana Republic for their casual clothes. The transfiguration of safari clothing into urban wear was managed over successive collections that were focused—and right on target. To be sure, there was a connection across the decades, and each successive collection at Banana Republic reflected the cool metallic hues and the minimalist androgynous lines often associated with Giorgio Armani and futuristic space travel.

One need only look at the bland but "repositioned" Banana Republic catalog. The fabled catalog of Mel and Patricia Ziegler had, of course, been abandoned in 1987 and was revived eleven years later in 1998. The new Banana Republic catalog, however, was a far cry from the original one. Jeanne Jackson's version of the catalog was, arguably, an uninspired piece of work. The look was reminiscent of the failed Aca Joe foray into supersonic expansion that faltered in the late eighties.[3] The content resembled what might occur if the closets of J. Crew were to meet the closets of Prada, if one can imagine what the offspring of such a union might look like. One need not imagine, however.

Consider the logical conclusion of the emerging gay urban vision of the future for a moment. The clothes found in the Banana Republic catalog now are invariably described as "urban" and "metro." They are the contemporary uniforms of American urban gays presented in the industrial hues of black, gray and blue, traditionally associated with the emergence of the Industrial Revolution and so often seen throughout the corridors of corporate America since the fifties. Indeed, in the first Banana Republic catalog of the year 2000, there it is for all to see: for women one finds the lightweight wool zip jacket (page 13), the hidden zip leather jacket (page 15) and the silk hook and eye shirt jacket (page 22); and for men there are the leather zip front jacket (page 55), the snap front drawstring shirt (page 60) and the sueded knit seamed polo (page 62). Each and every piece of clothing resembles the stark and minimalist cuts so familiar as futuristic perceptions in popular culture. Anyone from the cast of *Star Trek* or *Lost in Space* (or *Planet of the Apes* for that matter) could very well saunter aboard any spaceship and fit in perfectly. These clothes are the mainstream versions of "circuit party" wardrobes popular among gay men.

Voila!

These are smart wardrobes of quality materials, pleasing to the eye in the sedate colors appropriate to an urban cityscape. The fashionistas may not have been impressed at Banana Republic's imitation Gucci collection of clothes, but each and every piece is the *prêt-à-porter* clothing Roddy McDowall—or any chimpanzee on the *Planet of the Apes*—would be proud to wear. Or, for that matter, young urban professionals of either gender and every sexual persuasion.

"What we are finding," Jeanne Jackson said, "is that we are having a difficult time keeping up with the customer demand in the larger urban markets. The lines we are introducing are so well received it is making it difficult to serve customers adequately."[4]

Banana Republic was imitation Prada and Gucci at a lower price point— and it was hot once more. It had not seen this kind of excitement since the early days when Mel and Patricia Ziegler carried on in their delusional high jinx reminiscent of Victorian imperialism and social Darwinism. Who would have thought that Roddy McDowall's vision of the future had been right on the mark, for it was he, of all people, in his life-long role of *homo fashionus*, who turned out to be Banana Republic's missing link?

The cash registers at the repositioned Banana Republic in fact begin to register—after six dismal years—the kind of success that pleased Donald Fisher. Indeed, Banana Republic was on the road to a winning formula. Within the first year, sales shot up almost 10 percent, and kept shooting up at healthy clips throughout the remainder of the nineties.

"We are back on the right track," Donald Fisher said, summing up his assessment of Jeanne Jackson's accomplishments at "repositioning" Banana Republic. "We've come a long way," he added. "We are closer to achieving our goals. We are very pleased with the strides made by everyone at Banana Republic."

That these were clothes inspired by chimpanzees for made-to-order contemporary urbanites was beside the point: the financial results at Banana Republic emboldened Donald Fisher and Mickey Drexler, both of whom became much more enthusiastic about the division. In the first quarter of 1997 Gap, Inc. announced that Banana Republic would add thirty new stores, including four large showcase stores that would carry new products available only at "flagship" stores. To sustain the excitement generated, flagship stores were opened on Michigan Avenue in Chicago, King Kalakaua Plaza in Waikiki, Sutter and Grant streets in San Francisco, and Caesar's Forum in Las Vegas.

There was still, however, an unspoken separation between Banana Republic and the other Gap divisions that first began in 1989 when Tasha Polizzi launched the homoerotic "My chosen family" campaign. When Jeanne Jackson took over Banana Republic the consensus was that it had to remain "youthful"—a code word for young and straight. But the evolving urban metro "look" of Banana Republic, particularly since 1997, became so homoerotic that it was completely embraced by the gay subculture with such enthusiasm that it became a stereotype.

"There's been a dramatic change [in San Francisco gay bars]," said Morgan Gorrono, the owner of the gay/biker/leather bar A Hole in the Wall, speaking about the changes he implemented when he bought the San Francisco Eagle, a gay leather fetish bar that is an institution, and converted it into the Eagle Tavern. "The leather curtains have come down. We're now dealing with people who court on computers and then come to the bars to meet. Bars are more socialized and mixed. You can have a guy in full leather next to someone in Banana Republic."[5]

Within the gay subculture, fetish, kinky sex is associated with a leather uniform—leather chaps, harnesses, boots and jackets—and at the other extreme is the "vanilla" sex of twinkies, who are best portrayed by the gay characters on the television sitcom *Will & Grace*. The banality of the latter's uniform *de rigueur* comes off the rack from Banana Republic.[6]

That Banana Republic had come to occupy such a central place in the gay universe was not lost on Gap executives, who feared this fast association with homosexuality was beginning to alienate heterosexual men. "This has nothing to do with homophobia, but there is a decorum that is missing," an insider explained. "At Abercrombie & Fitch, the salesmen act like men and the saleswomen act like women. But at Banana Republic, it's a different world altogether."

Whatever reservations Gap executives might have had vanished like the city's early morning fog for the simple reason that Jeanne Jackson's strategy was an undisputed winner. Banana Republic flagship stores were beautiful settings with vigorous sales, to be sure. Their locations were also blessed with high visibility. The tremendous foot traffic allowed Jeanne Jackson to implement a broad strategy of "relationship marketing" that consisted of upscale product lines and related accessories to develop Banana Republic into a "brand" unto itself that could be nurtured and cultivated. The idea that Banana Republic customers would want throw pillows and throw blankets made of the same suede and cashmere as the shirts and sweaters they bought proved irresistible. Banana Republic Home, then, would capitalize on making the connection from clothes to the bedrooms and dining rooms of its customers.

If there was glamour now associated with Banana Republic this is largely credited to the personal style of Jeanne Jackson. The stores benefited tremendously from excellent locations in happening real estate urban markets. There were flattering comparisons to other notable American icons of the twentieth century—Katharine Hepburn and Lauren Bacall—that generated tremendous excitement among the Banana-Republicans. "She made Victoria's Secret exciting," an employee at the Rockefeller Center Banana Republic explained. "And she's making Banana Republic just as sexy and hot!"

Jeanne Jackson, not unlike Katharine Hepburn and Lauren Bacall, is blessed with an exquisite bone structure that allows a weathered face to look elegant. The aging process is evident in her face, but it serves to give her a certain aura of a bygone, more athletic, era. It was on this accidental genetic good fortune that her personal glamour and success spilled over onto Banana Republic.

"Jeanne Jackson is a living diva within this company," a Banana Republic manager at the flagship store in San Francisco said. "She's our inspiration, a mythic combination falling somewhere between Martha Stewart and Lauren Bacall!"

And like Martha Stewart, she has the persuasion, charisma, and work ethic necessary to make Banana Republic into an appealing brand and the Banana Republic division into a profit center within Gap, Inc.'s corporate structure. It is fortuitous, for if Banana Republic had once attempted to emulate Ralph Lauren's "Safari" lifestyle with the original vision of its founders, through Jeanne Jackson—Donald Fisher was convinced—it was now possible to expand the emerging collections of clothes into a broader brand by developing complementary lines of products that capitalized on the brand's signature aesthetics. The personal confidence Jeanne Jackson exudes, coupled with her glamorous social life, created the kind of buzz and excitement about Banana Republic that no advertising could secure.

Through the sheer force of her presence, her design teams would develop home lines to broaden the Banana Republic brand. The idea of this kind of "relationship marketing" came into vogue throughout the nineties as a way of expanding the breadth of a brand by offering increasing lines of related and complementary products. If Banana Republic is introducing suede shirts, why not make suede throw pillows as well? If Banana Republic is introducing a full line of underclothing, then why not provide plush towels too? And leather desk accessories? And china and crystal? Drapes, perhaps? Christmas ornaments? Japanese teacups? Why not?

Why not, indeed?

This strategy was pioneered brilliantly by Ralph Lauren, who, through his home line, tapped into the insecurities of up-and-coming professionals whose business success surpassed their confidence in their own middle-class or middle-brow taste. Ralph Lauren quite simply made furnishing one's home effortless. One had simply to wander in and there—years before Martha Stewart arrived on the scene—one found everything in one place, coordinated and presented in a disarming mix-and-match setting. And it was all tasteful. The Banana-Republicans sought to duplicate this success on their own terms: buy clothes, pick up a few towels, some china, shoes and beauty products with the full confidence that everything was perfectly matched, refined and consistent in the look and image conveyed.

The intent was to create an identifiable Banana Republic "look" that would distinguish it as a recognized "brand."

To create the kind of buzz and excitement necessary, however, the terms of retailing had to change. In the same way that in the early seventies the Gap stores evolved to reflect the "look" of the *Sonny & Cher Show*, at the end of the nineties, Banana Republic had to convey a differentiated brand recognition. This could best be done by making the shopping experience into a singular event. Thus, in a stroke of genius Banana Republic sought to differentiate itself from all the other stores pursuing similar strategies by restoring singular pieces of American real estate as master showcases.

Banana Republic sought out properties of *historic* significance and propelled them to an entirely new level in terms of retailing. That Banana Republic was able to establish stores in historic buildings in Rockefeller Center on Fifth Avenue in New York and at the former Chase Manhattan bank building on Lincoln Road Mall in Miami Beach was astounding. Both stores restored the art deco beauty of former bank buildings, transforming the shopping experience into nothing less than outright theater, evoking not only the glamour of the Hollywood forties, but also winning kudos by refurbishing properties of importance to American culture that had long languished from benign neglect.

"All the top honchos from the San Francisco offices have been here," a source at the Rockefeller Center Banana Republic stated. "They have been so excited with how the store looks, especially since this is the epicenter of the American experience today! We are around the corner from the NBC *Today* show and across the street from Saks Fifth Avenue and St. Patrick's Cathedral! *Banana Republic* is part of *Rockefeller Center!*"

The Rockefeller Center Banana Republic boasts on-line terminals that allow customers to place Internet orders directly, the new trend in expanding the "bricks-and-mortar" symbiotic relationship between mail order, traditional retailing and virtual catalog on-line shopping. The strength of American capitalism made manifest and the elegance of another, more genteel era are present in Banana Republic—while moving into the future of retailing at a warp Internet speed!

The Miami Beach store does not afford customers the use of computer terminals, but it compensates by having a splendid home accessories section on the second floor that is second to none. With inspired touches— dressing rooms are in the bank vaults—the restoration of this structure lends vitality and vigor to the entire historic art deco district of South Beach. Once, on Lincoln Road Mall, designer Gianni Versace made the observation that South Beach would lose its appeal if ever any of the Gap's divisions were "allowed" to open here. "The day a Gap store is opened on Lincoln Road," Versace prophesied, "then that's the day Miami Beach will become a sandbar."

What Gianni Versace alluded to—that the Gap's contribution to society resided in the restoration of historic *buildings* and not in the history of *fashion*—is not lost on Gap itself, so tremendous is its effort at architectural restoration. Nevertheless, the gentle marriage between shopping and historic preservation does create a sort of Disney-like atmosphere of contrived effort, particularly in locations such as South Beach where young people on roller blades, wearing frayed Abercrombie & Fitch caps zigzag their way between couples of aging baby boomers, their bodies sagging as they carry shopping bags with the Banana Republic and Gap logos on them. The message is clear: Gap is for the middle aged, not the young.

If youth is wasted on the young, then purchasing power is squandered on the old.

This is the way of the world, but it does raise certain questions about Banana Republic's price point in its relationship marketing program. Taken together, however, the high visibility of Banana Republic stores in historic buildings is instrumental in consolidating the image of the brand, and it is the kind of positive corporate good deed that provides a cultural service to society.

Image and altruism, however, only go so far. It is true enough that Jeanne Jackson deserves much credit for masterminding the stunning turnaround at Banana Republic, which thrives on the urban professional with significant discretionary income. Then again, disposable income is one thing, and being gouged is another. Consumer resistance to Banana Republic's home lines is classic price elasticity in action. This is not to say that all strategies to create a fusion between clothes and housewares are doomed to failure. But "relationship marketing" by Jeanne Jackson had thus far failed to differentiate Banana Republic as a distinct brand.

"Our strategy is about extending our brand into the lifestyle products our customers want," Jeanne Jackson stated in the spring of 1997. "We will do as many lines as we can without compromising our core apparel business."[7]

Three years later (in the spring of 2000) it would appear to any casual shopper that pillows, desk blotters and similar "accessories" were of little interest to Banana Republic shoppers. For example, Banana Republic employees confirmed that the home divisions in all the Banana Republics in Miami had been closed but the one in the Miami Beach store remained opened. Consumers saw little "relationship" between patent leather shoes and expensive patent leather desk accessories being sold under the same roof.

"Actually, even with the employee discount, it's still a rip-off," a Banana Republic employee at the Miami Beach store said. "See these Christmas ornaments? We sell them for $7, but you can get them across the way at Pottery Barn for $4."

They went on sale for $2, a markdown of more than 70 percent. If the Banana Republic home line was stagnant, products from other divisions also languished. In fact, the other startling blemish at Banana Republic stores was the lackluster performance of the beauty and toiletries line; they were unexceptional products that customers politely looked over and then passed on. The stores, moreover, that carried the home product line and other accessories had been reduced to setting up displays for discounted products.

"Certain things don't move out the door without a little push," one employee at the Chicago Banana Republic admitted. "The stuff is beautiful, but way over-priced and people who can afford to spend that kind of money tend to want better names like Ralph Lauren or Versace or Waterford or whatever. The glasses and dishes we have are about twice what they should be considering they're like what you can get at Crate & Barrel and Pier 1 Imports. It isn't as if this is stuff on the same level as Williams-Sonoma. People do like it, but just because our customers have that kind of disposable income, doesn't mean they don't want value. Our home products don't deliver the right kind of value. The Williams-Sonoma crowd isn't going to come here to shop for their table settings just yet. But we'll be that fabulous one day."

If there were problems with the "relationship marketing" program at Banana Republic, that was because consumers resisted the idea for all Gap, Inc. divisions. Old Navy had failed miserably to sell nonclothes items and the Gap was notorious for its exceptional fiascoes when it introduced anything that defied its antifashion "basic" mentality. While Jeanne Jackson had been frustrated by her failure to make her "relationship marketing" product lines take off, the success with the core clothing business at Banana Republic was such that it afforded her tremendous room in which to navigate.

Despite the problems making relationship marketing work, Banana Republic's seeming embrace of homosexual sensibilities broke new ground in unexpected ways. Consider once more *Planet of the Apes*. One of the most striking things about chimpanzees is that, compared to human beings, secondary sexual traits are not pronounced in adults: it requires reflection to determine whether it's Cornelius or Dr. Zira flashing across the screen. For humans clothes have served to offer protection from the elements as much as they serve to send gender signals. The androgynous ambiguity of Banana Republic's "unisex" look has had marketing advantages; it has helped Banana Republic position itself as urban and futuristic. That this "look" also happens to conform to the aesthetics of gay subculture as presented by gay catalog companies, such as International Male, is not lost on executives who court the homosexual community.

Indeed, the gay community responded with enthusiasm to the fashion philosophy advanced by Banana Republic. The social impact of this merchandising formula, ironically, has been to blur the differences in how men and women shop. One characteristic of homosexual men is a greater sense of style than their heterosexual counterparts. In this sense, then, gays approach the shopping experience not like straight men, but like heterosexual women. Paco Underhill describes the traditional differences between men and women shoppers this way:

You'll see a man impatiently move through a store to the section he wants, pick something up, and then, almost abruptly, he's ready to buy, having taken no apparent joy in the process of finding. You've practically got to get out of his way. When a man takes clothing into a dressing room, the only thing that stops him from buying it is if it doesn't fit. Women, on the other hand, try things on as only part of the consideration process, and garments that fit just fine may still be rejected on other grounds. In one study, we found that 65 percent of male shoppers who tried something bought it, as opposed to 25 percent of female shoppers. This is a good argument for positioning fitting rooms nearer the men's department than the women's, if there are shared accommodations. If they are not, men's dressing rooms should be very clearly marked, because if he has to search for it, he may just decide it's not worth the trouble.[8]

Now consider the Banana Republic experience, which, by catering to a disproportionately homosexual clientele defies convention. "We've been very successful in getting men to buy more than one item," Jeanne Jackson said, adding, "we've finally convinced men to browse, take their time and try on more than one combination of clothes. Overall, this has helped them find entire outfits, which has helped sustain growth."

In other words, in the nineties Banana Republic has succeeded in getting their customers—male and female alike—to shop in the way women have traditionally shopped. This peculiar gender-bending achievement notwithstanding, Banana Republic has not changed how heterosexual men shop. In the first decade of the twenty-first century, however, where baby boomers and Generation X-ers are concerned, Banana Republic's gay aesthetics are nevertheless becoming "mainstream." This has not been without its comic effect. Consider the homosexualized wardrobes of not only characters of popular sitcoms but also throughout the corridors of casually attired corporate America. These clothes have raised more and more eyebrows of senior executives, many of whom are now advocating a return to a more professional dress code.[9]

When I wandered into the Banana Republic flagship store, I spoke to a few of the salesmen to determine if Jeanne Jackson was correct in asserting that male shoppers were, in fact, spending more time shopping than retail anthropologists had indicated. "I haven't really paid much attention to how long male shoppers are actually in the store," one salesman said. "But they do take their time and they make sure to browse all over the men's department." When pressed further, he waxed loquacious and offered a more precise statement. "Well, to be honest about it, sometimes it seems like they're in here for *hours*—but that's great because some of these guys are real 'eye candy.' In fact, it wouldn't be a bad idea to open up a coffee bar, some guys who work close by just want to hang out here for their lunch hour. If we had a coffee bar *and* a gym, then these queens would be here all day."[10]

Men, at Banana Republic, shop like women.

Commercial success selling clothes is not analogous with bravos from spectators looking up at the runway at fashion shows, however. One can sell clothes without the clothes being "in fashion." For one thing, there was no runway. Banana Republic refused to hold fashion shows or present its collections before the fashion community. While Banana Republic generated a buzz on Seventh Avenue, it was more for the marketing genius that had revitalized a languishing brand, not for the clothes themselves.

"Banana Republic can't very well have a fashion show, really," a critic for a fashion magazine stated. "How could they? On a catwalk their entire collection would be laughed at for looking so derivative of last season's Prada or Armani. I mean, their stuff is nice—for office workers, but it's, it's very utilitarian in a minimalist sense or something. But whatever you can call it, it's not really, well, it's not *fashion!*"

What this fashion maven wanted to express is the essential fact that, after the Industrial Revolution, workers' clothes in urban centers throughout the Western world aspired to be "urban camouflage." Under the guidance of Jeanne Jackson, the "Manhattanization" of Banana Republic was, in essence, based on Anglophile aesthetics taken from the Edwardian period and reinterpreted via *Planet of the Apes* for American urban professionals at the dawn of the twenty-first century. A tortured journey, undoubtedly, but this is how Alison Lurie described British workers' clothes:

City clothes [in the United Kingdom] are most often made in colors that echo the hues of stone, cement, soot, cloudy skies and wet pavements: black, white, navy and the darker shades of gray. . . . These subdued and gloomy hues . . . are brightened here and there with color: the red of a pillar-box or a tie, the orange and yellow of a bed of marigolds or a flowered blouse. . . . [The purpose of this approach is] to make the naturally rounded human figure seem more rectangular, helping it to merge into the urban landscape.[11]

Think of the drab advertisements highlighted by hot pink in the Banana Republic's advertising campaign first launched for Valentine's Day in 2000 to see more clearly the Banana-Republican interpretation of the Anglophile take for urban corporate wear.

But if the Banana Republic collection could be summarized as uninspired knockoffs of the minimalist European designers and one that made their customers blend in nicely with the bank building down the street, it didn't matter in the slightest to the accountants. Sales were growing at steady clip, and under Jeanne Jackson's direction the Banana Republic embarked on the fastest expansion program in its history. But commercial success is one thing, and critical acclaim is another. Banana Republic may no longer be disparaged as "rags for fags," but it is dismissed as gay urban wear.

There have been some accolades along the way, however. This praise may not have been for the fashion style of Banana Republic clothes, but it was welcome praise nonetheless. Indeed, Banana Republic won kudos for the *architectural* restoration and *interior design* of its showcase stores. The combination of wood, steel, glass, granite, color and lighting of Banana Republic's interiors was singular. The meticulous care and attention to detail at restoring historic buildings to their original state were heralded as both innovative and groundbreaking. The signature look of Banana Republic in its 32,000-square-foot flagship store in downtown San Francisco was duplicated uniformly throughout the chain's other stores.

Whatever style the clothes lacked, the shopping experience more than made up for it. Consider the Banana Republic on Michigan Avenue in Chicago. Housed in Chicago's prime shopping district, the store blends marvelously among other swank retailers that straddle Magnificent Mile, but the moment one steps in, the entire look of the store is undeniably Banana Republic. The Zen-like use of glass, wood and steel is splendid. Whatever style and fashion the clothes leave to be desired, the stores themselves more than compensate by providing an exciting shopping experience. The combination of wood, glass and steel, coupled with the use of light and space, creates a splendid environment that is singular and energized—and rendered seductive by such thoughtful and pretentious touches as an in-store concierge to make the shopping experience more pleasant. The interior design of all Banana Republic stores, in fact, is so admired that decorators and architecture students make pilgrimages to study how materials and light-ing are used to create a retail sensation.

"There are times when people will walk through only to look at the store," a manager at the Banana Republic store on Lincoln Road Mall said. "They have no intention of shopping for anything; they just wanted to see if we were true to the original design of the bank—and they want to see how the vault was converted into a dressing room."

Enough people do end up shopping to make up for the curious wan-dering though. Compare the Banana Republic on Michigan Avenue in Chi-cago with the struggling Ralph Lauren store down the street, for instance, and it is easy to see how Banana Republic has become a retailing sensation. "Jeanne Jackson has outdone herself," an editor at an industry publication said. "Forget how she transformed Victoria's Secret! What she has done to that Banana Republic—which was one enormous mess when she took over—has won her the respect of the entire industry. Don Fisher and Mickey Drexler are very, very fortunate to have her in charge of that store."

In a few short years two of Donald Fisher's goals had been met: a home run at the cash register in an upscale store and disposing of the disposable incomes of young urban professionals. As for respect from Seventh Ave-nue, well, Jeanne Jackson was still working on that one. And Donald Fisher has had to settle for the admiration from a few of the historic preservation societies scattered throughout the country. Other retailers took notice and as the nineties ended the uniform look spread across retailers—Armani Ex-change, J. Crew, Banana Republic, Gap, Abercrombie & Fitch, Ann Taylor, Structure (Express Men's), Club Monaco, The Limited, Eddie Bauer, Ken-neth Cole, Guess and North Beach Leather—all looked like each other. The Gap, stunned that its signature look had been plagiarized so completely, sought out unique properties of historical or architectural distinction in which to showcase its undifferentiated and unexceptional clothes.

"I see people wander throughout the store and stroll by the home prod-ucts without pause," a Banana-Republican at the San Francisco flagship store said. "Their eyes just glaze over things, as if the stuff were rejects from Gump's."[12]

It can be argued that homosexuality represented a manageable market niche for Gap, Inc. executives; the success of Banana Republic in attracting gays into sales at the cash register was too lucrative to pass up. Gap, more-over, continuing to struggle at its core division, could only look on with envy as Jeanne Jackson revolutionized how clothing was merchandised to men.

Jeanne Jackson was unable to get everything right during her tenure running Banana Republic. Fashion mavens were right to say that Donald Fisher and Mickey Drexler were fortunate to have her, and it was certain they would miss her. In her five years at Banana Republic sales almost tri-pled from $650 million in 1995 to $1.8 billion in 1999; sales approximated $2 billion in 2000. Jeanne Jackson resigned as president of Banana Republic in March 2000 in order to head Wal-Mart.com, with the mission of expanding the world's largest retailer's presence in e-commerce.

Her departure created significant problems for Gap, Inc. Mickey Drexler found himself stretched too thin. With the continuing problems at the Gap's core business and the rapid implementation of "related" product lines throughout the company's divisions, there were concerns that the successful growth Jeanne Jackson had nurtured would not be sustained. The only criticism that could be made, in fact, was the disappointing results from relationship marketing. There was speculation of possible conflicts with upper management or that Jeanne Jackson had become "fagged out"—a term used to describe an individual who simply grows tired of being surrounded by certain kinds of homosexual men. In one of the few interviews she gave after settling in at Wal-Mart.com, however, Jeanne Jackson recited the reasons for her frustration at Banana Republic, "There was no where else for me to go within the Gap's organization. Mickey [Drexler] is young and he's not going anywhere, unless he gets hit by a bus." Then again, sometimes all we need is a little push.

Under Jeanne Jackson's management the only challenges that remained to moving forward with the establishment of Banana Republic as a brand unto itself were to overcome consumer resistance to the price point of the relationship marketing lines and to generate the kind of buzz that will make Seventh Avenue industry observers sit up and take notice. The former goal is bound to be easier than the latter. Few critics believe Seventh Avenue will overcome its resistance and forgive Donald Fisher for having launched and celebrated the antifashion revolution. As for the former challenge, it is clear that consumers have some sort of psychological block that turns them off to shopping for homewares when they are shopping for clothes; neither Banana Republic nor Old Navy are "department" stores, so the presentation of incompatible product lines throws consumers off.

Within Banana Republic, however, there was a certain resentment, a feeling that Jeanne Jackson had not been as loyal as she should have been. Mickey Drexler took over her responsibilities, ordered to stay the course and let the months drift by, unable to find a replacement capable of picking up where she left off. "You know what the problem is?" one Banana-Republican offered by way of assessing the state of affairs at the post-Jackson Banana Republic. "It is this: Dr. Zira was no Martha Stewart!"

Catty comments aside, what no one can deny is that what Jeanne Jackson managed to accomplish in turning that hapless division around was nothing short of revolutionary, which is what one often associates with the other kind of banana republics.

7

THE CANNIBALISM OF OLD NAVY

When Gap Warehouse became Old Navy in March 1994, the purpose was to compete with discounters like Wal-Mart and Target in order to gain market share in the lower-end market. What no one expected was for Old Navy to cannibalize the Gap. Every time the cash register at Old Navy went *"ding!"* that's one sale Gap or Gap Kids or Baby Gap did not make. Old Navy's *explosive* growth corresponded to an *implosion* at the Gap.

In Greek mythology Neptune devoured his children, a ghastly scene of infanticide immortalized by the Spanish painter Francisco Goya. At the end of the nineties another scene, of equally monumental terror, unfolded in corporate America as Old Navy—in a heinous act of parricide—began to devour its corporate parent: the Gap.

The higher sales at Old Navy *soared*, the lower sales at the Gap *dived*. Another way of looking at these developments is by noting that by the time the year 2000 rolled around, Gap, Inc., in essence, was only selling Gap-style merchandise at a discount—and under the Old Navy label. The impact of Old Navy on the Gap's core business—Gap stores, Baby Gap and Gap Kids—can be summed up in one word alone: catastrophic.

"Sluggish" was the kindest adjective used by investment and retail analysts to describe sales of the Gap at the end of the millennium; "faltering" was the word on many analysts' lips when describing the situation at the Gap's core business. This only underscored the frail loyalty consumers had for the Gap as a brand, and it further substantiated the price elasticity in the American economy for apparel that is relegated to everyday wear.

"The Gap's in a difficult situation," a fashion executive admitted as 1999 came to a close. "If you are wealthy, you can afford to dress your infants and children at Brooks Brothers, Giorgio Armani and Bergdorf Goodman. Everyone else is opting for the great values at Old Navy. Where does that leave the Gap, Baby Gap and Gap Kids?"[1]

Adults were divided between those who could afford the upscale Banana Republic and those who defaulted to Old Navy.

"The only difference between these corduroy pants from Old Navy and the ones from the Gap is the price," a woman shopping for her twelve-year-old twin sons' school clothes in the fall of 1998 pointed out. "And if it isn't Old Navy, the boys want Abercrombie & Fitch. So I'm compromising: three pairs each from Old Navy and one pair each from Abercrombie & Fitch."

And nothing from the Gap, alas. As Banana Republic had the hold on the upscale market, the danger was not the notion that "creeping homosexuality" would "contaminate" the other divisions, but rather that the impact of Old Navy on the lower end of the market would be of such magnitude that it would cannibalize the Gap's core apparel business with relentless speed. The dilemma confronting Donald Fisher and Mickey Drexler was that Old Navy was more successful in unexpected ways. It was certainly making inroads against competitors like Wal-Mart and Target, but it was also wreaking havoc on the Gap's core business.

"It comes down to this," one retail analyst said. "American families are buying their Monday-through-Friday wardrobes for their kids at Old Navy and the kids are spending their own allowances or earned money on the nicer clothes from Tommy Hilfiger and Abercrombie & Fitch. That leaves the Gap stores in a very difficult position."

In five years Old Navy grew at such a pace that, by the close of 1999, its sales equaled those of thirty-year-old Gap stores. Old Navy surpassed the Gap division in the year 2000. This was as much evidence of the seismic shift in the terms of trade between consumers and retailers—where "sale" prices were everyday prices—as proof of the Gap's humiliating failure to connect with the 70 million members of Generation Y who rebelled against the antifashion conformity of the Gap.

Old Navy, on the other hand, was not the Gap. Old Navy was Old Navy and Old Navy was unstoppable. When, in the fall of 1999, Old Navy opened its mammoth 102,000-square-foot flagship store in downtown San Francisco on the corner of Market and Fourth streets, however, one could not have discerned a care in the world on the face of Donald Fisher. Old Navy had arrived and not even the several dozen protesters outside—naked men and women who, under police protection, were shouting anti-Gap slogans to protest the plight of women and children who worked in factories throughout the Third World to make Old Navy clothing—could detract from the festive mood of the revelers gathered for this frivolous occasion. And momentous occasion it was, indeed, made more so for senti-mental reasons.

Long before Donald Fisher went into retailing, he was a real estate devel-oper. His brother, William Fisher, owns and operates the privately held Fisher Development Inc., which is the general contractor for many Gap stores. In the wake of the ouster of Banana Republic founders Mel and Pa-tricia Ziegler, there were accusations of nepotism: Over the years there has been grumbling about the preferential treatment Gap, Inc. has given Fisher Development, Inc. on many contracts. No one, however, has substantiated any financial improprieties, but it cannot be denied that Fisher Develop-ment, Inc. has undoubtedly benefited from a steady stream of contracts from Gap, Inc. over the years.

There is no harm in any of this, of course, other than occasional appear-ances and rumors. But there are times when there are unexpected plea-sures. The grand opening of the Old Navy flagship store on October 20, 1999, provided one such pleasure. That building, the Pacific Center, was originally built by Don Fisher's grandfather, Moses Fisher, in 1908.

"My grandfather built this building shortly after the earthquake in 1906," Donald Fisher said at the ribbon-cutting ceremony for Old Navy in 1999. "I'm extremely proud of this whole building and proud that we've made this major investment in San Francisco."

Gap, Inc. had just celebrated its thirtieth anniversary. Old Navy had lifted the firm's fortunes tremendously. Donald Fisher was being praised for restoring an architectural gem for the people of San Francisco. Old Navy's presence in the heart of the South of Market district constituted an anchor in the revitalization of this part of town. No other private citizen in San Francisco stood out as a benefactor as did Donald Fisher.

The Pacific Center was one of San Francisco's first concrete-reinforced structures. The nine-story building, graced with a terra-cotta facade of red on the lower floors and pale green above, is an inspired Victorian legacy. The building sat mostly vacant after the 1989 Loma Prieta earthquake. A decade later it had been splendidly restored to its original state. The bottom four floors house Old Navy while the remainder of the building is occupied by the understated Hotel Palomar.

For the Fisher family, it was an emotional moment to witness in such a breathtaking juxtaposition their family's bond to the city of San Francisco's past and future. A historic building his grandfather had built was now, al-most a century later, at the heart of the invigoration of the booming South of Market district, crowned with a landmark retail operation that was pio-neering merchandising at the dawn of the twenty-first century.

"This is like a dream," Don Fisher said as he looked around.

It was a sight to behold! Spread out throughout four floors, Old Navy boasted four foot-long helicopters, a 350-foot-long conveyor belt, and hot air balloons rotating around platforms. The actress Morgan Fairchild spun the Big Deal Wheel and gave out prizes to shoppers. An old-time tin toy of Magic the Dog, with a rocket pack, flew through the air. There were dirigibles, seaplanes, biplanes and even a flying saucer prominently displayed. And there were shoppers and clothes and cash registers working nonstop.

The principle of entertainment, first initiated by playing rock music at the Gap in 1969 and transforming the store's decor to mimic the colors, designs and imagery of the *Sonny & Cher Show*, had come to its logical conclusion: shopping *as* entertainment.

The difference between the Gap and Old Navy was that the former was an efficient and simple place to shop while the latter was becoming a fun place for prepubescent kids to hang out. The same phenomena that Barnes & Noble had stumbled into—by serving Starbucks in their in-store cafes—was now happening here at Old Navy. Generation Y teenagers now had a place to meet, see and be seen—Old Navy was fast becoming a hangout for the twelve-and-under crowd. In terms of sheer entertainment value Old Navy, in fact, now rivaled the video arcade.

How did Old Navy come so far so fast? And more importantly, what did its success portend for the future of the Gap?

"When we started Old Navy, we sat around and we talked about what we didn't like about discount stores—poor quality, colors that are always just a hair off. We really thought, 'What do we not want to be?' and took it from there," Jenny Ming, the president of Old Navy, said in an interview with *Fortune* magazine.

What the Gap didn't really like about discounters was how they were gaining market share at the Gap's expense. What Old Navy really didn't want to be was what it has become—the chief competitor for Gap, Gap Kids and Baby Gap. No one saw it this way, however, back in 1993 when the Gap opened forty-five Gap Warehouse locations throughout the United States to compete against Target, J.C. Penney and Wal-Mart among others. Before there was an Old Navy there was a Gap Warehouse. And Gap Warehouse offered a wider selection than any other store and the prices—about a third less than Gap—were exactly the right price point.

"When I accidentally stumbled into a Gap Warehouse, I had just bought clothes at J.C. Penney," a middle-aged man from Berkeley said. "Then I realized that it was almost exactly like Gap, but at reasonable prices. I always thought Gap was over-priced for what they offered, but Gap Warehouse was Gap without the mark-up."

Gap Warehouse as "Gap-without-the-mark-up" became an overnight sensation. Sales far exceeded projections and Gap executives thought they had hit a winning formula to compete head to head with the discounters.

"It was like 1978 all over again," Donald Fisher recalled, referring to the wave of competition in the jeans business after the Federal Trade Commission ruled Levi Strauss & Co. could no longer set the retail price of its jeans.

"Everyone was coming out with knockoffs of our clothes, but at a lower price. We had to compete in the lower-end market."

But if Gap Warehouse was to become the definitive rejoinder to the unprecedented competition Gap felt in the early nineties, it would need a *distinct* identity. The idea behind Old Navy, "making shopping fun again," was an attempt to engage heterosexual men in the shopping experience. If Banana Republic had succeeded by catering to gay men, could Old Navy appeal to straight men with similar success?

Paco Underhill reported the undeniable gender difference in how men impact negatively on a woman's shopping experience:

Here's the actual breakdown of average shopping time from a study we performed at one branch of a national housewares chain:

woman shopping with a female companion: 8 minutes, 15 seconds
woman shopping with children: 7 minutes, 19 seconds
woman alone: 5 minutes, 2 seconds
woman with man: 4 minutes, 41 seconds

In each case, what's happening seems clear: When two women shop together, they talk, advise, suggest and consult to their hearts' content, hence the long time in the store; with the kids, she's partly consumed with herding them along and keeping them entertained; alone, she makes efficient use of her time. But with him—well, he makes it plain that he's bored and antsy and likely at any moment to go off and sit in the car and listen to the radio or stand alone and watch girls. So the woman's comfort level plummets when he's by her side; she spends the entire trip feeling anxious and rushed.[2]

Old Navy had to find a way of engaging fathers and husbands—or entertaining them—to reduce the level of stress women feel when shopping with their male parents, boyfriends, or spouses. "The last thing we wanted," Jenny Ming said, "was to jeopardize Gap, Gap Kids and Baby Gap by having everyone flock to Gap Warehouse. We had to create a distinct division directed exclusively at a lower-priced market segment. We wanted to make this a shopping experience for the *entire* family."

To accomplish this goal, three stores, all different from the Gap, were opened around San Francisco in 1994 under the name "Old Navy Clothing Co." The stores were immensely popular. In a few months' time, Gap Warehouses vanished from the American landscape and were replaced by Old Navy. An additional fourteen stores opened throughout the country, bringing the total of Old Navy stores to 59 by the end of 1994. Those three wait-and-see experimental stores in March 1994 had become a nationwide chain a mere nine months later.

It also offered compelling evidence that consumers were responding to price almost exclusively. No one at Gap, Inc. thought Old Navy represented any serious competition for the Gap brand. What executives saw was a winning formula for putting the Wal-Marts and Targets of the world out of the clothing business.

"What a thrill it was," Jenny Ming said, "to see Old Navy shopping bags everywhere as soon as we opened a store."

The Wal-Mart and Old Navy shopping bags became familiar sights in parking lots in suburban shopping centers in short order. That Old Navy sought to create a marketing campaign modeled on memories of the fifties gave it a certain edge that consumers liked. Old Navy's early success resided in its use of time-tested, family-oriented marketing. Cookies and balloons created a small town feeling that delighted children and grandparents. Sponsoring ball games and having female celebrities attracted families, with fathers eager to participate.

"When Cindy Crawford threw out the opening baseball at Candlestick Park—it was Old Navy Day at Candlestick—that was tremendous," Richard Crisman, an executive at Old Navy recalled.

After the game, baseball fans followed Cindy Crawford to the Old Navy in Colma where she signed autographs amid the baseball-themed decorations scattered throughout the store. It was healthy, old-fashioned family fun. It was not without its critics, however. "Brash hucksterism," John King of the *San Francisco Chronicle* characterized it. Handing out cookies and giving away cups of lemonade and helium-filled balloons was innocent and amusing. Critics complained that because of these ploys, few of the shoppers realized that Old Navy's cookies and cupcakes were not baked by some grandmother somewhere but were instead paid for by Gap, Inc.[3]

"The clothes are a little better quality than Wal-Mart and the prices are better," a sixty-eight-year-old grandmother said, standing outside the Old Navy store in Chicago. "I don't feel like I'm really on a budget at Old Navy—although I am!"

The phenomenal growth accelerated in 1995, with six stores opening every month somewhere in the country. In March 1995 the "item of the week" was introduced. In self-standing displays, graced by flashing, matinee-style marquees, these promotions enticed customers to buy an array of items, from cargo pants to "performance fleece" sweaters, for men, women, children or infants. The campy tie-ins, in the retro spirit of the sixties, were hits; Old Navy paired up with General Mills's Cinnamon Grahams to promote "Breakfast and blue jeans better together" in September 1997; there were contests for trips to Hawaii.

In the fall of 1995, Magic the Dog, Old Navy's scruffy mascot, was introduced. Richard Crisman noted that Magic was "everyman's dog" and, as such, Old Navy was "everyman's store." The endearing dog—"discovered" at an animal rescue facility—immediately became a star, requiring staff members to take care of the "fan" mail he was receiving. When *Entertainment Tonight* adopted him in the nightly birthday announcements two years later, Magic the Dog had arrived! It was all tremendous fun and Richard Crisman was right on the mark: Magic was everyman's dog and Old Navy was everyman's store.

The following year, in 1996, Old Navy's growth accelerated with five stores opening every month, an unprecedented rate of growth for a clothing retailer, particularly one that was expanding into what could only be described as slapstick *I Love Lucy* retail entertainment. The antics were something one would expect if Lucy Ricardo were put in charge of running a clothing store for children: mayhem.

This slapstick hucksterism was, of course, silly, but it delighted shoppers. When Old Navy stores celebrated their "birthdays," for instance, oftentimes they would hand out cupcakes or balloons to customers. Old Navy had prizes and games, it hosted sports celebrities who signed baseballs and footballs. In an act of inspired silliness it introduced a delectable Old Navy Chocolate Bar. On any given day in 1996 a hapless customer could walk into Old Navy, be handed a cupcake, see children waiting to have a football signed by Buffalo Bills' quarterback Jim Kelly and be asked if he wanted to enter a contest to win an Old Navy Chocolate Bar. Or perhaps, he might be asked, Would you like to "Beat the Clock" for a shopping sweepstakes?

How about if one simply wanted to buy clothes in peace? Oh, well if you must.

It was evident that this sort of nonsense could only have been dreamt up in San Francisco. But it was working. The management team at Old Navy consisted of Richard Crisman, Kevin Lonergan, Jenny Ming and Jeffrey Pfeiffle, who together reflected accurately the sensibilities of the northern California experience.

Shopping as entertainment—and entertainment through vaudeville—was particularly resonant to the very young and the very old. Thus by 1996 the definitive profile of the Old Navy customer began to emerge with precise clarity: kids spending their allowances, retired folks with more grandchildren than discretionary incomes, and working-class families trying to stay within their budget. Alan Millstein of the *Fashion Network Report* summarized it thusly: "Old Navy combines fashion, food and entertainment at prices that are affordable for the teenager and the geezer."

If unkind with his characterization of senior citizens, he was also mistaken about the age of the youngsters running through the store—most were pre-teens; and of the teenagers, well, a disproportionate number were teenage *parents* trying to survive.

The question Gap executives asked each other remained unanswered: Where was the rest of Generation Y? Neither the Gap nor Banana Republic registered highly on the radar screens of their lives; other brands were "cooler" to their way of thinking. And the only time they ventured into Old Navy was when they were broke and had no other option. Generation Y was shopping primarily elsewhere.

Generation Y-ers, in fact, were imitating the happening styles of the young groups appearing on MTV. There was a staccato of inexplicable visual noise from bands with unpronounceable names, of gender-bending qualities, but dressed in signature styles that caught everyone off guard. They were repudiating the notion of antifashion with which they had grown up, caught up in a Jamesian conflict between the egalitarianism of American life and the European sensibilities for style and glamour. They were fantasizing about the boys and girls they saw in the pages of the Abercrombie & Fitch catalogs, teenagers whom they idolized and wanted to emulate. Those fantasies reverberated throughout the Gap stores with the same chaos that an appearance by the Backstreet Boys stops traffic in Times Square in front of the MTV studios.

Compared with the has-been celebrities Old Navy thrust upon them, or the mannerisms affected in the "Everybody the same" Gap ads, Abercrombie & Fitch, more than any other retailer in the nineties, presented models who looked like hip teenagers. Whereas Calvin Klein, Tommy Hilfiger and Ralph Lauren offered girls who were too thin and too pretty and boys who were too muscular and too handsome, Abercrombie & Fitch, as well as the increasingly popular J. Crew, presented images that reflected the heterosexual nature of their teenage lives.

Old Navy was overflowing with people, even if their demographics weren't what retailers would necessarily covet.

"Hey, a warm body with a pulse and a valid credit card is better than standing around all day in an empty store," one Old Navy manager told me, comparing his store with the Gap down the street. "As long as we're selling, so who cares who the buyers are?"

The executives at Old Navy should have cared, but they were oblivious to any of this for they were too busy ordering cupcakes by the thousands and figuring out how to entertain little old ladies who had ventured on over to Old Navy just to see what amusing mischief was going on over at that carnival of a store.

"Oh, it's so much fun to see so many people out—and so many kids!" an older gentleman in midtown Manhattan said. "I'll buy little things for the kids in my life at Old Navy, and it's enjoyable to see youngsters having fun and staying out of trouble."

The curious, fortunately, became shoppers. Old Navy's calculated seductive charm readily won over millions. With relentless confidence, Old Navy forged ahead, indifferent to the shifting markets now emerging. With the arrival of 1997, the pace of expansion increased by 50 percent: 89 Old Navy stores were opened nationwide. By the end of the year, sales at Old Navy surpassed the $1 billion dollar mark. Whereas in 1994, Old Navy represented only 3 percent of Gap, Inc.'s worldwide sales, by 1997 that percentage was almost 20 percent.

In other words, in 1994 each Old Navy store sold about $2 million and three years later, each store was selling over $4 million. It was now that Old Navy's impact on the fortunes of the Gap stores emerged: Old Navy's phenomenal growth was coming, to an undeniable extent, at the expense of the

Gap. There was no way to deny this—unless one argued there were millions of nudists in America who suddenly decided to wear clothes—from Old Navy exclusively.

This was evident in the crisis that struck the Gap in 1996. It was that summer that Mickey Drexler was forced to cancel his vacation, work June through August to "reposition" the core apparel business of the Gap, and hope this would be enough to rescue the spring 1997 season. Mickey Drexler also replaced Donald Fisher as CEO of Gap, Inc. that same year.

Old Navy was, a few observers conceded, "out of control," which is to say that it had taken on a life of its own. If Donald Fisher had feared losing control of Banana Republic and thus pulled the plug on Mel and Patricia Ziegler's *Trips* magazine, then in Old Navy he had unleashed a creature that Gap, Inc. could not control. It bears recalling that in 1987 the Gap stores dwarfed Banana Republic and Donald Fisher could launch a coup against the founders of that wayward division without a qualm—or shareholder backlash. A decade later in 1997, on the other hand, it was the start-up that was overtaking the Gap—and Gap Kids and Baby Gap—with breathtaking speed. The corporate narrative was filled with provocations and challenges: it was the Gap stores that were faltering and it was the Gap stores that would have to reposition, if not reinvent, themselves in order to keep up. A Banana Republic–style coup against Old Navy was no longer an option.

Within the corporate offices of Gap, Inc. executives conceded that Old Navy's momentum was enormous and it was "unstoppable." In 1998 the pace of expansion accelerated even further with almost ten Old Navy stores opening every month. There were almost too many openings for Gap executives to keep track of—and Old Navy's total sales were fast approaching that of all the Gap stores combined.

"There were rumors at one point about perhaps spinning Old Navy off, because their success made the Gap, Gap Kids and Baby Gap look so terrible," a Gap watcher said. "When Old Navy's sales surpassed the $1 billion dollar threshold, I wondered, Will this turn out to be Don's Billion-Dollar Boo-Boo?"

Mothers and fathers didn't have to be sold on Old Navy for the simple reason that the prices were all they needed to see to be convinced to shop there. Old Navy, however, needed to cultivate an image; its success would not be sustainable if it competed exclusively on price. To differentiate itself it needed to excite youngsters who would cajole their parents into going to Old Navy and appeal to the growing ranks of senior citizens in this country who were living longer—and thereby living to shop for more and more grandchildren and great-grandchildren.

In a stroke of marketing genius, Old Navy brought aboard Carrie Donovan, a former fashion editor of the *New York Times Magazine*, in April 1997 to introduce Old Navy's "item of the week." A woman of an older generation who identified with Youth Culture, with a definite authority and a celebrated campy delivery. Carrie Donovan became to Old Navy what Diana Vreeland was to Andy Warhol's Factory: a living dinosaur that amused kids, but made them sit up and take notice nonetheless. She energized the image of Old Navy from bargain-basement to campy chic.

"Di-*vine!*" Old Navy's diva declared as she beheld the world through retro-round black glasses, wearing pearls and pronouncing innocuous items—like cargo pants—as "fabulous!" Carrie Donovan was a septuagenarian selling to consumers who had been conceived at the time when Nancy and Ronald Reagan danced at the White House during the Reagan inaugural ball in January 1981.

It was her tantalizing presence in Old Navy's advertising that further fueled the chain's growth. In the spring of 1997 Carrie Donovan was first introduced to the American public in full-page ads in the *New York Times*. That summer she appeared in television commercials with second-tier celebrities, like Jerry Hall and Marcus Schenkenburg, to ignite interest in Old Navy's celebrated "item of the week." Carrie Donovan became a sensation that fall. She was making news herself and articles about her appeared in *TV Guide*, *Vogue* and *Entertainment Weekly* among others.

Old Navy was steamrolling ahead at full speed. For the 1997 Christmas season, "performance fleece" clothes were the thing to have. Television and print ads contained campy spots featuring the likes of Morgan Fairchild and the Smothers Brothers. At the center of these campaigns was Carrie Donovan holding court, accompanied by Magic the Dog. Watching Carrie Donovan's rapport with Magic the Dog had an undeniable chemistry that energized the commercials. No doubt Carrie Donovan's contribution to the Old Navy ambiance was reminiscent of seeing Mrs. Vreeland swing her arms in the air and gyrate her hips as she danced—without ever moving her feet—at Studio 54 while Steve Rubell and Halston snorted cocaine behind her.

Well, not quite exactly, but close enough.

In 1998 the pace of growth continued at the rate of about ten new stores each month, and sales throughout the chain almost doubled to $2.3 billion. Celebrities and former celebrities were recruited to make a pitch for Old Navy, everyone from Dr. Joyce Brothers to Joan Collins, Sherman Hemsley and Isabel Sanford to the Smothers Brothers. If it was kitsch, it was Old Navy. If it was Carrie Donovan, it was camp. With one complementing the other the combination proved irresistible.

The populism extended beyond advertising, to be sure. In April 1998 Old Navy at Bat debuted at forty minor league ballparks, winning over little leaguers throughout the country. The cupcakes and contests and prizes characterized the opening of more and more stores through the end of 1999. As the century drew to a close, Old Navy had 528 stores throughout the United States with total sales of $3.3 billion, meaning an average Old Navy store was selling $6¼ million a year. The sales projections were dwarfed by the actual figures coming in and Old Navy accounted for 30 percent of Gap, Inc.'s worldwide sales.

But the concern on analysts' minds, that Old Navy was gaining market share at the expense of Gap, was readily dismissed by Old Navy officials. "If we really felt [Old Navy] is cannibalizing, why would we be opening stores down the street from Gap and in the same mall?" Old Navy president Jenny Ming answered when asked at the opening of the flagship store in San Francisco in October 1999.

Is the answer, *The better to eat the Gap with, my dear?*

Or, perhaps the Gap is in denial as to what Old Navy is doing to its core business? Or, perhaps Old Navy is fueled by its own internal combustion that is completely apart from that of the Gap? Or, perhaps Old Navy considers the Gap just another competitor to be afforded no special treatment?

Jenny Ming posed that last rhetorical question to reporters on October 20, 1999, from her vantage point, a vantage point that sounded like the B-52's singing the chorus from their song, "You're Living in Her Own Private Idaho."

Nine days later Gap, Inc. announced the resignation of Robert Fisher as president of Gap division. The story was carried on the first page of the *New York Times* business section. After a surge in sales in 1997 and 1998, Gap was once again confronting a crisis of such severity that top management at the Gap stores changed.

While admitting "sluggish" sales at its core business, which were described as "faltering," "distressed" and "stagnant," Gap, Inc. said that Robert Fisher's decision to resign was for "entirely personal reasons," adding that he wanted to spend more time with his family.

It was not clear, however, that *anyone* could reverse the devastation unleashed upon the Gap by the success of Old Navy. Indeed, Old Navy employees, from Jenny Ming down to part-time store clerks, were either in denial about the impact their division was having on the Gap, or they refused to accept the corporate parricide that they were committing.

Old Navy's cannibalistic impact on the Gap stores was nothing less than shocking. In 1997 *Advertising Age* had named the Gap as "Marketer of the Year," bestowing honors and praise and kudos, but less than twenty-four months later, the Gap was in a free fall. Gap was once more in the throes of a management shake-up and was forced once again to "reposition" its core apparel business.

"Old Navy's like a runaway locomotive that crashed right into the Gap at full speed," an executive at Levi Strauss & Co. noted with delight upon learning of the announcement that Robert Fisher was stepping down as president of the Gap division. *"Old Navy cost Don Fisher's son his job! Wow! That blows my mind!"*

Gap, Inc. announced simultaneously that Mickey Drexler would take over the day-to-day operations of the Gap stores effective November 15,

1999. It would be another five months before Gap, Inc., named Ken Pilot president of the Gap division, on April 5, 2000, an announcement made on the same day that the Gap revealed a sales decline of almost three times what analysts expected, sending shares plummeting more than 10 percent in one day.

"We have to get back to our basics. The Gap now has to focus on simplicity of its basic clothing line," Mickey Drexler said at that time.

Thus another "repositioning" at the Gap was underway. All together now: *reposition!* It would be an ineffective repositioning, however. In August 2000 when Gap, Inc. reported its second-quarter earnings, it reported that sales at its core business and Old Navy were down dramatically. "Dragged down by sagging performance at its once-stellar Old Navy chain," the *San Francisco Chronicle* began its report, noting that "[s]ales at Old Navy stores open a year or more ... declined a dramatic 17 to 19 percent in the four weeks ended July 29[, 2000]."[4]

The only good news was rather indifferent, Banana Republic's sales were flat. Wall Street reacted by sending the Gap's shares plunging 20 percent, falling 7¾ to close at 30³⁄₁₆ on the New York Stock Exchange, near its 52-week low. Analysts attributed the stock's weakness in part to warnings that figures for the third and fourth quarters would, only with great effort, come in at the lower end of expectations.[5]

"In the summer of 1999 the Gap was trading around this level and Robert Fisher resigned a few months later," one analyst at Merrill Lynch said. "This stock is now back where it was in November 1998. It's clear that we're into the second half of 2000, Ken Pilot's proving to be in over his head at the Gap stores, and Mickey Drexler's magic touch is gone. These were terrible results, just terrible. I don't know where the Gap is going. I don't think they know where they are going. It's going to take some hard thinking and hard decisions before the Gap turns around. How could things fall apart so quickly for them?"

Heidi Kunz, Gap chief financial officer, explained that "in any month or quarter there are lessons learned." Gap officials have argued that the late Easter, unseasonably cool weather throughout the country and executive turnover accounted for the disappointing sales in 2000. When on August 10, 2000, Gap expressed "concern" about the trends at both its core business and Old Navy, the price of its shares plunged an additional 14 percent, closing at 27³⁄₁₆. The Gap, a year after the resignation of Robert Fisher, was in a crisis.

Confronted with lower than expected sales in 1999 and 2000, Gap executives concentrated on reducing marketing expenses and studying ways of doing cross-promotions between Gap, Old Navy and Banana Republic. Kunz admitted, however, that for the Gap and all its divisions, the year 2000 "was a confusing time for us."[6]

"We still have room to grow in clothing," Jenny Ming said the same week the first disappointing quarter results were announced, speaking of her own plans to expand further the number of Old Navy stores. "We think we can grow to 1,000 stores. Everyone is looking for great value today. What Old Navy attracts the most is the value segment because they're starved for something like what Old Navy offers. Great prices. Fun shopping."

The implied criticism, therefore, is that the Gap has lousy prices and boring shopping, which is why it is starved for customers. "If we [at the Gap] don't get it together already, we won't have to 'reposition' itself," an executive said. "We'll be 'repossessed' by Old Navy."

This is not to say that everything always went according to plan at Old Navy. Not unlike Banana Republic, Old Navy was discovering that "relationship marketing" was easier as a concept than as a reality. The secondary product lines brought in, like the home lifestyle products of the Banana Republic, were a hard sell for Old Navy customers. The accessories product line—flippant touches that turned out to be duds—was one stumbling block. These blemishes didn't faze anyone, particularly given the sensational growth Old Navy was enjoying.

"We've made a fair amount of mistakes over the years, but that's part of taking risks. The thing about our company is that we learn from our mistakes," Mickey Drexler explained, by way of excusing the problems with relationship marketing at Gap, Inc.'s divisions. "Taking risks and learning from mistakes are part of our corporate culture."

Good enough, but why repeat the same mistakes over and over again? Old Navy launched its body care line in October 1996, despite the mediocre performance of Gap Scents, which, since its inception in 1994, had failed to generate outstanding sales. Banana Republic Body Care did not generate enough sales to warrant opening a stand-alone division. (The following year Gap launched its signature fragrance—Blue No. 655—the sales of which made executives, true to its name, blue with disappointment.)

If Old Navy has made one glaring mistake it is that, as Mickey Drexler phrased it, "the tchotchke business at Old Navy hasn't worked out well."

This was an understatement. The "tchotchke business," of course, referred to Old Navy's efforts to expand its brand through the "relationship marketing" of seasonal and impulse items, which is the merchandise usually found by the cash registers and in free-standing displays near the grocery store–style check-out counters.

"Those aluminum watering cans were a total bust," one Old Navy employee said. "They went on sale really fast. And the alarm clocks. The mugs do okay, but they're, like, almost a joke. I mean, so many get broken, is there a profit in selling them? It's like those restaurants that want to sell you a mint for 10¢ after you've spent $20 for lunch: why be so petty about it?"

Old Navy thus confronted the same consumer resistance that frustrated Banana Republic, but on a different level: Banana Republic had trouble

moving the patent leather desk sets and Old Navy ended up having to discount the aluminum watering cans. These are undeniably two different
markets altogether, but that shoppers ignored the disposable alarm clocks
at Old Navy as they did the over-priced purses at Banana Republic is indicative of a basic psychological barrier that consumers have when they think
about the Gap as a brand. That this stands in sharp contrast to the experience of other brands, such as Ralph Lauren and Martha Stewart.

Ralph Lauren can put his name on anything and it's instantly upscale.
Martha Stewart does the same and it thus becomes part of her "gracious living" philosophy—and a natural tie-in for whatever is the current season or
theme in her magazine or on her television show. This is evidence that both
these brands are clearly differentiated in the minds of consumers—and that
each holds intrinsic value. The brands of Gap, Inc.'s divisions, however, do
not enjoy this advantage, which suggests their brands are neither mature
nor valued by consumers.

"I know my girls," a man in his forties shopping at the flagship Old
Navy store said of his two daughters, one twelve and the other fourteen.
"They don't care if its Gap or Old Navy. It's basically the same to them. I
care because there's a big difference in the price. But I will tell you this,
though, they go crazy over Abercrombie & Fitch, ever since they started
coming out with that catalog that's as thick as a phone book for a small city."

The notion of brand loyalty is an interesting one among American consumers. People are loyal to either Coke or Pepsi to a surprising degree, but
they find 7–Up and Sprite interchangeable. Generation Y identifies healthy
lifestyles with Tommy Hilfiger, Calvin Klein, Ralph Lauren and Abercrombie & Fitch in ways that Gap and Old Navy can only envy.

"It's a good price-value," one Wall Street analyst says. "But have you
seen Old Navy stores? It's cute at the beginning, but after a while you see it
for what it truly is: a schlocky store disguised as fifties pseudo-fifties retro.
It wears out fast."

It was a prescient observation. What Old Navy thought was hip, most
others considered juvenile. "Old Navy is the first Manhattan retailer to outfit employees with headsets," Old Navy officials boasted. "Employees say
the headsets 'make the job easier and they look cool.' "

They looked cool for a few months. Then sales clerks in every other retail
store in New York and Los Angeles were sporting the same headsets and it
suddenly reeked of corporate oppression.

"Old Navy's employees looked like asexual worker bees in a corporate
beehive," said a manager at a Banana Republic on Fifth Avenue in New
York. "Can you imagine the humiliation we have to endure just being associated with that kind of store? It's too unfabulous to even think about."

This conversation took place in November 1995 when Old Navy opened
a 30,000–square-foot store on Sixth Avenue at 18th Street in Manhattan.
Rock star Chris Isaak was the featured guest at a party for which thousands

of people showed up, resulting in "the largest single-day sales performance in Gap, Inc.'s twenty-six-year history." The bargain-starved New
York multitudes flocked to the opportunity to buy clothing at a reasonable
price without having to make a pilgrimage to outlet malls hours away in
upstate New York or neighboring New Jersey. That Old Navy store expanded its floor space by 15,000 feet within a few months to accommodate
the traffic. It was a stupendous hit—but only because people who live in
Manhattan find things like, say, a K-Mart to be a novelty.

Not everyone was impressed by the invasion of the bargain hunters, par-
ticularly in New York. The novelty was short-lived, as much because Old
Navy relied on a contrived formula because of the jaded nature of New
Yorkers whose curiosity for the new is insatiable.

The *au courant* "industrial" look of Old Navy with its raw concrete floors,
chrome and particle-board fixtures, exposed pipes and factory lighting has
a way of looking interesting at first, but quickly comes off as "cheap." That
might very well be consistent with Old Navy's need to keep overhead low,
but it is odd that so much effort goes into the cheesy—and expensive—gimmicks, from the grocery-store refrigerator cases with stacks of T-shirts in
shrink-wrapped packages to the Torpedo Joe's cafe—which may very well
contribute to ambiance, but all this distracts from the merchandise.

"I go to [New York's] Chelsea [district] and look around and think, *Ho
hum, another industrial floor, another plywood wall. Fine. Could you please lac-
quer this entire thing and I'll adore it,*" Isaac Mizrahi, a designer, is quoted in
Esquire. In his one-page essay he argues that antifashion has run its course
and people in the twenty-first century crave style.[7]

"Do you really want to have all these kids running around?" an Old
Navy employee at the Chicago store asked. "If they're unsupervised, they
can become a disciplinary problem for us, but the last thing we want to do is
throw kids out of the store. Not that we don't want to. But we just can't."

Instead of giving away sugar-enriched cupcakes that make the kids even
more hyperactive, another employee suggested later on, perhaps Old Navy
should hand out Ritalin.

There was a certain fatigue setting in, of course. Old Navy's advertising
was as clever as it was ubiquitous—and it quickly became as tiresome.
When arbiters of taste, like Isaac Mizrahi, reduce one's company to catty
one-liners and television skits on *Saturday Night Live* portray a firm's employees as slaves to mindless drudgery, this kind of mockery and ridicule
cascades down through society. In no time, people of all walks of life began
to dis the Gap.

"Old Navy's cheesy and the appeal of cheesy fades fast," one former Old
Navy employee said. "How many times are I *Dream of Jeannie* and *The
Jeffersons* going to generate the interest necessary to build brand loyalty?"

This disdain accelerated when an embarrassing—and inexplicable—
marketing problem emerged: both the Gap and Old Navy were coming out

with the same featured items. In the course of 1999, for instance, both divisions launched campaigns to promote vests—"Everybody in vests" at the Gap and "performance fleece vests" at Old Navy. This was repeated shortly thereafter with the emphasis this time around on corduroy pants.

"Great minds think alike," a spokesman for Gap, Inc. explained, adding that both divisions develop their lines independently of each other and these two campaigns were just a coincidence.

"See, man?" a male member of Generation Y in New York pointed out to me. "The Gap's ripping off Old Navy's style."

Perhaps not, but it is perception that counts. Even if, as Gap, Inc. executives claimed, these coincidences were the product of great minds thinking alike—and not mindless acts of desperation by the Gap trying to play catch up—such similarities were detrimental to the Gap nonetheless. Consumers would drop by the Gap and see virtually the same vests they had seen at Old Navy—for almost twice as much. This confirmed what consumers already believed to be true: the Gap was a ripoff, and if Old Navy could sell and make a profit, then that was proof that the Gap had been gouging their customers all these years.

The Gap overestimated the value of its brand. Americans are not prepared to pay a premium just to have the word "Gap" on the inside label of their clothing. This is not exclusive to the Gap, of course. "[W]e are witnessing the erosion of the influence of brand names," Paco Underhill notes. "Not that brands don't have value, but that value is not the blind force it used to be. A generation or two ago, you chose your brands early in life and stuck by them loyally until your last shopping trip."[8]

When Old Navy and Gap both came out with vests and cords simultaneously, Gap officials dismissed the coincidence as "great minds thinking alike." What consumers saw, however, was that the merchandise at Old Navy was essentially the same as that at the Gap, except that at Old Navy it was 40 percent less. When the sales at the Gap plummeted, it was clear that the Gap had overestimated the value its brand held for members of Generation Y. "That means," Paco Underhill continues, "that while branding and traditional advertising build brand awareness and purchase predisposition, those factors don't always translate into sales."[9]

Great minds do think alike. So do stupid ones.

The intensifying "Gap-lash" impacted the Gap and loomed ominously over its marketing campaigns. Consider that in November 1999, at the height of the longest economic expansion in the history of the United States, and while Gap, Inc. was opening stores throughout the country at an unprecedented pace, same-store sales for the Gap stores were declining.

In 1999 same-store sales at the Gap were flat or down for the seven months before Robert Fisher stepped down. Indeed, prices at the Gap had been slashed drastically beginning in March 1999 in an effort to revive sales in the wake of Old Navy's impact. Gap executives were quick to point out that these price "adjustments" were necessary, not because of Old Navy's cannibalism, but rather because of "certain fashion mistakes," which defied belief, for it was in 1997 that, after disposing of Maggie Gross, Mickey Drexler had personally supervised the much-heralded return to "basics," a bold affirmation of the antifashion philosophy. It was too soon for the Gap to have gone "astray."

What no one at Gap, Inc. wanted to discuss was the possibility that the Gap's core business was rapidly being cannibalized by Old Navy. And even the rate of growth at Old Navy was slowing; in the third quarter of 1998 same-store sales at Old Navy grew in the mid-teens but a year later, the growth was in the single digits. The overall performance of all the Gap, Inc.'s divisions was a same-store increase of about 5 percent, approximately the pace of growth of the national economy.

"Banana Republic has the high end and Old Navy has the bottom end," explained a manager at Nordstrom. "That leaves the Gap struggling to hold on to the middle."

In a misguided attempt to capture that elusive middle, however, the Gap accelerated its coarsening of American life. As the twentieth century drew to a close, critics watched in horror as vulgarity suffused American life. If *Vanity Fair* under Tina Brown had been a magazine of well-written articles that trashed people, Gap under Mickey Drexler was a company offering well-constructed clothes that made people look trashy. This process was now accelerated in unexpected ways: walking into the Gap and expecting to find tastefulness was like opening the pages of Tina Brown's *New Yorker* magazine—where she introduced her panache for vulgarity that she had refined while at *Vanity Fair*—and finding Paul Theroux's article about a dominatrix staring you in the face.

The unprecedented success of Old Navy was the triumph of the lowbrow: taste had been replaced by vulgarity, discernment buried by popularity. The egalitarian antifashion clothes of the Gap found wild commercial success in the crass and vulgar offerings of Old Navy. In a world where commercial success was the highest cultural value, some social critics argued Old Navy's stellar rise meant that the Gap's core business was now under siege—and by the hand of its own thankless child. Gap's philosophy, that the world should be without hierarchical distinctions, had fostered a relentless embrace of what was expedient, without regard to anything other than economics. Robert Fisher thus struggled to grab hold of the middle—only to find that in 1999 there was very little middle left in the middle.

By the time the year 2000 arrived, tensions were rising between the competing demands and rivalries between Old Navy and Banana Republic.

"Each division is pulling Gap, Inc. in opposite directions," a fashionista in New York observed. "What's it going to be? Highbrow or lowbrow?"

These divergent paths reverberated throughout the company, a reflection of how San Francisco itself was changing in response to that community's diversity. Consider how City Hall adopted terms in common usage in Standard Queer English (SQE) into its official language. When city officials, for instance, argued, in a value-neutral way, for the establishment of a commission on "Queer Youth," words that had once been derogatory became bold affirmations of identity and pride. Gap, Inc. became one of the most visible corporate citizens moving *beyond* politically correct speech in its efforts to embrace and empower diversity in the workplace— and there was a backlash.

Banana Republicans were embarrassed by the "cheap clothes" for "breeders" (read: heterosexual youth) sold at Old Navy stores. Old Navy employees retaliated by railing against those "stuck up faggots ruining Banana Republic for normal people" (read: gay aesthetics that alienate mainstream heterosexual consumers). These words, consistent with community standards, however, had been deprived of their derogatory connotations. Gay rights activists used the pink triangle—an emblem used by the Nazis to identify and humiliate homosexuals and sexual deviants—into a symbol of gay and lesbian pride in the seventies. Now in the nineties, in San Francisco, words such as "queer," "fag," and "dyke" were empowered as honorifics by public officials, consistent with SQE usage. But on a corporate level, Gap, Inc. found itself confronting a dualism it had never experienced before, one that introduced an element of racism and bigotry through speech that was, politically, beyond reproach.

Consider something as innocuous as security and inventory control. The silent cameras that monitor retail stores throughout the various Gap divisions are used to combat "shortage"—an industry euphemism for shoplifting—and to provide videotape evidence in instances where there may be liability, such as an injury to a customer or an employee. When security personnel at stores were interviewed and asked to discuss in general terms what their experiences working for these divisions were, the responses were consistent with the rival perceptions expressed by division employees themselves: Old Navy is on the lookout for inner-city youth shoplifting and Banana Republic is mindful of customers having sex in the dressing rooms.[10]

Old Navy's success loomed ominously over the Gap. It was not lost on Donald Fisher that Old Navy's sensational growth was evidence of the Gap's vulnerability. If Old Navy could become larger than the Gap in only six years, then *any* competitor with a winning formula could eclipse the Gap as well. After all, what if Old Navy belonged not to Gap, Inc. but to a well-financed competitor? Where would the Gap then be if that were the case?

Levi Strauss & Co. had never forgotten its "betrayal" by Donald Fisher. "We worked together for almost a decade," a former Levi Strauss official said, "and together we made the Gap into the largest retailer of Levi's® in the world. Then when the profit margins are squeezed, we are shown the door."

In the second half of the nineties Levi's entered into difficulty as it slashed production, closed factories and laid off thousands of employees. "Think about it," one executive at Levi Strauss & Co. fantasized out loud. "With the right formula and the right price point, it only takes five or six years to eclipse the Gap's core businesses. Old Navy's a bold experiment that demonstrates that the Gap's Achilles heel is *price point*. And that's because the Gap has no intrinsic value as a brand by itself!"

Selling more is the biggest revenge in corporate America. If out-selling is revenge, then why was Old Navy, through the sheer power of its commercial success, exacting such cannibalistic vengeance on its parent company? How long could this go on?

These questions emerged around the same time that Old Navy opened its flagship store in San Francisco. It was, curiously, around this time that analysts and industry observers began to wonder about the sustainability of Old Navy itself as a brand. For four years straight Old Navy recorded double-digit growth, far exceeding projections. In the second half of 1999, however, for the first time in its brief history, its growth was only in the single digits, albeit the high single digits.

"Old Navy Brand Losing Steam?" *San Francisco Examiner* reporter Victoria Colliver asked on November 5, 1999, noting that actual same-store sales fell far short of the projected 12 percent increase.

"October [1999] retail sales figures show the tide may be turning on Old Navy," she reported. "For most of the year, Old Navy's phenomenal sales have been boosting sales at San Francisco–based Gap, Inc., dragged down by declining numbers at the company's namesake store. . . . Some analysts have questioned whether Old Navy has been cannibalizing the Gap by luring shoppers away with lower prices than Gap store."

The embarrassment of riches at Old Navy was not guaranteed, investors suddenly realized. This was becoming more evident as more and more people wondered what the profit margins were for a store that was selling T-shirts for $7.50, khaki pants for $22.50 and wool cardigans for $32.

"I believe in strong marketing," Jenny Ming said. "We hit the customer over the head. This is what it is. Our margins are slim. That's why we have to move volume."

If the margins are too slim, or even negative, then the more volume sold, the greater the losses are down the road. It seemed very unlikely that Old Navy represented an attempt to sell at a loss in order to drive competitors out of the market—and then raise prices once the competition had been decimated. Such pricing would run afoul of the principles of fair competition, of course, and in Old Navy's case it could very well prove fatal to the Gap's core business as well.

"I don't want our customers to buy one item. I want them to buy outfits," Jenny Ming explained. "Our prices are that competitive."

Price point, however, is not always enough. Fashion mistakes and flawed merchandising turned consumers off to Old Navy throughout 2000, particularly Generation Y-ers. By the fall of 2000, Old Navy sought to attract customers by distributing a $10 gift certificate on the purchase of $50 or more, in effect giving customers a 20 percent discount just to come in and buy something. Old Navy was cognizant of its diminished popularity among Generation Y, for it launched contests to give away $100 gift certificates in magazines such as *Teen People*, *CosmoGirl* and *People*. It reached out to all kinds of demographics—launching its Holiday 2000 promotions on commercials aired during *Will & Grace* as it sought to associate the Old Navy brand with Karen Walker, the wisecracking fag-hag character on that television show.

With this strategy Old Navy encountered several dilemmas. It was only able to sustain revenues by concentrating on price points. But for profits to be reasonable and prices to be kept this low, the costs had to be slashed. The only way to accomplish this was to rely even more on producing garments in developing countries where workers' incomes were depressed, either through weakened currencies or exploitative wages, or both. Such a strategy carried with it the danger that civic-minded members of Generation Y, as well as seasoned activists, would take a stand against the inherent inequities in such a corporate strategy. Of greater concern, moreover, was the decision of Old Navy to follow the Gap's lead and begin to associate its brand with Banana Republic's gay aesthetics. Whether or not this would prove to be a prudent course of action would only be known as the 2000s unfolded.

8

BRIDGING THE GAP TO
GENERATION Y

On January 1, 1992, thousands of youngsters throughout the United States turned thirteen. The first members of Generation Y thus became teenagers. Every day their ranks grew, resulting in a demographic shift. For the first time since 1975, the U.S. Census Bureau reported, the percentage of teenagers in the United States increased. The coming-of-consumer-age of the members of Generation Y occurred during the worst recession in recent memory. "It's the economy, stupid," the ingenious slogan coined by James Carville became the compelling theme of Bill Clinton's successful presidential campaign to defeat George Bush in the 1992 elections.

The recession impacted Gap in stunning ways: Gap slashed prices, profits plummeted, its stock price lost half its value, troubled divisions— Banana Republic and Gap Shoes—continued to flounder despite all efforts to reverse fortunes. Competitors, from J.C. Penney to Ralph Lauren to Armani Exchange, also reeling from unforgiving economics, launched "basic" lines of their own. While Gap officials looked on in horror, the same kind of "basic" clothes they had begun to introduce in the early nineties was suddenly found everywhere.

"Our 'basics' line was successful and everyone was imitating it," one former Gap executive said. "It was as if each of our competitors had gone to the nearest Gap, bought one of everything, and then copied it. I know imitation is the greatest form of flattery, but this was terrible!"

Perhaps, but then again, perhaps not. It is possible that apparel companies were not consciously imitating the Gap, but merely responding to a fundamental psychology of the human mind. The simple clothes presented as interchangeable and available in an ordinary selection of hues, accompanied by a mix-and-match dullness appropriate to their cookie-cutter antifashion styles, once pioneered by the Gap, were now found in stores everywhere.

Was the world in fact copying the Gap, or was there something else going on? Alison Lurie offers the following insight:

> Plain, unimaginative clothes in neutral colors, euphemistically referred to at the time as "classics," are the sign of periods of economic and social anxiety and depression. . . . In anxious and conservative times there is a preference for solid value in all areas. Expensive garments . . . are advertised not as thrilling luxuries but as "good investments," talismans that will give the wearer "a sense of security."[1]

If it was "the economy, stupid," then that accounts for the rush to come out with "classic" lines of clothing that offered "value." The Gap was therefore responding to the same social anxiety and uncertainty at the end of the Bush administration as was everyone else. It might very well have been that the Gap was ahead of the social curve, but the probability was greater that the Gap was the first to introduce a collection of plain, unimaginative clothes because it was more anxious than other retailers about its own future.

There were, of course, valid reasons for social and political anxiety across the spectrum. The economic recession was exerting tremendous pressures on the bottom lines of firms throughout the entire economy. George Bush's run for a second term was faltering, and a new generation of consumers—70 million strong, whose impact on society and culture was an unknown—was entering the marketplace, armed with $200 billion in purchasing power. The nation, confronted with anxiety about the future, unconsciously and naturally gravitated toward dress that promised "value."

There was, however, something of equal consequence: the Gap misunderstood Generation Y. The ease with which the Gap had reached out, and seduced, Generation X in the eighties fostered a false sense of security—and arrogance. "Kids are kids and we thought we *knew* kids," one Gap employee said, characterizing the problems the Gap encountered in the early nineties.

The eighties were not the nineties, however. In the early eighties, when *Risky Business*, the film that made Tom Cruise a star, was being promoted, David Geffen, the producer, was the one who, over the studio's objections, decided what the poster would look like. Tom Cruise was posed wearing a white T-shirt and blue jeans—from the Gap—as he looked over the top of a pair of Ray Ban Wayfarer sunglasses, which had been made popular the year before when Jack Nicholson had worn them to the Oscars. David Geffen instinctively realized that the Gap's interpretation of James Dean's rebellious attire had become the quintessential uniform of suburban American youth. The clothes were important, and so was the egalitarian nature of who manufactured them.

The year was 1983. This was when the Gap's antifashion philosophy was christened as cool by Hollywood's biggest star, thus ushering in the Gap as the destination store for Generation X. The "look" Tom Cruise projected in *Risky Business* was a combination of the James Dean look of the fifties and a sanitized American version of the skinhead uniform popularized in the seventies in Britain. This is instructive for it illustrates how street culture develops styles that are subsequently devoid of their political context and mass-merchandised in a different context. George Marshall explains the history of the how the skinhead uniform in Britain evolved:

> The jeans to be seen in were Levi's red tags. They had been popularized by the mods earlier in the [sixties] because they were more expensive than your average pair of jeans and therefore more exclusive. Skinheads liked them for much the same reason. . . . Another thing about Levi's was that they were meant to be worn on the hip, but everyone pulled them up to the waist—hence the need for something to hold them up and the addition of braces to the skinhead wardrobe. . . .
>
> Soon however two styles had emerged as definite favourites. One was the collarless union shirt in plain colours or occasionally in stripes. And the other was the classic American button-down, as championed by the mods in the mid-Sixties. . . .
>
> And that was you. Dressed in the height of working class fashion and ready to take on the world. All you had to do was tap the old man for a few bob and it was off down the road to meet your mates.[2]

What would otherwise be interpreted as "threatening" and "menacing" was sanitized and transformed into the uniform of choice of American suburban adolescents via the Gap. But if it was in the eighties when Generation X-ers ruled, and it was the Gap that outfitted them, as a generation they remained so few in number and so old for the digital revolution that their influence would be short-lived.

The generational embrace of the Gap by Generation X nonetheless represented a stunning success for Donald Fisher: the same daring that bridged the Matures and baby boomer generations was used to bridge from the baby boomers to Generation X. Generation X-ers, it is clear, were so timid compared to the baby boomers who preceded them and the Generation Y-ers who followed them that the Gap's non-threatening skinhead look was their idea of social rebellion.

For the Gap, fast becoming the largest clothing retailer in the United States, the gentle incorporation of Generation X fit in handsomely with the changing preferences of the baby boomers, who themselves were now middle-aged men and women. That the baby boomers were now sensible adults and that Generation X was timid and complacent created the social context in which the Gap established itself as the retailer of choice.

It is clear that if other retailers adopted the basic line introduced first by the Gap, it was as much a response to the same set of social factors as the desire to imitate the line of a successful competitor. How these economic fears, at precisely the moment when a new generation was becoming teenagers, would impact retailers was a much-debated question by marketers. Donald Fisher, of course, had successfully bridged the gap between his own generation and the baby boomers. Mickey Drexler, too, had then helped the Gap co-opt the passive and compliant members of Generation X quite effortlessly.

But what was one to make of Generation Y-ers?

They were twice as many as Generation X-ers in number. And they baffled retailers, marketers and corporate executives alike. They were the first generation of American consumers raised in the milieu of corporate "branding," MTV and the Internet. They were coming of age during a recession that had challenged, for the first time in the twentieth century, the very idea about consumer *loyalty*.

Nowhere was this more evident than on April 2, 1993, known in the retailing world as "Marlboro Friday." Philip Morris announced that day that it would cut the price of its Marlboro cigarettes by 20 percent in order to compete with *generic* brands of cigarettes that were cutting into its market share. "Study after study showed that baby boomers, blind to the alluring images of advertising and deaf to the empty promises of celebrity spokespersons, were breaking their lifelong brand loyalties. . . . The bargain craze of the early nineties shook the name brands to their core," writes Naomi Klein in *No Logo*.[3]

The intensity of Generation Y has been commented upon by corporate America. Michael Wolf at Booz-Allen & Hamilton, in his trademark hyperbole, sums up Generation Y as being "Generation X on steroids."[4] This may be as much a reflection of the interactive approach to life taken by members of Generation Y as it is being compared with the passive members of Generation X. That Generation Y-ers have come of age at a time when technological innovations are changing the way the world does business and how human beings interact with one another heightens their sense of purpose. The optimism of youth makes young people believe they can make a difference, whether it is at the cash register, polling booth or demonstrating against the establishment. Management consultants who make careers trying to help the business community understand these forces are themselves struggling to identify the points of reference that can help put things in perspective. Thus throwing one's hands in the air and saying that an entire generation of American consumers are on some testosterone high is a fair summary of how bewildered corporate America is, in fact.

"There was no loyalty to the Gap," Donald Fisher said, recalling that tumultuous period in the seventies for apparel retailers. "People went out and bought Levi's® at the store that had the lowest prices. We had to compete with everyone on price—and you can imagine how profit margins suffered for it. If we had relied on just selling Levi's®, it would have been over for us."

That sense of consumer disloyalty resurfaced once more. For Donald Fisher, the dread of having to compete exclusively on price points was felt once again in the early nineties as consumers shifted away from the Gap in favor of the lower prices for casuals introduced at stores such as Wal-Mart, K-Mart and Target. The last time there had been anything like this was back in 1978 when Levi's® were first discounted. The Gap's sales figures in the first half of the nineties told the story in an arresting way: in 1991 and 1992 same-store sales grew by a meager 5 percent; in 1993 and 1994 growth had slowed to 1 percent in each of those years; and by 1995 there was no growth at all. The Gap was in a crisis at a time when multitudes of Generation Y teenagers were coming into their own as consumers.

"I remember the first time I went to my dad's office," a young man named David who was fifteen in 1995 explained to me. "Everyone was walking around in Dockers® khakis, knit polo shirts and sneakers. Or loafers. That's what people wear to work. That's why the baby boomers are called 'baby' boomers, because they are adults who still look like babies. Who wants to dress like big babies?"

If in the sixties young people declared that no one over thirty could be trusted, in the nineties Generation Y teenagers proclaimed that no one over thirty could be trusted to have any fashion sense. That the Gap had pioneered the antifashion revolution now created an obstacle that made it difficult to bridge the current generation gap. In the historical context of the second half of the twentieth century, Alison Lurie explains the phenomenon in this manner:

Then, in the early sixties, a new wave of romantic enthusiasm and innovation—political, spiritual and cultural, or rather countercultural—broke over the Western world. . . . Youth Culture. . . . The fashionable appearance for women became that of an eight-to-ten-year-old child, with a child's wide-eyed pouting face and a child's figure. . . . Women's clothes, too, were those of children. Men . . . also readopted—or refused to give up—the clothes of their childhood . . . jeans, cord pants, sneakers, sweaters, T-shirts, turtlenecks and windbreakers. And, like little boys, they preferred bright colors.[5]

Maturity was a casualty of a society where "casual Friday" had become every day of the week. A sense of decorum and pride in one's self were other casualties of the antifashion revolution, which was to be expected when one had an entire generation of adult men and women pretending to be little boys and girls.

"All my life I've worn white tube socks," a young man who became a teenager in 1997 explained to me. "Do you know how I felt when I wore 'real' socks for the first time this year? I wasn't a kid anymore! I felt grown-up for the first time in my life! I felt like an adult! I felt like a man! Why did it take this long?"

In the first decade of the new century, the Gap was in the absurd position of renouncing "ambiance" when it had been its close identification with Youth Culture that had brought such spectacular success. The Gap had lost its hold on the imagination of young people. Ralph Lauren had snapped up Club Monaco and a revitalized Gucci was leading the return of style and fashion to the delight of Generation Y. Retailers from J. Crew to Levi Strauss & Co. studied carefully the Achilles heel Old Navy's cannibalism had exposed.

"Now [in the twenty-first century], I love looking at girls who have matching shoes and handbags, looking at men who are wearing pochettes," Isaac Mizrahi wrote in *Esquire* magazine in the year 2000. "I could not stick one in my pocket for ten or fifteen years, and now I want to wear a pocket square. It's like, *I'm gonna flaunt this in your fucking minimalist face. I'm gonna flaunt this damn bit of finery.*"[6]

Is this, then, what the spiritual mentors and idols of Generation Y are advocating to America's youth? Are they imploring that Generation Y counter the counterrevolution the Gap represents and rebel against the triumph of the antifashion philosophy?

It is, indeed.

Now that the nineties are history, the one guiding principle of Generation Y's *zeitgeist* has been reduced to this succinct mantra: *Flaunt fashion in the Gap's minimalist face.*

One unintended consequence of the proliferation of Youth Culture was the triumph of the "infantile wardrobe," one in which adults lived their entire lives dressed as over-sized children. The frustration felt by Generation Y was echoed in the media at the end of the nineties: MTV personalities decried the tiresome "sameness" of everyone dressing alike by pointing to the ubiquitous Gap advertisements at the end of the nineties. "Casual clothes are for children," Wendie Malick, who portrays the character Nina Van Horn on the hit NBC television show *Just Shoot Me*, proclaimed to the world, rolling her eyes in disgust on December 21, 1999.

Generation Y knows that instinctively. One of the more popular shows on MTV is the *House of Fashion*, which is, in essence, a primer on how youths can repudiate the Gap's antifashion tyranny.[7] Youth rebels against the conformity the Gap has imposed on America much the same way youths in the sixties railed against the Eisenhower world of the Matures generation. It was one thing, recall for a moment, for baby boomers to rebel against the conformity and rigid rules of dress that prevailed in the fifties by dressing down and another thing for Generation X-ers to assume the casualness they inherited as their very own. The baby boomers had collective memories of being forced to wear school uniforms in the fifties and early sixties. They had been traumatized by being forced to learn to wear ties, instructed on how to groom their hair, told to tie laced shoes and been taught to wear different clothes for different occasions. These "dress codes" particularly affected women. Discipline and discomfort are a faint and distant memory to most consumers at the dawn of the twenty-first century.

Consider, however, how Alison Lurie describes how women were liberated by the simple act of wearing pants:

In the late 1960s trousers for women finally became elegant as well as respectable, and underwear vanished or mutated into harmless forms. Even before the second wave of women's liberation got underway, the long struggle for comfort and freedom in female dress seemed to have been won at last. The introduction of panty hose freed women from the ugly and often painful rubber and metal and plastic hardware they had been using to hold up their stockings. It was again permissible to have curves below the waist as well as above; and millions of girdles went into the trash bins. . . . During the 1970s pant suits and slacks were worn to work, to parties, to the theater, in elegant restaurants and on international planes, by women of all ages.[8]

The Gap ingeniously catered to the first generation of Americans who were discarding the restrictive clothing styles of the past. The women's movement as much as the triumph of Youth Culture created new styles that dismantled the very idea of fashion; clothes were for living realistic lifestyles that were active, modern and fun. But if the baby boomers had cause to righteous rebellion—and Generation X simply went along for the ride— by the nineties, this had been reduced to some ancient history that was best forgotten and meant nothing to Generation Y.

Indeed, in the sixties, James Dean wore blue jeans and T-shirts and by so doing made a statement on social, cultural and political terms. By the time the nineties rolled around, Jerry Seinfeld, on the other hand, wore the same clothes—and he ended up blending into a nondescript background like dull wallpaper. Whereas James Dean's wardrobe was sexually charged in its visual impact as a rebellious act against authority and a stand against conformity, three decades later, Jerry Seinfeld's wardrobe was remarkably generic and antisexual and not worthy of comment. That the same clothes that on James Dean exuded raw sexuality have come to represent the mundane and ordinary on Jerry Seinfeld is proof of the enormous power to desensitize through cultural repetition of images over time. What once was evidence of potent sexuality had become a mundane uniform devoid of the power to arouse or seduce. Of greater importance, however, was whether this seduction was straight or gay.

Was the Gap, by reverting to an androgynous look for its print advertising, in danger of turning away Generation Y?

This perception is not meant to be argumentative. It is offered, however, as a mindful commentary on the importance for retailers to maintain a positive balance in how a brand is perceived by the consumers they court. There is, after all, a difference between pushing buttons and tipping the scale. The history of Benetton and Diesel stores bears repeating. First, consider

Benetton. In its campaign to stir political controversy, Benetton, the Italian retailer with stores around the world, inadvertently pushed the wrong buttons among American consumers. The stark advertisement featuring a black woman breast-feeding a white infant caused a maelstrom among Americans. The Italians were trying to juxtapose random images by putting people of different races and cultures together as part of their notorious "United colors of Benetton" campaign. That single image, however, resulted in impassioned and furious denunciations throughout the United States precisely because of America's history of slavery. That this image constituted a graphic reminder of a social injustice greatly harmed the Benetton brand. The history of the United States, in which generations of women of color neglected their own children because they were forced to make a living by taking care of the children of whites, was not what Americans wanted to see staring back at them from the pages of fashion magazines.

Now let us turn to how Diesel, which in an effort to make social commentary, similarly tipped the scale against it by being identified as "too" homosexual. In full-page advertisements that featured two gay lovers, body builders dressed up as sailors, who were embracing and passionately kissing, Diesel alienated straight young men. That the men featured, Bob Paris and Rod Jackson, had become celebrities within the gay community and were featured in a best-selling homoerotic book of photographs made Diesel's fast identification with homosexuality an aberration to many younger Americans. Diesel, based in the United Kingdom, terribly underestimated the backlash it subsequently suffered by embracing this kind of commercial sexual deviancy with such enthusiasm.

As a consequence of these miscalculations Benetton and Diesel both lost significant market share in the United States. Brands that were once hot are now difficult to find. Banana Republic itself stood at a crucial crossroads, one in which it ran the risk of diminishing further the value of its brand. Reflect for a moment on something as innocuous as how the public perceives the little details. In early 2000 Banana Republic introduced the idea of featuring a color in its seasonal collections. Pink was the color for the spring of 2000, an appropriate enough selection, considering the campaign was launched in time for Valentine's Day. There were, in fact, three different shades of pink. Their names were simple enough: "light pink," "pale pink" and "pink."

Six months later, as the fall collections began to arrive at stores, the featured color was green. But this time, instead of having, say, "light," "pale" and "standard" green, Banana Republic could not resist being fabulous and campy. The three shades of green were named "lettuce," "kiwi" and "avocado."[9] What kind of straight young man is about to walk into any Banana Republic and ask to try on the shirt in the window in the hue of kiwi?[10] The sight of two gay lovers kissing resulted in "straight flight" from Diesel. Banana Republic began to experience the same phenomenon from the members of Generation Y who were straight males. Banana Republic, indeed, followed in the missteps of both Benetton and Diesel in how it devalued its brand among the straight male members of Generation Y.

The Gap was not far behind in pushing the envelope similarly. To understand this clearly, it bears pointing out that clothes have always been used to send gender signals for attracting the attention of potential suitors and romantic partners. Alison Lurie elaborates upon this point:

> Some modern writers believe that the deliberate concealment of certain parts of the body originated not as a way of discouraging sexual interest, but as a clever device for arousing it. According to this view, clothes ... are a tease, a come-on. It is certainly true that parts of the human form considered sexually arousing are often covered in such a way as to exaggerate and draw attention to them. People done up in shiny colored wrappings and bows affect us just as a birthday present does: we're curious, turned on; we want to undo the package.[11]

In the nineties as Generation Y reached puberty, one could only pity young people who had been deprived of the skills necessary to use their dress for romance and in courtship: there was no "package" to undo. Clothes that made it impossible to signal gender proved one of the most infuriating consequences of the antifashion revolution at the end of the twentieth century.

"Life in the twenty-first century is more complicated when it comes to relations between the sexes," Donald Huber, a New York designer, explained with authority. "In those old MGM romance musicals from the forties, the plot was so much simpler. Boy meets girl. Boy loses girl. Boy gets girl. But now, the plot can be summed up this way: Boy meets girl. Girl thinks boy is a fag. Boy loses girl until boy comes to his senses and throws all his Gap clothes in the garbage. Boy, then dressed like a boy, gets girl—which means boy gets laid before girl gets dumped."

The apparent repudiation of the Gap by heterosexual members of Generation Y was swift. Sales at the Gap fell immediately after that advertising campaign (its androgynous look) was launched. That "sale" signs were prominently displayed in Gap stores in the spring and summer of 2000 was proof of how badly Mickey Drexler had stumbled once more in his attempt to make the Gap a place where consumers went to purchase something that was thought of as fashion. Indeed, if at the end of the twentieth century, Banana Republic had become "too queer for words," then at the beginning of the twenty-first century, the Gap was fast becoming too androgynous to wear. The Gap brand was fast becoming, to a disconcerting number of self-respecting members of Generation Y—and to the complete horror of Donald Fisher—a store that lost the masculinity that other brands projected. To the question, *Quién es mas macho?* the answer was Abercrombie & Fitch, J. Crew and Marc Ecko.

The mounting male heterosexual Generation Y-ers' repudiation resulted in tremendous turmoil that reverberated throughout all the divisions of Gap, Inc. There is even now a certain cognitive dissonance among Gap executives when explaining the schizophrenic performance of the various divisions. By the mid-nineties it was clearly evident that the situation at Gap, as Nina Munk, a reporter for *Fortune* magazine phrased it, had gone "from bad to dreadful."[12]

If Isaac Mizrahi's directive to Generation Y was to flaunt fashion in the Gap's minimalist face, then Charlize Theron was the "ambassador from the future," demonstrating in no uncertain terms everything that American womanhood could strive for—and achieve. The dreams and aspirations voiced by disenchanted young men and women, resentful of the antifashion philosophy that has dominated their lives with relentless tyranny, were validated in the way true fashion, which is to say, fashion as it had once been presented by visionaries like Diana Vreeland, was being embraced by role models. Indeed, it was Charlize Theron's style, her elegance and the way she carried herself that, on Oscar night in the year 2000, made manifest the yearnings of Generation Y.

Consider that as early as 1993, *Saturday Night Live* ridiculed the Gap in skits featuring the "Gap Girls." That same year's "Who wore khakis?" campaign was mocked, pointing out that, in addition to James Dean and Jack Kerouac, the Italian fascist dictator Benito Mussolini also "wore khakis"—and so did, we soon learned, Charles Manson. The Gap was mentioned in mundane episodes of *Seinfeld* on network television, and being a manager for a Gap store was portrayed as the metaphor for a life not worth living in the successful film, *Reality Bites.*[13] Seven years later, *Saturday Night Live* intensified its ridicule of the Gap in mock commercials that had grossly obese dancers parodying the Gap's 2000 campaign with the tag line, "When you're XXXL," and the logo "Gap Fat" flashing across the screen.

This "Gap-lash" of sorts continued throughout the nineties, culminating in a startling sight. Rage Against the Machine, a rock band whose fortunes and popularity soared at the end of the nineties with the release of "The Battle of Los Angeles" on Epic Records, in their concert performed in the fall of 1999 in Mexico City, and subsequently televised on MTV, railed against the Gap brand and everything it represents by denouncing what it labeled as the Gap's "immoral consumerism" while the audience cheered approvingly. Then Rage Against the Machine raged against the Gap in an onstage protest that culminated in a Gap advertisement being destroyed while the band decried to the audience, "Everybody in denial!" The music of Rage Against the Machine was a classic snubbing of the lowbrow antifashion philosophy of the Gap, which was now equated with the pornography of materialist consumption.

The cheering kids at the Aztec Stadium went wild.

This social repudiation and mocking of the Gap affected how Generation Y perceived the Gap brand. The impact on the Gap was undeniable and there was something erratic about how the company continued to perform throughout the nineties. It was hot one season, then cold the next. Sales rose, then plummeted. Prices had to be slashed—only to be raised again. Despite the seesaw performance of the Gap stores, no one dared question Mickey Drexler or Donald Fisher. *Fortune* magazine's Nina Munk reports that "Drexler's control over every aspect of Gap is legendary. He's known for sudden bursts of temper when things go wrong. 'Nothing gets by Mickey. His attention to detail is extraordinary. He looks at the threads, buttons, everything, . . .' explains Jim Fielding." Then, in the same article a few pages further along, Nina Munk points out, matter-of-factly, that "[o]ne day in the summer of 1996, Drexler wandered slowly through a Gap store and was shocked. The clothes were ugly, the carpet was frayed, the fixtures looked cheap. Simplicity and cleanliness had been forgotten."[14]

Forgotten? Forgotten by whom?

Which is it then?

How can one reconcile Mickey Drexler the control freak with the Mickey Drexler who wanders through a Gap store and is disoriented—and shocked—to see what he finds there, because it's all new to him? How can one insider report that Drexler obsesses about buttons and threads, only to learn that in 1996 Drexler didn't go on vacation and, in order to get re-acquainted with the Gap's line of clothing, he "spent 2½ months, from June to August, going through every item of clothing in the line—clothes that were to hit stores in the spring of 1997?"

This paradox was the natural result of the Gap pushing the right buttons with baby boomers (who now had children of their own and shopped at Baby Gap, Gap Kids and Gap) and Generation X-ers (who remained faithful to the antifashion style of Gap), but then failing miserably to connect with the pulse of Generation Y. It was apparent that the turnaround of 1988, when Mickey Drexler was showered with praise for being a wonder boy who made the Gap the envy of retailers throughout the nation, had fizzled to nothing by the end of 1993.

From bad to dreadful, which is to say, less than zero.

To be sure, the Jekyll-and-Hyde personality of Gap, Inc. manifested itself in other areas also. Consider its advertising, for a moment. Stuart Elliott, who covers advertising and the media for the *New York Times*, reflected on the irony that Gap was capable of producing both the "best" and the "worst" in its in-house advertising simultaneously. "Kudos to Nike, V.W. and Gap; Catcalls to AT&T, Ford and Gap," he wrote in December 1999, summarizing the year's best and worst in terms of advertising.

How is it possible that Gap could be the best and the worst at the same time? The schizophrenic nature of Gap's personality in the nineties was summarized by Elliott when he pointed out that "Gap, Inc. delighted consumers with a khaki campaign, this one a sequel to 'Khakis swing,' perhaps the best spot of 1998. As attractive dancers sashayed to go-go, country and soul tunes, viewers wondered whether 'Khakis waltz' or 'Khakis polka' would come next. Gap's holiday campaign also used music and dance to good effect as models cavorted to an odd medley of 'Sleigh Ride' and 'Ice, Ice Baby.' " The same in-house staff that won such accolades was then admonished by Elliott, who wrote, "Not every Gap campaign was a winner. Commercials urging 'everybody' to wear cords, leather and vests were as dispirited as their khaki and holiday counterparts were energetic. The casts behaved like zombies who had exchanged their personalities for Gap gift certificates—or jobs at Gap stores."[15]

Stuart Elliott's praise and condemnation, curiously, appeared in the same article.

"Look at those boys," said a young African-American woman, age seventeen, who looked at a photograph of an "Everybody in vests" Gap advertisement launched in 1999. "They don't look like they have dicks!"

The entire "zombie chic" cast of young men and women, of various races but the same age group, wore identical khaki pants—rumpled and wrinkled and a size too large—and pastel T-shirts as tops. The clothes were interchangeable, and it looked like they put on the first thing they grabbed from the first dryer they reached into at some campus laundromat somewhere in collegiate America. The disinterested expressions on their faces and the indifferent poses further highlighted a certain detachment, ennui—and irrelevance.

These advertisements of "dickless" youngsters, so freely derided by members of Generation Y in both their adoration of MTV videos that ridiculed this campaign as much as in their categorical aversion to purchasing any of these clothes, were the brainchild of Jim Nevins. Changes in the perceptions of the Gap as a brand accelerated once Maggie Gross had resigned. The care with which she had created a uniform brand image for the Gap was systematically undermined. Compared with the meticulous craftsmanship employed by Maggie Gross to nurture a coherent branding for the Gap, Jim Nevins flippantly characterized Gap's new approach by stating that "we don't think things through too hard."

Obviously, as the results show vividly. Indeed, the "sale" signs that mushroomed throughout the Gap stores were but one stunning consequence of the "thoughtlessness" of the new approach to the Gap's brand.

"I guess you could say we sort of guess about these things," Jim Nevins is quoted as saying about the Gap's approach to advertising as the nineties ended. It is as disingenuous as it is discomforting to think that "Gap"—the corporate brand—is treated with such casual disregard. There is comfort in knowing that fiascoes such as "Everybody in ... " and the capri pants were not thought through carefully. What appeals to the homosexual market—which remains a niche market, however visible it might otherwise be—does not appeal to mainstream. There's nothing wrong with that, except that the Gap aspires to be in everyone's closets.

It would be appalling to think that Gap executives held meetings in which, for instance, the announced agenda was nothing less than to decide how to spend millions of dollars in advertising for the expressed purpose of alienating members of Generation Y, exposing the firm to public ridicule, developing a line of clothing so shunned by consumers that to move them out of the stores would require steep discounts and, finally, sit back and, without much thought, watch the company's stock lose half its value.

That, however, is what might as well have happened. Of course the gaily whimsical advertisements designed by Jim Nevins were not entirely to blame. Old Navy's voracious cannibalistic appetite could not be satiated. What was clear, however, was that, confronted with management that didn't really think things through, shareholders were not so nonchalant about plummeting sales and stock prices. The accidental attitude put forth by Jim Nevins, to a considerable degree, is an attempt at damage control. Gap does think these things through, but sometimes its thinking is irrational.

Gap, Inc. was not the only consumer company confronting the fallout when many members of Generation Y turned away from the Gap and embraced other labels they associated more firmly with "healthy" masculinity, to be sure. Throughout the marketing departments of corporate America there was great concern about what was commonly referred to as the "erosion of masculinity."

Firms from across the economic spectrum, since the mid-nineties, have been confronted with the unprecedented challenge of reaching young heterosexual men. The erosion of masculinity specifically refers to the increasing difficulty corporate America has in attempting to reach heterosexual male consumers between the ages of eighteen and thirty-five. The proliferation of the androgynous clothes that eliminated the differences between the sexes had resulted in the unprecedented fragmentation of young men as a target audience, a target audience that proves quite elusive to reach with general interest advertising. This isolation of men, which is the ostracism of the male ego, has required corporate America to make significant investments in market research and focus groups. One result, confirmed by cigarette companies and soft drink makers alike, was that, at the beginning of the twenty-first century, one of the few remaining undiminished bastions of "masculinity" was race car driving. This sport continued to score very high among consumers in its fast association with male heterosexuality, which resulted in an explosive interest by marketers to strengthen their sponsorship and association with this sport.

The fear among marketing executives was that the present situation was one in which they had inadequately considered the impact of gay aesthetics on mainstream consumer behavior. There was a realization that male members of Generation X had been feminized by the sweeping cultural forces that presented sexual deviance as innocuous, but Generation Y-ers repudiated the fundamental assault on healthy and undiminished masculinity. Companies like Philip Morris and Coca-Cola had no alternative but to invest millions of dollars in campaigns associated with race car driving and similar activities to reach straight young men.

In the nineties, because of companies like Banana Republic, it seemed as if American men were a bunch of eunuchs. Corporate America was forced to spend billions of dollars in research to understand how the erosion of masculinity tore asunder time-tested marketing strategies. This fragmentation of the male market represented nothing more than a generational conflict in which heterosexual Generation Y-ers felt left out. Female Generation Y-ers bemoan the "dickless" boys they see plastered in advertisements all around them. Executives throughout corporate America are stunned at how the fallout from the erosion of masculinity undermines their marketing campaigns.

"What *is* their strategy? Does Gap *have* a strategy?" one fashion diva observed, scoffing at the ludicrous capri pants on an enormous billboard in downtown San Francisco. "If Maggie Gross were around, she wouldn't stand for this nonsense. And all this stuff they're coming out with is the empty-headed nonsense."

There definitely was a problem. Advertising campaigns developed by Jim Nevins, such as the "Everybody in . . ." and the *West Side Story* campaigns proved to be arresting visually, but they did little to lift sales. Even after Jim Nevins left, Gap not only struggled to understand why consumers rejected its brand but also compounded its errors by bringing back failed fashion ideas and blurring distinctions between its brands. The disastrous Capri line of clothing of 2000, for instance, was reintroduced in 2001 as a "boot cut" Capri. To make matters worse, conflicted marketing blurred the distinctions between the Gap brand and Old Navy when Old Navy launched its own line of "boot cut" Capris. Gap executives were beside themselves, longing for the return of Maggie Gross whose brilliance was ever the more evident in the series of missteps that characterized the Gap in her absence.

"Did you ever see the movie *The Time Machine* on television?" a young Asian man who is a member of Generation Y asked me rhetorically, referring to the 1960 film directed by George Pal and based on the Jules Verne novel of the same title. "Well, the Eloi were a race of young people who dressed in stupid pastel-colored clothing and walked around completely oblivious to the fact that the Morlocks bred them only for food—just as if they were cattle! There was no *civilization* for the Eloi, no *history* of any kind and they were *passive agents in their own destruction*. They lived their lives as if they were cows! That's what the Gap wants us to be: cows who follow the herd, don't make any waves and then let the Morlocks from the Gap slaughter us to feed their evil corporate machine!"

Then I am informed, in no uncertain terms, that *The Time Machine* is a nothing but a vivid metaphor for Gap, Inc.—and that Donald Fisher and Mickey Drexler are the Morlocks who breed the Eloi, which are the whole of American consumers, for their own selfish benefit.

"The Eloi look exactly like the stupid kids in the Gap ads on television and in magazines, staring out as if they were in a trance with their unquestioning stupidity and completely ignorant of the fact that they exist only so the Gap brand can feed off them! That's what the Gap is doing to my generation: killing off our creativity with their corporate violence."

The world is rediscovered by every generation, of course. And as each generation, individual by individual, discovers life, there are certain cycles inherent in our nature. Think back on your own experience. A three-year-old at the beach will delight in running after sea birds, but is ever mindful to stop, turn around, and make sure that a watchful parent is there. Fast forward a mere decade, and that same child will look back to make sure a parent isn't around. Three year olds who held their parents' hands as they walked onto the beach become teenagers who, reminding their parents not to embarrass them in front of their friends, look back to ensure their parents are nowhere in sight.

This is the natural process of establishing our independent and separate identities and of becoming our own persons. For generations this "rebellion" has had social consequences. If, as a group, they think they "know" things, there is a tendency to see the world in shades of black and white. It is only as one matures that one is struck by how many shades of gray there are in this world. If Generation Y-ers—and their voice against the Gap embodied by Global Exchange—can be faulted, it is in the irony that this generation has benefited from technological advances and material wealth never before experienced by humanity. They rage against it without understanding fully the complex nature of how it is precisely globalization that has made so many cherished aspects of their lives possible.

Rock concerts, cell phones, MTV and the Internet—the staples of Generation Y's world—are all the products of the materialism of relentless corporate discipline, innovation and hard work. On Monday morning it is the members of Generation Y who go on-line or pick up the newspaper to read the box office sales, measured in the millions of dollars, of movies over the weekend. And throughout the week, they look at the relative ranking—winners and losers—of music, whether it is the weekly Top Forty on the radio or the daily *Total Request Line* on MTV.

This is the natural evolution of merchandising—and selling. The advantage that Generation Y enjoys is how fast technological change has revolutionized the art of selling. Edward L. Bernays, whose career began in earnest in the twenties, is largely credited with inventing the art of public relations, an instrumental profession that helped transform retailing. Larry Tye summarizes Edward Bernays's approach in this manner:

Bernays's first rule: Public relations is a two-way street. On one side the PR man interprets his client to the public, presenting as upbeat an image as he can. It is equally important to interpret the public to the client, telling company executives what people want and need, and altering the behavior of those executives just as he did that of the public.

To do the job right, Bernays believed, the PR man not only needs to be smart and intuitive, he needs to understand psychology, sociology, and enough other social sciences to get under the skin of the public and the client, to know what makes them act the way they do and how they can be enticed to act differently. Realizing this second goal, he added, required poring over books and journals, interviewing experts, and doing all the other research a social scientist would do.[16]

Thus the father of spin argued that successful companies are the ones engaged in nothing less than *social engineering*, with all the Orwellian implications this kind of marketing holds. Members of Generation Y, by pointing out that the Eloi did not even possess cell phones (to speak nothing of lacking any common sense) are using these very arguments in their relentless deconstruction of the Gap.

To understand the predicament confronting the Gap, consider the following experiment. *YO!*, which stands for "youth outlook," is a monthly newspaper publication of the Pacific News Service in San Francisco that is written, edited and produced by and for high school students throughout California and beyond.[17] The young journalists, reporters, writers and editors reflect the cultural, racial and sexual diversity that constitutes contemporary California.

In several discussions with these civic-minded members of Generation Y, I spoke about the "coolness factor" of Gap and its various divisions. It was clear that the Gap presented ethical problems for these young people, who were representative of the protesters likely to show up at a demonstration against the Gap a few blocks away. These were the savvy consumers who equated the casts of the "Everybody in cords, leather and vests" campaigns to be as idiotic and catatonic as the Eloi in *The Time Machine*.

"How can you compare these boys in these Gap ads," a Generation Y female mentioned to me with a longing look in her eyes, "with the Backstreet Boys?" The Gap presented a group of young men who, despite the fact they were of different races, wore interchangeable clothes, alluding to indiscriminate and blasé personalities. Each member of the Backstreet Boys, on the other hand, wore a different outfit, one that revealed as much about his individual style and personality as it did about the public image each wanted to present to the world.

The comparison is arresting. Whereas the Gap offers an Orwellian vision of totalitarianism, where the masses are dressed in drab uniforms issued by omnipotent state authorities and where individualism has been forbidden, the Backstreet Boys, defiantly and exuberantly celebrate, through their clothing and in their grooming, the distinct personalities of the individual young men who make up the group. As the nineties ended, the Youth Culture of Generation Y craved sophistication and originality in their clothes.

To understand why Generation Y feels betrayed and deprived, a simple experiment is in order. I took four members of Generation Y shopping individually.[18] A couple of blocks from Pacific News Service one finds a Gap store on the intersection of Powell and Market streets in front of the cable cars. Directly across from the Gap, on the corner of Market and Fifth streets, one finds the San Francisco Centre, where the Nordstrom department store occupies the top four floors. The experiment conducted on each occasion was the same, and the results were identical each time.

Upon arriving at the Gap, each teenager was told to pick out two outfits, consisting of two tops, two pairs of pants and whatever accessories (belts, socks, etc.) each desired. Then we crossed the street and went to Nordstrom to shop for two additional outfits. At the Gap, each teenager meandered about the store, picking what he or she liked, in the familiar sizes and colors, for the most part on his or her own. But once we crossed the street and took the elevators to Nordstrom, *what a difference tailoring makes!*

One of the young men had never realized that shirts were sold by neck sizes when we arrived at the Men's Department at Nordstrom. "I thought it was just 'S, M, L or XL,' " he confessed. The other had never been measured by a tailor to make sure the inseam on his trousers was the proper length. Both young men had never been in a situation where salesmen took precise measurements of their necks, arms, waists and inseams and then proceeded to present "appropriate" selections for each young man to consider. Shoes that matched the belts, and socks that matched the outfit, were brought over; these gestures were a novelty to these members of Generation Y. Each stood on a small platform while pins were used to adjust fit, tailors armed with tape measures and chalk were bent on their knees to ensure proper fittings.

The following week when the clothes were ready, it was astounding to see the reaction of these members of Generation Y to how spectacular they felt to wear clothes, for the first time in their lives, that had been tailored exclusively for them. The clothes were "restrictive," by which they meant the clothes fit them snugly, but when they saw themselves in the mirror, they were as delighted with their clothes as with their appearances.

"Hey, I'm 'styling,' " one of the young men said. "I look great!"

The transformation for the young women was not as dramatic or, as one phrased it, as "mind-blowing." Both admitted that they had long agonized over their appearances in the mirror and that they had owned "real" dresses before. The attention lavished upon them by the saleswomen at Nordstrom, however, was a singular experience for the young women. Both had never been in a situation where they were helped as much to find dresses and outfits that approximated what they wanted and were flattering to their individual features and make-up.

"I felt like Jennifer Lopez," one of the young women said, referencing the stylish Puerto Rican actor and singer whose first album lingered at the top of the charts for most of 1999, after two saleswomen were through with her.[19] "Jennifer went from looking OK to looking beautiful after she got a personal trainer and a makeover, you know. But I've never looked so beautiful!"

If television sitcoms joked that casual clothes were for children in the nineties, then what Generation Y wanted more than anything in the first decade of the twenty-first century was to be grown up.

This is readily understandable when one considers that Generation Y-ers never had the choice the baby boomers took for granted: the ability to rebel against the rigidity of tailored clothing by virtue of having lived their entire lives in casual wardrobes. They harbor a certain resentment to having been raised wearing exclusively blue jeans, T-shirts and sweats, a resentment that is directed on the Gap brand.

"It isn't that I want to dis the Gap," a young woman who was born in 1987 explained. "But it's that all their clothes are so everyday. Only Banana Republic has interesting-looking stuff, but it's for old people, you know, people in their thirties. And the clothing for guys is really for gays. But I see what role models from my generation are wearing and it's so different from anything you see in Gap ads. I see the stylish clothes Missy [Misdemeanor] Elliott and Tionne [T-Boz] Watkins and Mary J. Blige and Jennifer Lopez wear in their videos and on television and you know that not one of them went shopping at the Gap for anything in their wardrobes! How come no one ever taught us how to dress up and be sexy?"[20]

It wasn't only members of Generation Y who had grown tired and disaffected with the impact of the Gap's antifashion doctrine on American society. Grown men and women longed for a certain decorum that was missing in American life. This coarsening of public life was reflected as much in how people dressed as in the embrace of the vulgar by the American public. Generation Y-er's lament that they had never been taught to dress—and had therefore been deprived of a fundamental right to civility—found resonance among older Americans who waxed poetic for the quintessential American elegance that so captivated the world in the forties and fifties.

"Witness the élan with which Cary Grant comports himself in 1957's *An Affair to Remember*, leaning suavely against the cruise-ship railing in a gray three-button jacket, light-gray tie, and French cuffs, charming Deborah Kerr into dinner. . . . Of course, it's facile to argue that people dressed great then, that style is dead now, and that the Gap is to blame," Ted Allen wrote, lamenting the Gap's particular form of American juvenilia in *Esquire* in the year 2000.[21]

It's facile, but it's also true. Ted Allen, however, was not alone in being fed up with the vulgarity the Gap's antifashion marketing had unleashed upon the land. "It's like a plague seeing the way our people dress," a partner at Goldman Sachs confessed. "But if we don't let them dress like adultchildren at day camp, they'll just go work for some Internet start-up some-where, where they can wear sweats and T-shirts—and turn their offices into kennels."

One man's lament is another's opportunity. Gianni Versace recognized he could establish his brand in America by satisfying the desire for fine tai-loring. "The Gap has mass-marketed the most boring clothes in the history of the world," he said at his home in Miami Beach in 1992. "Americans are starved for style, for tailoring, for anything that gives them a sense of ele-gance, of finery, of things that will [make] them beautiful. But they don't know how to become beautiful women or handsome men. American women walk city streets wearing Nike sneakers and Gap jeans! This is too horrible! If I had to live my life in clothes from the Gap, I would die of shame. I love America *too* much to let Americans dress like *peasants* any lon-ger. No! No! No! The Gap is like a biblical plague!"

If the Gap's effect on the way Americans dressed was indeed a plague upon the land, there were those ready to step forward and rescue corporate America. Brooks Brothers, along with other New York haberdashers, em-barked on a proactive campaign to reverse this trend. If it all began when Alcoa first allowed "casual Fridays" in 1991, then the natural antidote would be a "dress-up Thursday."

"Casual dress fatigue" became a question for the entire country to pon-der out loud when in the summer of 2000 the national newspaper, *USA To-day*, featured as a cover story, "Companies rethink casual clothes." Whereas in 1998, 97 percent of companies throughout the United States allowed their employees to dress casually, in 1999 that figure dropped to 87 percent and throughout the 2000 more and more companies pulled back from lib-eral dress codes, citing falling productivity and concern that the more ca-sual work environment might contribute to corporate liability in sexual harassment cases. "Concerned that laissez-faire policies on casual dress un-dermine professionalism," the mass-market daily reported, "many em-ployers are asking workers to dress up instead of down."

This sentiment resounded more and more throughout the fall of 2000, when dressing up was the thing to do in corporate America. When Bill Gates, who had long been dismissed as "an overgrown kid with a Gap charge card," began wearing tailored suits to denote his change in attitude in the aftermath of Microsoft being found guilty of engaging in predatory mo-nopolistic practices in the summer of 2000, the unequivocal message that business is best left to men and women who dress like adults was down-loaded throughout the corridors of corporate America.[22] "The Justice De-partment's proposed breakup of Microsoft is a serious matter," a spokesman for Bill Gates replied when asked why Bill Gates, for the first time in his pro-fessional career, had begun to dress in tailored suits. "Bill Gates wants his dress to reflect the gravity of the matter at hand," he added.

GQ, the influential men's magazine, simultaneously applauded what it titled "The Return of the Elegant Man," telling readers that, commencing with the fall 2000 clothes, it was "time to dress up again." The magazine informed American men that it, once more, enthusiastically embraced "the lost art of manly elegance," ruefully jesting that had this casual wear nonsense pioneered by the Gap continued much longer, the magazine would have been forced to drop the word "gentlemen" from its name.[23]

Thus "dress up Thursday" became a bold and welcome experiment to rescue American style and elegance in September 2000 when participating companies in New York began to encourage workers to dress up—at least *one* day of the *damn* week—on Thursday (not unlike the way children had been encouraged to wear their Sunday best in generations past). It gained the stature and acclaim of a national response that rebuked the decade-long antifashion revolution unleashed by the Gap. There were empirical data to support the misgivings senior managers felt. City Personnel Group, a human resources organization, conducted surveys among the 230 member companies in which executives reported that their companies experienced no advantage at all from adopting dress-down policies. In fact, human resource officers throughout corporate America noted that dress-down policies generated more complaints than plaudits from employees who were confused or offended by their co-workers.

Wearing one's best on Sunday was not in the life experience of most Generation Y-ers, however. If the Gap brand was now identified with an oppressive force, it bears recalling the purpose of "brands" in the first place. "Familiar personalities such as Dr. Brown, Uncle Ben, Aunt Jemima, and Old Grand-Dad came to replace the shopkeeper, who was traditionally responsible for measuring bulk foods for customers and acting as an advocate for products," Ellen Lupton and J. Abbott Miller explained while discussing how products were marketed at the end of the nineteenth century in the United States.[24]

Thus as the Industrial Revolution took firm hold in America and transformed the economy throughout the 1880s, consumer goods were now, for the first time, mass-produced and packaged in cans and boxes that bore corporate names such as Campbell's Soup and Quaker Oats cereal. Soon thereafter hundreds of other consumer goods were similarly packaged. That they were merchandised under corporate names that were "trademarked" instantly transformed these products into "brand" names.

One hundred years later at the end of the twentieth century this process had evolved to the point where, as Naomi Klein writes, we "[t]hink of the brand as the core meaning of the modern corporation, and of advertisements as one vehicle used to convey that meaning to the world."[25]

While Gap aspired to become a brand the way McDonald's has become the quintessential purveyor of hamburger fast-food, there was widespread resistance to such a notion among members of Generation Y in the mid-

nineties. Donald Fisher and Mickey Drexler were oblivious to all of this because they were distracted. Both men were absorbed by the tumultuous
events swirling around the Gap in the early nineties. When Gap Shoes
closed in 1994—after two years of floundering—it came as no surprise to
anyone. "Sometimes it seems like Fisher and Drexler stumble into these sit-
uations," an executive at Gap said. "I mean, Mickey Drexler approached
the entire concept of Gap Shoes as if they were shirts—have small, medium
and large shoes—but of course it failed. We can get away with selling shirts
that don't fit exactly, but when you even *think* you can try to merchandise
shoes that way, it's ridiculous, simply ridiculous. There's a difference between taking risks and being reckless; Don and Mickey don't seem to know
that every so often unfortunately."

Gap shoes were sold in standard sizes, to be sure, but the cookie-cutter
designs with a certain androgynous style failed to catch consumers' attention long enough for them to take a second look. By 1995 the Gap experienced zero growth. Old Navy and Gap Scents had both been launched the
previous year, even as Gap Shoes closed shop. Banana Republic was still in
the throes of yet another overhaul, one that would not be completed for another two years. In 1996, while he worked through his summer vacation,
Mickey Drexler announced that Gap would "reposition" itself once more,
returning to its "basics" line of clothing.

"Gap is a value-driven company, and our focus is on solid values in basic
staples of clothing," Mickey Drexler explained to the press in the fall of
1996, oblivious to what this revealed about the anxiety at Gap, Inc. over its
chosen line of basics—and to how such a strategy would alienate further
the disenfranchised members of Generation Y, who were staying away
from Gap stores in droves. "We intend to establish 'Gap' as a brand, one
which will be recognized by consumers without a doubt whatsoever."

"Where's the fun?" one corporate executive who is no longer with Gap,
Inc. told me over lunch. "Everyone at the Gap was in a panic mode in the
mid-nineties. We had failed with Hemisphere and Banana Republic. Gap
Shoes was a fiasco. Sales were flat at Gap and we had just launched Gap
Scents and Old Navy. It was all stress and no fun. Everyone was in such de-
spair, no one really wanted to wake up in the morning and go work for the
Gap. How could you not expect this bad karma not to keep customers out
of the stores?"

"We're not in the business of selling ambiance," Donald Fisher had declared at a press conference in 1988 when Mel and Patricia Ziegler were
ousted from Banana Republic.

How could he, in hindsight, have said this? It was precisely by evoking
the magical ambiance created by the *Sonny & Cher Show* that gave currency
to the Gap's connection with Youth Culture in the seventies. It was the playful incorporation of music and pop culture that made young people see the
Gap as "hip," "happening" and "cool." It was this ability to move to the

rhythm of young consumers that had been the secret of the Gap's success at the cash register. It was the revolutionary way in which Donald Fisher had packaged "ambiance" that had extended the Gap's presence across the American landscape.

"Why buy knockoffs when you can get the real stuff," a member of Generation Y who is also an industry observer explained. "Club Monaco is the new Gap. Gucci is the new Banana Republic. And nothing is the new Old Navy because Old Navy is worthless."

America fell out of the Gap once the Youth Culture of Generation Y discovered the wisdom of Vivienne Westwood's observation and embraced it as its own. "It is elegance that is subversive, elegance in a world of vulgarity," she argued. The moment Oldsmobile ridiculed the Gap during a Super Bowl half-time ad in January 2000, with its speeding car almost running down the "zombie chic" kids mocking a Gap ad, the antifashion philosophy of the Gap was christened as the epitome of the vulgarity of contemporary American life, the end of the exaltation of the lowbrow as a cultural ideal. The Oldsmobile tag-line was "It isn't what everyone else is doing." If Oldsmobile wasn't what everyone else was doing, then the Gap was in big trouble. The Gap became, at that precise moment, passé.

The dissing of the Gap by Generation Y stunned corporate executives, who grew frustrated at their failure to seduce the new generation of American youth. Were it not for Old Navy—which was successful for the ghastly reason of price point—it would have been impossible for Gap, Inc. to keep up appearances. The problem was, however, that that appearance was one of the vulgarity of materialism. Stacks of clothes abounded in piles everywhere, but there was no single article of clothing that offered refined elegance.

Succumbing to the cannibalism of Old Navy was the only logical conclusion for the Gap's "Old Navy as Gap Warehouses." The cultural excitement of Old Navy faded fast as the century turned and the Gap brand itself was ignored by the youngest, hippest consumers. For Donald Fisher and Mickey Drexler now to throw their hands in the air in exasperation was as ridiculous a sight as Paul Lynde singing "What's the Matter with Kids?" in *Bye-Bye Birdie*, the early sixties musical that was a send-up of how members of the Matures generation were confused by the baby boomers' embrace and celebration of that inexplicable cultural phenomenon known as rock 'n' roll.

"Kids! What's the Matter with Kids?"

As 1996 drew to a close, however, the Gap was engulfed by turmoil— Donald Fisher said they weren't selling ambiance, but then again, they weren't selling anything else either—as executives ran down the corridors of Gap, Inc., screaming at each other "Reposition this! Reposition that! Reposition everything in sight!"

"Matures! *What's the matter with* Matures? Baby boomers! *What's the matter with* baby boomers?"

Donald Fisher and Mickey Drexler themselves resembled no one more than an exasperated and overwhelmed Paul Lynde, but in the new century, their fear could be summed up in Matchbox Twenty's lyrics, "I'm so scared I'll never/Get put back together." It was clear that in 2000, Donald Fisher and Mickey Drexler had faltered once more by failing to bridge the gap to Generation Y.

9

BY THE SWEAT OF
(SOMEONE ELSE'S) BROW

The world is full of sweatshops.

The world is full of women and children exploited everywhere day in and day out. The world is littered with the Dickensian factories, the means of production where knockoffs of Gap and Old Navy can be produced in a snap of a finger, a fax or an e-mail. In the amoral world of corporate accounting—where the bottom line is the bottom line—there is surprisingly little moral accountability. This is why the labels of Gap, Banana Republic and Old Navy clothes carry the names of the Third World nations where anonymous multitudes are exploited in order to make shopping fun again.

Youth Culture is also about idealism and activism. In 1969 when the Gap first opened its doors, Levi's® jeans were made in America. Sweatshops were a distant concern. In 1999, however, the world had changed and almost nothing sold at the Gap, Banana Republic or Old Navy was made in either the United States or in countries where garment workers' incomes provide a decent living for a family, as understood by American standards.

Old Navy and Gap held equally little resonance for the current generation of American youth, a further cause for alienation. To Generation Y-ers, Old Navy was for the kid siblings who didn't know any better, or for old people who knew even less. It wasn't that shopping wasn't fun, but that the Gap and Old Navy simply weren't where fun was happening. And that was precisely the reason behind the disappointing figures at Gap as the twentieth century drew to a close. Old Navy as retail entertainment for the masses was right on target, but it wasn't retail shopping for the hip members of Generation Y.

Those protesters assembled at the opening of the Old Navy flagship store on the corner of Market and Fourth streets were mostly members of Generation Y. The previous summer they had marched in an anti-Gap parade through the streets of San Francisco. Now they stood naked, mocking the celebration in front of the Old Navy store. Whereas in the summer they would only carry an effigy of Donald Fisher, they now had him within shouting distance. Above the carnival atmosphere that accompanied the inauguration, above it all, reminding the world that a protester is a protester no matter how small, the voices of Generation Y, with the stakes now raised higher, denounced Gap, Inc.

"Our message is this!" one naked female member of Generation Y said. "As long as the Gap makes its money by exploiting the peoples of the Third World, we will never stop denouncing them! We don't want the Gap! We don't need the Gap! We don't want Old Navy! We don't need Old Navy!"

The protest was organized by Global Exchange, an organization with a long history of activism in San Francisco. Concerned at the sweatshop conditions in factories under contract to manufacture clothes for Old Navy in the United States territory of Saipan, the Generation Y activists participating in the demonstration shouted, "We'd rather wear nothing than wear Old Navy."

This being San Francisco, some of the spectators walking by saw the commotion, agreed with the sentiments of the protesters and then proceeded to join the rally—by stripping their clothes off as well. The police were forced to close access to Old Navy for about ten minutes before order and unfettered passage was restored.

"We believe people have a right to express themselves," Old Navy spokeswoman Maria Hoyer-Angus said. "Sometimes they happen to protest in front of our stores."

Gap, Inc. officials rushed over and quickly began to distribute fliers to shoppers, the press and pedestrians stating that it was their policy to forbid forced child labor and coerced adult labor in any factory producing clothing for any of their divisions. Gap, Inc. claimed that it periodically sent monitors to visit the factories randomly to inspect for compliance. Gap, Inc. stated it was proud to be providing employment to the residents of Saipan who would otherwise not be able to provide for their families.

There was confusion at Old Navy, however. Old Navy employees spoke into their headsets and tried to keep the protesters at bay. The results were mixed. Most shoppers were indifferent to the disruption. San Francisco police Officer Kevin Gotchet told a reporter that "More people wanted to go into the store than to see these people naked."

But others were swayed. Katie Emans, a woman shopping at Old Navy who was not aware of the Gap-Saipan connection, is reported to have said, "My shopping experience definitely was affected. I will think twice before buying clothes here." She left without making a purchase. Passersby who witnessed the protest were of different minds over the matter. "*Naked* people protesting a *clothing* store," George Andrews, a tourist visiting California for a month from London, said, "how bloody clever."

San Franciscan taxpayers were less amused at times. "How much overtime is the city paying," Belinda Griswold opined, a bystander who stumbled upon this scene, "to protect Old Navy and their minimum wage jobs? It's a disgrace."

Those protesters were naked not because they were exhibitionists, but because they were making the point that we cannot clothe our bodies in warmth through the exploitation and suffering of others. Generation Y-ers were brazen and self-assured about taking a stand on moral issues. Generation Y-ers were more sophisticated than the flower children of the sixties or the antiwar demonstrators of the seventies.

One way of making sense of these demonstrators stripping naked for their cause is to note the tongue-in-cheek humor of American writers. "American style is wearing what needs to be worn to get the job done best, and nothing else—unless dressing up simply happens to please you," Ted Allen wrote in "In Search of American Style," in *Esquire* magazine.[1] Wearing what needs to get the job done, Generation Y-ers know, sometimes means wearing nothing at all.

That this protest could occur in the first place was astounding. On an emotional day filled with family memories and personal achievements thirty years in the making, Donald Fisher was repudiated publicly by the new generation of Americans who were hostile to everything he represented. This was a seismic shift in the relations between America's youth and the man who had first embraced the commercial implications of Youth Culture.

As the year 2000 unfolded, Gap experienced dismal results. Robert Fisher had resigned too late to salvage its spring 2000 collection, and sales continued to fall and expectations were lowered time and time again. For the first quarter, analysts expected Gap to grow at the modest rate of 3 percent. Instead, Gap stores were off between 1 and 3 percent, sending shares tumbling almost 8 percent when the news reached Wall Street. Mickey Drexler's repositioning had not reversed the cannibalism at the hands of Old Navy. Gap was destined to spend the year 2000 thinking how it could reinvent itself. This meant cleaning house. "Gap Is Making Management Changes to Fight Sales Slump," the *Wall Street Journal* reported on November 7, 2000. The article noted that Gap "may be in its deepest slump yet," one reason why it had been quietly making management changes. The article recounted the departures of Lisa Schultz (executive vice president of product design and development, Gap brand), Scott Olivet (senior vice president of real estate), Charles Ferer (vice president of finance at Old Navy), Jim Nevins (executive vice president of marketing for Gap) and John Wilson (chief operating officer of Gap) within a six-month span. *Wall*

Street Journal reporter Calmetta Coleman speculated that "with the stock relatively out of favor and no clear end to the sales slump in sight, others [on Wall Street] are concerned that executives might begin bolting on their own," which would complicate matters even further. There was a widening generation gap that threatened to become an unbridgeable abyss as the Gap, Inc. confronted a management crisis.

The Gap had to differentiate itself and make its brand have resonance with Youth Culture, but the questions remained: Did it have the managerial wherewithal to do so? Did it "get it" as far as Generation Y was concerned?

One characteristic of Generation Y that proves so seductive is its absence of arrogance. Whereas other generations of youth were so self-assured—recall the righteous indignation of the antiwar protesters in the sixties, the anti-Watergate protesters in the seventies and the anti-Reagan protesters in the eighties—Generation Y understands instinctively that the world is in perpetual flux. Perhaps this is attributable to the nature of the technology: upgrades can be downloaded continuously since nothing remains the same for more than a few months before it becomes, if not obsolete, then at least not current.

James Gleick writes that

[i]nstead of distinct, tested, shrink-wrapped versions of software, manufacturers distribute upgrades and patches that change within months or even days. They simultaneously offer official versions and more advanced versions still undergoing testing. With the Internet removing delays from the promotion and distribution processes, software manufacturers began to think in terms of six-month product cycles.[2]

This is the mental timeframe through which Generation Y-ers view the world. It is, in other words, a world where there is no permanence and immediacy shapes their fluid view of the world. Within this cultural context, what is striking is that, while Generation Y-ers have firm principles and convictions, they are no more rigid in their methods than they are in their disposable software.

In one of my interviews with Leila Salazar, who runs the campaign against the Gap for Global Exchange, I noticed how things changed when she turned things around and began to ask me questions. It is not uncommon for interviewers to be interviewed by their subjects, but seldom do the questions reveal moments of self-doubt. "Do you think our campaign against the Gap is having an effect?" she asked, after pointing out that Global Exchange's efforts were five years old in 2000. "You know so much about the Gap. Do you think that our campaign to educate consumers has an impact in their corporate decisions?"

That she felt comfortable asking these questions was evidence of an inquisitive and open mind, something so often missing when people who hold opposing views are engaged. An admirable characteristic of Generation Y-ers—often confused with being jaded—is that they don't know all the answers. Unlike, for instance, the anti–Vietnam War protesters who were so smug and intolerant, confident in their moral superiority, Generation Y-ers understand that, in the age of the Internet, there are always "upgrades" that have to be "downloaded" and that therefore there is never such a thing as the final word.

Global Exchange, I opined, was on the right wavelength with the political and social concerns of the members of Generation Y. Her efforts had been successful in building a generational network that distributed its message about sweatshops abroad and unfair labor practices at home. She had successfully orchestrated impressive showings at the Seattle protests against the World Trade Organization and the Washington, D.C., demonstrations against the World Bank and the International Monetary Fund. It is worth noting that Global Exchange, in the spirit of Generation Y, organizes its protests by disseminating information via Majordomo, a software that allows for multiple e-mails to subscribers around the world. Leila Salazar listened intently, making a few comments that revealed a subversive intelligence. The clear-headedness of their approach elevates their campaign. The members of Generation Y, firm in their principles, recognize with lucidity that continuing need to "download" and "upgrade" their methods to achieve their goals.

"Old Navy and the Gap! We don't need this kind of crap!" was the slogan shouted that crisp fall day in San Francisco by America's disbelieving youth. When Gap president Robert Fisher stepped down in 1999, anti-Gap activists felt vindicated and "victory" speeches were made at anti-Gap rallies. When the spring 2000 collection flopped, it galvanized even more protesters. And when the *New York Times* characterized the Gap's performance as the "biggest disappointment" of all clothing retailers, on May 5, 2000—Cinco de Mayo—pitchers of margaritas fortified with twice the tequila flowed as Generation Y activists in San Francisco celebrated their "triumph" over the "moral depravity" of Gap, Inc.

The Gap had lost Generation Y, which was a monumental defeat, for never in the history of the world had there been a generation as hip and as wealthy as Generation Y. The truth was now as jarring to behold as seeing a nudist standing in a crowded clothing store: While Generation Y didn't need the Gap, the Gap did need Generation Y.

Who would have thought that the line in the sand in the struggle against the exploitation of women and children in Third World sweatshops would be drawn between the stacks of neatly folded Gap T-shirts?

That it has been is a curious development, one that stands in stark contrast with the corporate culture Gap, Inc. has embraced, championed and cultivated as its own. If the unpleasant experiences with Levi's and the Zieglers were what convinced Donald Fisher that the Gap would only sell what the Gap made, he failed to consider that, by virtue of contracting its private-label products to foreign companies dedicated to fulfilling garment orders, Gap, Inc. was, in essence, dealing, once again, with "middlemen" of sorts. That Gap did not own the factories that made Gap jeans, or Banana Republic's gay urban wear, or Old Navy's Wal-Mart knockoffs meant it had to contend with the realities of managing suppliers. The question of ethics became all the more troublesome when one considers that when Gap, Inc. adopted a voluntary code of ethics for how workers in these overseas garment factories were to be treated, the implementation of this code was completely out of the Gap's control.

"If everyone in corporate America exploits people in the developing world," a sympathetic executive on Seventh Avenue remarked, "why can't the Gap?" The Gap is no worse than any other clothing manufacturer—and it has striven to be better. The Gap has honestly tried to present itself—and become—a company with a conscience. But it exploited its sales clerks by striving to emulate the pioneering McDonald's in hiring the very young and very old in the American labor force. The Gap was fast becoming a lightning rod for critics on the Left, who envisioned multitudes of women and children being forced to work for meager wages in factories around the world.

To understand why the Gap has become a target, consider the manufacturers of casual footwear. Reebok, Puma, Nike and a host of other firms all produce their sneakers and sports shoes in factories scattered throughout the Third World. But activists, knowing that to be more effective they should concentrate their efforts on one single company, have pounced on Nike. That made Nike an example for the entire industry. This has been the fate of the Gap. While Tommy Hilfiger, Ralph Lauren, Liz Claiborne, Donna Karan, and hundreds of other clothing manufacturers have their garments made in similar factories, activists have targeted the Gap, if for no other reason than the Gap has over 3,700 stores around the world in front of which, theoretically, they can protest—and Gap, Inc. has its headquarters in San Francisco, where labor activists abound.

Visibility is visibility—and visibility is not always good as the Gap was soon to find out. Indeed, if one walks into any of Gap's divisions, from Old Navy to Banana Republic to Gap Kids, a casual perusal of the labels reveals the names of country after country where people are exploited in factories to bring these clothes to the American consumer. Labor activists claim that the Gap's stores reveal the roster of the United Nations' member nations of the exploited. "Millions of workers around the world [are exploited] so that Donald and Doris Fisher can be billionaires," explained a member of Generation Y, who participated in the protest in front of the Old Navy flagship store on opening day. "It's sick."

Organized resistance to the Gap had its origins in San Francisco. In 1984 a band by the name of Negativland coined the phrase "culture jamming" to describe efforts to subvert corporate intrusion in our lives through the ubiquitous advertising that punctuates public space. Negativland held up the efforts of groups such as the Billboard Liberation Front—also from San Francisco—which had been altering advertisements since 1980. "Joe Camel" became "Joe Chemo." Apple Computer's logo became a poisoned apple with the phrase "Think different" replaced by "Think doomed." This resistance, most often carried out by members of Generations X and Y, sought to bring voice to the people in a democratic resistance to the invasive force of corporate America and the government and the loss of privacy facilitated by the advent of the Internet and other technologies capable of surveillance that impacts the lives of civilians.

Gap, whose strategy of "clustering" its stores had given rise to the concentration of its various divisions in neighborhoods, was scorned not because of its success, but because, by virtue of being based in northern California, it was held up to higher standards of corporate social responsibility. Naomi Klein writing in *No Logo* explains it thusly:

> We have heard the same refrain over and over again from . . . the Gap [among others]: "Why are you picking on us? We're the good ones!" The answer is simple. They are singled out because the politics they have associated themselves with, which have made them rich—feminism, ecology, inner-city empowerment—were not just random pieces of effective ad copy that their brand managers found lying around. They are complex, essential social ideas, for which many people have spent lifetimes fighting.[3]

It offends the enlightened sensibilities of San Franciscans to think that the corner of Haight and Ashbury streets has been desecrated by the presence of the "vulgar" commercialism of a Gap store. This intersection, which held sway over succeeding generations extolling cultural rebellion and creativity, was a sacred space. From Jefferson Airplane in the sixties to Third Eye Blind in the nineties, there was a tradition many felt was violated by the very presence of the Gap, with its middle-brow bourgeois wares and its offensive exaltation of the conformity of its "zombie chic" youngsters in its advertising.

Generation Y's Youth Culture has an added palpable energy like electricity. Youth's dilemma on how to resist the Gap pointed out the distinct differences between Generations X and Y. Generation Y-ers hold Generation X-ers with contempt. Think of the collusion between the tail end of the baby boomers and the Generation X-ers. In *The Brady Bunch*, Greg and Marcia were among the last of the baby boomers with Generation X-ers Jan, Peter, Cindy and Bobby standing in the shadows of the older two siblings. Pop culture reflects the vocabulary youngsters understand and speak. Generation Y-ers sought to give voice to the political idea that, having been raised in a era of unprecedented prosperity, they had the moral obligation to rise above the mundane things of life, such as putting a roof over one's head, clothes on one's back and food on one's table.

The material wealth of the American economy, which had been made possible to no small degree by corporate America, was a given. What now concerned this generation was the idea of justice. The point, after all, isn't that the Gap doesn't have a moral obligation to pay teenagers a wage that can provide a livelihood. These are members of the workforce, after all, who live at home, are clothed and fed by their parents and work part time. Their outrage is something else. What about the fifty-year-old woman of color who works forty hours a week at minimum wage? These are the multitudes of American workers who do not have the luxury to organize and protest. Yet these are the Americans who are entitled to this one justice: that anyone in America working at a full-time job should be able to live above the poverty line.

Generation Y-ers "got" it. That their immediate predecessor, Generation X, did not was an affront to their sensibilities. In fact, the passivity of Generation X-ers, complacent and undistinguished, is derided by Generation Y-ers.

Generation X grew up thinking Pac Man was cool; Generation Y is obliterating its way through Dungeons & Dragons. The former generation grew up thinking call waiting and faxes were hip; the latter can be reached at the beach on their own cell phones and download their homework assignments off the Internet, where they have their own home page. Generation X-ers would be suspended from school for spray-painting graffiti in school; Generation Y-ers are arrested by the FBI for unleashing destructive computer viruses by virtue of being the second generation of hackers.

"The Gap's 'zombie chic' is what X-ers think will make them Y-ers," one member of Generation Y explained, dismissing Generation X-ers as pretenders, or "wannabes." From lower Manhattan on the fringes of Chinatown to the street gangs of San Francisco, the visual immediacy of MTV characterizes the lives of Generation Y. How can the Gap appropriate and regenerate that kind of energy and excitement?

The Gap has become the lightning rod for all the criticism of, and anger to, the shortcomings of the globalization of commerce. It was one thing for a band to pronounce "culture jamming" as the highest degree of Generation Y's social value. Then again, it is another for the antics of the Billboard Liberation Front to be institutionalized through *Adbusters*, a journal devoted to reporting, organizing and instructing on "subversion" by "using the momentum of the enemy"—the advertising paid for by corporate America— against the enemy. Noble as this youthful rebellion may be, in practical terms, petty vandalism for political ends is a nuisance for corporate America—and not much more.

Unlike the largely complacent members of Generation X, who contributed little in terms of social activism, Generation Y-ers brought an optimism. The culture jamming first identified by Generation X-ers of Negativland matured in the early nineties through a global movement known as

RTS, short for Reclaim the Streets. This movement focused on reclaiming public space for the public. As much artistic expression as protest, the RTS movement relies on a democratic activism.

This is how it works in its most basic manifestations: at a predetermined time, people gather at a certain location, such as an intersection at a busy downtown street, and then proceed to set up speakers and hold an ad hoc celebration, blocking traffic and reclaiming the streets as pedestrian thoroughfares for citizens at large. One of the earlier manifestations of the RTS began in San Francisco in 1992 when commuters, fed up with Friday rush-hour congestion, organized bike runs in the city's financial district on the last Friday of each month. In due course, the number of cyclists participating surged to such numbers that they *became* traffic, spilling onto the sidewalks, bringing intersections to a standstill, forcing cars to surrender the right of way to cyclists, thus snarling traffic for miles in all directions. This reclaiming of the streets of San Francisco for pedestrians and cyclists meant bringing cars and buses to a virtual standstill.

The movement, called "Critical Mass," an apt description of the impact thousands of cyclists had on rush-hour traffic, progressed as a nonviolent civil protest that demanded more bicycle lanes and greater public transportation to reduce the congestion brought about by multitudes of cars. This movement grew peacefully over the course of several years until 1998, when Critical Mass erupted in violent confrontation. This occurred when San Francisco Mayor Willie Brown, hitherto oblivious to the existence of Critical Mass as a movement, was *himself* caught up in standstill traffic during a Friday rush hour. The infuriated and intolerant mayor then ordered the police to stop Critical Mass at any cost. They proceeded to do so the following month, by a show of force that resulted in hundreds of cyclists being roughed up and beaten by the police and hundreds of bicycles being "arrested" in the ensuing melee.

This being California, unbeknownst to the mayor and the police many of the cyclists were attorneys whose bicycles, costing thousands of dollars, were seized. They retaliated against city hall. A flurry of lawsuits for "unlawful seizure," "police brutality" and "violation of constitutional rights" followed. It was the kind of marvelous and inexplicable maneuvering of which only American attorneys are capable. The ludicrous confrontations between city hall and the people of San Francisco were eased somewhat through unspoken accommodations reached after many, many meetings. Commuters now know that on the last Friday of each month, one either leaves work early to avoid the mayhem, or stays late into the evening.

The RTS movement, however, is not confined to California—or the United States. From Tel Aviv to Sydney, from Vancouver to Prague, hundreds of RTS events over the past five years characterize the emerging citizen resistance to the globalization of trade and the growing presence of branded identities thrust into the lives of people the world over. In San

Francisco, however, the convergence of ideas and arguments put forth by Negativland and *Adbusters* have found resonance with Generation Y. Critical Mass—when hundreds of bike messengers join corporate lawyers in the same defiance of city government—galvanized, among other things, greater scrutiny of the Gap.

Gap, Inc., by virtue of being the largest private employer in San Francisco and because of its ubiquitous presence throughout the city, provided a microcosm of the globalization unfolding throughout the world. In 1995 "Gap-lash" began in earnest as a sustained movement of "resistance" to protest the Gap's ubiquity in the lives of Americans. San Francisco activists and local newspapers exposed abuses at sweatshops in the developing world under contract to the Gap. The *San Francisco Examiner's* investigative reports towered above the rest in covering Gap, Inc.'s abuses of workers in Central American sweatshops. Naomi Klein noted that

in August 1995, the Gap's freshly scrubbed facade was further exfoliated to reveal a lawless factory in El Salvador where the manager responded to a union drive by firing 150 people and vowing that the "blood will flow" if organizing continued.[4]

The viciousness of this embarrassing revelation—that blood will flow over a pocket T-shirt—was further aggravated when, later that month, at the invitation of church groups, union organizers and human rights groups, two teenage women toured the United States speaking out against working conditions at the factories that produced clothes for Gap, Inc. Claudia Leticia Molina, a seventeen-year-old seamstress from Honduras, and Judith Yanira Viera, an eighteen-year-old seamstress from El Salvador, spoke before crowds gathered in front of Gap stores. The inhumane working conditions described by these two members of Generation Y resembled those exposed by Charles Dickens when he wrote about the working conditions in England's factories at the end of the nineteenth century.

The conditions described by these Latin American teenagers echoed the conditions found in developing countries around the world where Gap, Inc. has its clothes produced. This process of exploitation begins with attempts to alleviate poverty and create jobs. Consider that

Wal-Mart and the Gap, for instance, contract out their production to [Export Processing Zones,EPZ] dotting the Southern Hemisphere, where goods are produced mostly by women in their teens and twenties who earn minimum wage or less and live in cramped rooms.[5]

Exasperated officials in developing countries and at international lending organizations, such as the World Bank, who are not entirely unsympathetic to the plight of the poor, throw their hands in the air at this criticism. Often claiming that *a* job is better than *no* job, short-term injustices are swept aside in grander macroeconomic schemes. Officials at the World Bank and the International Monetary Fund often fail to consider that if full employment is the sole measure of success, then one could conceivably solve the world's problems by bringing back indentured servitude and slavery.

This isn't an exaggeration to the multitudes of women and children around the globe caught in a Catch-22 dilemma. Consider the conditions under which these women and children labor:

> Many of the [EPZ] zone factories are run according to iron-fist rules that systematically break Philippine labor law.... Seamstresses at a factory sewing garments for Gap, Guess and Old Navy told me that they sometimes have to resort to urinating in plastic bags under their machines.[6]

The horrific descriptions of such outrageous exploitation were only topped by the bravura and arrogance with which Gap, Inc. spokesmen defended their practices. Gap officials remain unable to convince the California public of the sincerity of their excuses. Activists were not convinced by Gap's efforts to distance itself from the alleged exploitation it was inflicting on multitudes. What has made it impossible for Gap's aloofness to hold sway, despite the refined corporate image offered by its corporate marketers, is the wearing down on morale that these protests have caused. Generation Y-ers sit up and take notice when they see people their own age describe their exploitation by Gap, Inc.

This is how Karl Schoenberger describes the serendipity that put Gap and Global Exchange in direct conflict:

> Gap, Inc.'s phenomenal success placed it squarely in the crosshairs of human rights activists taking aim against the apparel industry. Gap was one of the earliest companies to draft a code of conduct covering contractors, but it had the usual problems with compliance, and it was heavily exposed to the stigma of bonded labor in Saipan. The company also had lots of centrally located storefronts that could be easily picketed for local television news stations. By most accounts, Gap's labor practices were no worse and no better than the rest of the apparel industry. But to maximize public awareness of their cause, the human rights community needed a brand that symbolized the sins of the entire industry, much as Nike was the whipping boy for sneaker makers. The notoriety that Levi's managed to avoid when it was at the top of the heap now visited Gap with a vengeance.[7]

The criticism was not forthcoming from a young malcontent who could be readily dismissed. Karl Schoenberger has a distinguished career in journalism that spans two decades. Currently the technology editor at the *San Jose Mercury News*, he has written for the *Asian Wall Street Journal* and taught as a fellow at Harvard University.

Other middle-aged and follicly challenged political commentators, too, joined the chorus of infuriated (and ungroomed) Generation Y-ers decrying the Gap. Consider the scathing ridicule delivered by Jim Hightower, who assessed the situation in this manner:

As for the Gap . . . and the other labels that profit from the exploitation [of workers in sweatshops], they claim to know nothing, *absolutely nothing*, about what goes on, and if anything does go on please understand that they find such goings on to be *absolutely deplorable*, not to mention being against their "corporate code of conduct," which is *absolutely firm* on the matter of opposing such gross exploitation, but you've got to understand that some of these foreign factory owners can be *absolutely unscrupulous*, so what's a company to do?[8]

Then he asks rhetorically: "Why do these corporations play such games, pretending that nothing is amiss here, and even if there is it's not of their doing? Because they desperately want the Saipan Sweatshop System to continue, since it's a bonanza for their bottom lines."[9]

To be sure, labor activists and political pundits were not the only ones becoming increasingly aware of the controversies surrounding Gap's labor practices abroad. The same moral outrage was felt by increasing numbers of American consumers, who were convinced that Gap was a company that had grown rich through the exploitation of sweatshop labor. The greater and greater use of assembly factories, beginning in the late sixties, had introduced a new term in American manufacturing: "Made in America" was replaced by "Assembled in [name of Third World country] of U.S. components." Whether it was a television set or a Kermit the Frog toy, the components were American, but the product had been assembled by underpaid workers overseas.

Gap, Inc. thus embarked on an ambitious campaign to lower costs, expand for the sake of expansion and to do it through the systematic exploitation of others. Donald Fisher, known for his staunch defense of free trade and globalization, apparently failed to consider the undeniable fact that, while the benefits of freer trade are real and enormous, in the short term, free trade often convulses entire nations into crises. Consider the devastating—albeit short-term—crisis that engulfed Mexico upon the implementation of the North American Free Trade Agreement with the United States and Canada.

For over four years Mexicans suffered from a recession and devaluation the likes of which Mexico had not experienced since the Great Depression. For five years, millions of Mexicans who had just entered the middle classes struggled to stay there and small business owners were deprived of credit to grow for the simple reason that the entire banking system was in such dire straits that it required a $68 billion rescue package. Is Mexico better off now? Of course. But the economic dislocation and human suffering have been tremendous. The long term is a piece of cake; it's getting through the short term that's wrenching. Indeed, there's probably a Nobel Prize in Economics awaiting the individual who can figure out how to make liberalized trade work without inflicting such a heavy price on the most disenfranchised members of any given nation.

The political argument offered by anti-Gap activists can be succinctly expressed in one statement: how Gap, Inc. metamorphosed into a company incapable of distinguishing the reality it created from the fantasy of its brand image. Refusing to admit the underlying connections between its corporate practices abroad and the aestheticized exploitation at home suggests a nihilism and moral bankruptcy that astounds. The Gap's treatment of workers in foreign countries has been compared to the worst excesses during the Industrial Revolution. Activists invoke a time when life for most people in Europe and America was so dreadful that Charles Dickens resolved to document the horrors of wretched capitalist excess in his novels and when an outraged Karl Marx published *The Communist Manifesto*. Capitalism, everywhere, was unkind to workers. The young activists seen on television protesting the globalization of trade argue that what Gap does overseas amounts to "imperialist" exploitation.

"Sweatshop imperialism," in other words, is the only appropriate characterization of how Gap employees were treated. In the eighties McDonald's was denounced for having created a company based on taking advantage of the very young and the very old—teenagers working for the first time and bored retirees returning to work for the last time—and these labor practices were refined by Gap, Inc. This is how Naomi Klein reported on the questionable working conditions at the Gap:

> For instance, the Gap—which defines full-time as thirty hours a week—has a system of keeping clerks "on call" for certain shifts during which they aren't scheduled or paid to work but must be available to come in if the manager calls. (One worker joked to me that she had to buy a beeper in case a folding crisis flared up in Gap Kids.)[10]

In other words, a single working mother with a high school education can work for the Gap "full time" and not be able to provide for herself and her child. There is a difference between giving people the opportunity to make money and depriving them of the opportunity to make a living. While the Gap defines "full-time" work as thirty hours a week, the law does not. Therefore, a "full-time" worker for the Gap does not meet the legal requirements to be entitled to health benefits, overtime, vacation and other rights afforded fully employed workers. This trend in corporate America— "permatemps"—is designed to exploit the inexplicable fact that, alone among industrialized nations, the United States does not give *every* worker equal access to health and employment benefits. The greed evident in this relentless pursuit of materialism creates a division within the American workers that frustrates efforts at fair compensation.

Gap, of course, is not alone in this practice. Microsoft was found guilty of depriving tens of thousands of its workers benefits by simply classifying them as "independent contractors," although they worked side by side and performed the exact duties of "employees"—as defined by the law.

That *Saturday Night Live* mocks the Gap and that films like *Reality Bites* portray the drudgery of working for the Gap in hilarious satire is now understandable within the context of culture jamming. The Generation Y groups that ridicule the Gap in their videos and reduced sales make sense. When Rage Against the Machine's rage against the Gap spills onto the stage at its concerts, the action is electrifying. It was at the Aztec Stadium, for instance, that Rage Against the Machine received the most enthusiastic response to its anti-Gap message, which at first appears odd considering there is not a single Gap store in Mexico City, the largest metropolis on earth. This is not to say that Mexican members of Generation Y are not familiar with the Gap: their mothers and sisters are the ones being exploited at the assembly plants throughout their country.

Leila Salazar describes Global Exchange's campaign against the Gap's presence in Mexico thusly:

In Mexico, Gap jeans that sell for $35.00 are made by young men and women for 50 cents per hour. This is not enough to meet their basic needs, and the needs of their families. [Conditions are] . . . not as horrific as working conditions on Saipan, a U.S. territory in the Pacific, where Asian immigrant women are making Gap clothing [and] work up to 12 hours a day, 7 days a week, for a fraction of U.S. minimum wage, often without overtime pay, but these workers are not paid living wages. They are denied the most basic human rights and live in overcrowded, unsanitary housing, surrounded by barbed wire, all of which has been extensively documented. Yet the Gap is allowed to sew "Made in the USA" labels inside their clothes, a deceptive and unethical practice that misleads consumers into thinking that American labor conditions went into the manufacture of these garments. The moral outrage is only heightened when one realizes that, according to *Forbes*, Gap, Inc. CEO Mickey Drexler made $172.8 million in 1999 and Gap, Inc.'s chairman Donald Fisher is worth an estimated $8 billion. Obviously, Gap, Inc. can afford to raise the wages of their workers in Gap factories and improve working conditions as well.[11]

It is in this context that the exhortations made by the member of Generation Y protesting at the Embarcadero Center—declaring that the Gap was "killing off [his generation's] spirit with their corporate violence"—are understandable.

The carnivorous *sangfroid* of Gap executives has enraged so many in San Francisco that there is now an organized, continuous campaign to expose the Gap's abuses and to raise the public's consciousness. Global Exchange spearheads full-time efforts against Gap, Inc. with such determination, in part, because both are based in San Francisco. Their demonstrations, spirited affairs that include effigies of Donald Fisher and nudists in front of Old Navy, have found a profound acceptance throughout San Francisco. The demonstrations described at the Embarcadero Center and at the Old Navy flagship store earlier in this book were organized by Global Exchange.

"If you think of sweatshops as concentration camps of forced labor," one Old Navy manager, frustrated with the politics of his employer, opined, "then that makes Donald Fisher a tyrant."

A harsh pronouncement in the extreme without a doubt. Gap officials are quick to point out that they are committed to "ethical" labor practices, but that's as facetious as saying I'm committed to stopping continental drift. None of the codes of ethics or principles of understanding developed by the Gap or by Nike—a firm that arguably is the most reviled for the sweatshop conditions under which its products are manufactured—are legally binding on the factories in the various countries where the Gap's clothing is manufactured. Gap, Inc. claims that copies of its code of ethics were distributed throughout the factories where its clothes are made, but activists claim that when they visited these work sites the only literature available was in the English language.

It is clear to Generation Y that these are *calculated* efforts at damage control for the consumption of the Western media and the American consumer. This seeming discrepancy is what many Generation Y-ers find infuriating. "We have to organize and take to the streets," a protester explained, adding that Seattle's protests against the World Trade Organization was only the beginning of his generation's campaign against Gap. "Fisher and Drexler are rich men from the work of someone else's brow."

Gap disagreed with this assessment. The company's official position on the matter stated:

> Gap, Inc. works with third-party manufacturers in more than 50 countries, including the United States, to make the products we sell in our stores.
>
> Though we don't own any manufacturing facilities, we developed a Code of Vendor Conduct to ensure the factories we do business with make our clothes under safe and humane working conditions. To do this, Gap, Inc. has a global network of more than 80 employees who must inspect and approve factories where orders are placed for the first time, and then monitor those factories on an ongoing basis. They inspect factory conditions, review payroll records, interview workers and meet with factory owners and managers to discuss and correct compliance issues.
>
> Most factories work hard to meet or exceed our requirements. If factories don't share our commitment to maintaining safe conditions and treating workers fairly, we stop doing business with them altogether. Today, we have the most comprehensive internal monitoring organization in the apparel industry, complemented by independent and external monitoring.

Leila Salazar, who heads Global Exchange's anti-Gap campaign, is unconvinced by the Gap's response. She explains her group's position as follows:

> Along with UNITE, Sweatshop Watch, and the Asian Law Caucus, Global Exchange believes that no one should have to toil under the conditions that workers in Saipan undergo. Like former Saipan sweatshop worker Chie Abad says, "No one

should be treated like a slave!" This is why we have filed lawsuits against Gap, Inc. and seventeen other retailers on the island of Saipan. We are calling on these companies to stop their misleading advertising and labeling practices, stop their use of the shadow contracts which workers must sign to waive their rights, to get rid of the exorbitant recruitment fees and to stop their violations of the federal law prohibiting the shipment of hot goods in interstate commerce. Global Exchange is also in the midst of a grassroots campaign to pressure Gap, Inc., as the largest manufacturer and retailer on the island, to settle the lawsuit and include a living wage in their Vendor Code of Conduct. We pressure Gap, Inc. through our monthly days of action (on the first Saturday of the month), civil disobedience, writing letters, faxes, call-in days, actions at store openings, shareholder actions, and by speaking out at many conferences and events. We are committed to putting pressure on Gap, Inc., specifically, until they adhere to our demands. It is ridiculous that Gap, Inc. has not settled yet, when so many other companies have already agreed to settle and improve conditions for their workers.[12]

Global Exchange's efforts are bolstered by its use of the Internet to mobilize Generations X and Y. Activists around the country and members of the public at large are able to receive periodic updates by e-mail about Global Exchange's efforts to expose labor practices at Gap, Inc.[13] In its hometown of San Francisco, Global Exchange holds the "Corporate Tour of Shame," which allows citizens to engage in an urban city tour of companies in San Francisco's financial and downtown districts that are alleged to engage in unethical corporate practices.

Gap, Inc. has explained that it refused to settle the lawsuit because its executives "believe the lawsuit against Gap, Inc. lacks merit, and we will continue to defend ourselves. We believe the facts will show that Gap, Inc. and our employees are committed to working with factories that adhere to our code of vendor conduct."

The civic-mindedness of Generation Y employs the strategic advantage of a horizontal structure, which stands in contrast to Donald Fisher's quest for vertical integration. The democratic nature of a horizontal organization is at odds with the hierarchical inevitability of a vertical structure. It's a question of a bottom-to-top democracy versus a top-to-bottom authoritarianism of civic economic life. Civic-minded members of Generation Y believe the Gap's corporate seed is evil. They argue there is enough in the world for everyone if we each keep our selfishness in check and it is the moral obligation of corporate officers to conduct themselves in socially responsible ways. In other words, men like Donald Fisher and Mickey Drexler are adults who, as children, were never taught to share their crayons.

The success of Global Exchange's resistance to the Gap may account for some of the plunging sales at Gap's core business. The massive advertising campaign to launch new "fashion" lines in the spring of 2000 were visually dazzling, but sales continued to fall as the year unfolded. Its dismal state of affairs was evident in a single fact: whereas in its first two decades, the Gap "repositioned" itself every seven or eight years, by the nineties that cycle had been cut in half. The Gap crisis of 1992—when it had been forced to slash prices to move merchandise out the door for the first time since 1987—resulted in a period of stagnation that culminated in zero growth by the end of 1995. Banana Republic remains "repositioned" once again and the Gap, as the year 2000 progressed, announced plans to refocus itself on "basics," oblivious to the subtext of economic insecurity and fear argued by Alison Lurie.

One strategy to stem the plunging sales—the Gap reported a stunning drop of 11 percent in same-store sales for the first quarter of 2000, news that sent its stock tumbling more than 10 percent—is, ironically, to increase the efficiency of its "sourcing" operations. "Overseas sourcing" is now an industry euphemism for "the management of sweatshops." In the spring of 2000 Gap, Inc. finalized negotiations with the city of Miami to relocate its sourcing operations from San Francisco to south Florida. Instead of managing relations with the factories that manufacture clothes for Gap, Inc. from San Francisco, Mickey Drexler wanted to move operations as far away from San Francisco as possible. This would not only take Gap officers charged with managing business relations with sweatshops away from protesters, but would bring them closer to many of the factories in Latin America that make clothes for the Gap, Old Navy and Banana Republic.

Gap, Inc. declined to comment on the whether this move was in response to the rising criticism—and demonstrations—in northern California. What is clear, however, is that the level of protests spearheaded by Global Exchange against the Gap had been so successful that Gap, Inc. decided it could not tolerate the disruptions that occurred when protesters took to the streets during the firm's annual shareholders' meetings. In 2000 Gap held its shareholder session in Gallatin, Tennessee, three time zones away from its corporate headquarters—and the familiar protesters who had embarrassed the Gap in previous years. Gap, Inc. subsequently announced it would continue to do so in future years in cities around the country.[14]

The Gap's realization that it was alienating many male members of Generation Y and the overwhelming proliferation of Old Navy have given rise to a definite "fatigue" among consumers. When sales of the capri and blasted jeans lines failed to move, the Gap responded with a media blitz—flooding the airwaves, filling all available billboards and side-swiping buses in cities across America—but to no effect.

In the course of traveling in the summer of 2000 to New York, Chicago, San Francisco, Miami and Los Angeles, seeing women wearing khaki capris was disconcerting. The first time I saw a young woman in Gap capris was at Miami International Airport. I was holding a place in line for a friend who was flying to Havana and the woman next to me was wearing a pair of capris. "Are those capris from the Gap?" I asked. She replied that they were, and wanted to know how I knew. I then mentioned that they looked very good on her—rather easy considering she had a svelte figure similar to Jennifer Lopez's. Then, after wondering what impact this fashion statement would have in the streets of Havana, I asked her, "Are they comfortable, because I've been told by several women I've asked that they really aren't." Then, with quintessential Cuban aplomb, she replied, "Being beautiful is more and more difficult all the time."[15]

"Beauty" is also being undermined by the Gap. What is astounding is to witness how the cyclical nature of certain trends in clothing reflect social mores. The continued economic expansion under the guidance of Alan Greenspan in the nineties was accompanied by a return of patriarchal values. A backlash against women's rights characterized the end of the twentieth century. Explaining the reason for this backlash against women, Alison Lurie states:

The fifties and early sixties were the years of the baby boom, togetherness and the feminine mystique; and, as usually happens in patriarchal periods, female and male clothes were sharply distinguished. The New Look Woman and the Man in the Gray Flannel Suit were almost as distinct in silhouette as their grandparents. Nevertheless, it was in this period that trousers for women began to edge their way into respectability.... The popular "toreador" or "Capri" pants, for instance, came in odd, glaring colors as if they had shrunk in the wash.... It was accompanied by shoes as narrow and sharply pointed—and no doubt as uncomfortable—as those fashionable in the fourteenth and fifteenth centuries.... [This represents an] ominous sign of retrenchment, and a counterrevolutionary movement seems to be gaining force. If one is pessimistic it is possible to see the sixties and seventies as merely a period of temporary victory. Indeed, the entire history of female fashion from 1910 to the present can be viewed as a series of more or less successful campaigns to force, flatter or bribe women back into uncomfortable and awkward styles ... and increasingly in order to handicap them in professional competition with men.[16]

American women resisted the capri fad in the spring and summer of 2000. The Gap's advertising campaign for these styles of clothing was seen by American feminists as a backlash against women's ascendance in corporate America. It was also a disingenuous affront.

Consider that the Gap's capri "assault" on America warranted its own op-ed piece in the *New York Times*. "At the Gap, the store I've relied on for years to supply me with blue jeans in progressively bigger sizes," writes Jennifer Moses, an aging baby boomer, "and white T-shirts in a seemingly inexhaustible variety, I could find nothing but capris—those tight, above-the-ankle pants that have spread from coast to coast like some terrifying virus."[17]

What Alison Lurie had argued two decades before her observations made news in the *New York Times* was validated further by Jennifer Moses, who continued,

The things weren't even comfortable to begin with, let alone cheap. And what was with my calves, anyway? Why did they look so—large?... But now I feel... what is the word? Old? Dowdy?... [S]uddenly, I saw capri pants not just in the mall, but everywhere: at the grocery store, on the mothers of my children's friends, on my neighbors.... Even my own 6-year-old daughter has a pair. Actually, she is the one person I know who looks good in them. After all, they were made for her.[18]

Feminist intellectuals argued that capri pants were designed to infantalize and handicap women, making them uncomfortable and objectifying their bodies, as Alison Lurie argued. What astounds, however, is that while Audrey Hepburn could make this style fashionable in the early sixties, things had changed in the first decade of the twenty-first century. While Jennifer Moses wrote her essay in Washington, D.C., a convention of nutritionists reported that for the first time in American history, more than half of the American population was overweight.

It may well have been that because American women (and men) are now fatter, the physiques flattered by capri cuts are slimmer. Most of the other women I stopped in public to inquire about their capris, however uncomfortable, confessed their pairs weren't from the Gap. The Gap was too expensive and they bought theirs from the Limited, Urban Outfitters, J.C. Penney and even Sears. As had been the case in previous attempts, fashion from the Gap was shunned by the consumer because of sticker shock. Thus, as the first summer of the new millennium arrived, the Gap found itself "repositioning" itself once more, as much from the capriciousness of its "fashions" as from the changing bodies of American consumers. This time, however, the "Gap-lash" was impacting the firm in fundamental ways. The departure of Jeanne Jackson at Banana Republic and Robert Fisher at the Gap division, the dizziness of the statements made by Jenny Ming at Old Navy, that Ken Pilot had taken over the Gap stores when sales were plummeting, speculation on Wall Street that Mickey Drexler was in over his head, and the aloofness of Donald Fisher's voice—all these created a sense of despair.

Five years of agitation by Generation Y activists were taking their psychological toll. "Isaac Mizrahi's comments in *Esquire* magazine hurt deeply," a gay employee at Old Navy's headquarters in San Francisco admitted. "All we're trying to do is be fabulous."

Then again, one person's fabulosity is another person's economic imperialism. Gap's decisions to cut costs, distance itself from its critics by relocating its sourcing operations and increase production from poor countries are desperate ones.

It is clear that the Gap confronted a dilemma: the more it is identified with the exploitation of multitudes in sweatshops around the world, the more it generates ill will from Generation Y. As store sales fall, the Gap cuts prices first, then reduces costs by shifting production to poorer countries. But as prices fall, the suspicion that the Gap is no longer cool is validated, making it even more uncool among young consumers. Meanwhile, the public's outcry over the working conditions of the Gap's contracted labor forces overseas grows louder—and the cycle is repeated. Both as a company and as a brand, the Gap loses.

What makes this dilemma the more exasperating is the hypocrisy of it all. If Donald Fisher, since the FTC Consent Order of 1978, has wanted to integrate his company vertically, then true and complete integration would entail owning and operating its factories. If Gap, Inc. were sincere in its "code of ethics," it could implement it at will.

Critics point to Donald Fisher's calculated callousness as the reason why Gap, Inc. is disingenuous. There is nothing, after all, preventing Gap, Inc. from doing what other multinational companies do—from Sony to Ford—and open its own factories in the developing world to manufacture its clothes exclusively. This would allow it to implement the labor practices that Gap, Inc. claims to espouse. Leila Salazar makes a strong case against Gap by pointing out that its "credibility is diminished by unconvincing arguments against owning and operating factories overseas."

Gap, Inc., so obsessed with total control that it refuses to let advertising agencies develop its advertising and instead produces everything in-house, has no convincing explanation why it refuses to apply this same discipline to how it manufactures the very products it sells. That Gap, Inc. does not end sweatshop conditions by owning its own factories is proof to activist members of Generation Y that Gap stands in opposition to their value system.

The question of the Gap as a brand is itself a curious one. Old Navy had demonstrated how little value Gap as a brand held for consumers. This was to be expected, after all. Mickey Drexler, in his zeal to increase market share, explained his approach by pointing out that "if you go to a supermarket, you would expect to find some fundamental items. You would expect to find milk: non-fat, 1 percent, 2 percent, whole milk. You would expect dates to be fresh."[19] Drexler argues that one would expect to find other staples, like eggs and cereal, and wondered why the Gap could not function in similar fashion. "Is a can of Coke less essential than a white Gap T-shirt?" he asked rhetorically.

But Coke is Coke and Coke is a patented formula. And milk and eggs are actual products, not brands, and most are procured by local and regional vendors. There is not "Milk" brand milk or "Eggs" brand eggs. There are dairy producers who advertise on a national level, but individual members are the suppliers. And the Gap owns no patent on denim jeans or T-shirts. This is why consumers refer to these other products by the kind of container in which they are sold: milk by the quart, eggs by the dozen.

On a fundamental level, confusing brands with products, as critics say, has substituted economic expediency with decency. Mickey Drexler's gross error was in believing that "Gap" as a brand had such intrinsic value in the minds of consumers that they would be prepared to pay a premium to have that label on the inside of their clothes.

This miscalculation—coined a generational phenomenon by Paco Underhill—is what made Old Navy's devastating cannibalism possible in the first place. And that Gap as a brand is devalued in the minds of consumers is what makes Global Exchange's well-orchestrated campaign to reclaim the conscience of corporate America such a success. It taps into the political activism of Generation Y, firmly building on the foundation established by the work of the Generation Y's Negativland and Billboard Liberation Front as well as the baby boomer student movement of 1968. The culmination of historic forces is of a cultural nature that has torn the Gap's New Age pretensions of enlightenment to smithereens—and sent store sales into a free fall.

10

FALLING OUT OF THE GAP

Time passes and we all age. In this process, first of maturation and then of decline, things go astray. Consider what happened when two political giants of the second half of the twentieth century met in Paris in March 1995. François Mitterand, the conscience of Western Europe's humanist approach to socialism, hosted Fidel Castro, a Communist dictator who has driven a stake through the heart of the Cuban family. Now, then, what does one suppose these two men, both past retirement age when they met, discussed in private?

The answer was, quite simply, their prostates. The world did not know it at the time, but François Mitterand was dying from prostate cancer. The ravages of time remain the same for all humanity. As Gap, Inc. celebrated its thirtieth anniversary in 1999, Donald Fisher was in his seventies. If aging reminds us of our mortality—and by implication of our humanity—it also burdens us with a certain, sadly undeniable, mindlessness. Fidel Castro and François Mitterand compare notes on how completely they can empty their bladders in the middle of the night.

And what weighs heavily on the mind of Donald Fisher, who, at the dawn of the twenty-first century, finds himself inching ever closer to life's door marked "exit."

"I've given up trying to find parking in downtown San Francisco," Donald Fisher is quoted as saying, by way of explaining that he is determined to help city government get more parking garages built. "There's no parking."

Donald Fisher, whose personal fortune is measured in the billions and who could afford a fleet of helicopters to shuttle him above the multitudes caught in traffic jams, is frustrated by the fact that, because he can no longer find convenient parking, he is forced to take cabs or be dropped off by his driver to keep his appointments about town.

Parking problems, prostate problems. *Whatever.*

Is the Gap "over"?

No, but America is over the Gap. What was once innovative is now common. What it once offered as unique is done better by others. Where once it had proved itself to be a retailing sensation, as the twenty-first century arrived, it had faltered and was struggling to regain its footing. The lessons Donald Fisher learned from observing Fred Pressman blunder were slowly being forgotten as he relinquished more and more of his day-to-day responsibilities. The Gap can no longer be hip simply because it is a mature business. If every generation of Youth Culture establishes its identity by standing against the status quo, the Gap is now the establishment that youth must resist.

Global Exchange, and not the Gap, is the heir to the groovy idea about which Doris Fisher boasted at cocktail parties in the waning days of the Summer of Love. This discussion, however, is not a chronicle of a bankruptcy foretold. As the nineties ended, the Gap failed to understand the tenuous nature of its brand and became the target of activists who equated the proliferation of its stores with pornography. In order to understand how, in a cultural context, America fell out of the Gap, three failures will be examined.

THE VULNERABILITY OF THE GAP BRAND

While brands may be recognized in market focus group studies, this recognition is not a guarantee of either approval or desirability. While Maggie Gross engineered a comprehensive branding campaign that created a coherent image of the Gap among consumers, subsequent efforts have done little to make the Gap premium in the minds of consumers.

The Gap, ever mindful of its brand recognition, chose to ignore that, and simultaneously, fewer and fewer consumers thought the Gap was "cool," a code word for premium. An explanation for this oversight might very well be Mickey Drexler's insistence on transforming the Gap into a "generic" product, best articulated in his analogy comparing the Gap with basic supermarket products. What astounds, however, is that the stunning success of Old Navy was evidence of how quickly consumers were prepared to abandon the Gap if another store—another brand—offered better value.

That Old Navy could cannibalize the Gap's core business solely on price meant, of course, that the Gap as a brand held little intrinsic value for consumers. The undeniable truth of the matter is that the Gap's urgent problem is not finding parking spaces; it is finding customers. By the time the year 2000 arrived the Gap had become a company with good products, terrific name recognition, excellent real estate locations. But it was also too dependent on one aesthetic; it had too few executives capable of managing a diversified portfolio. Additionally it was the object of mounting public outcry over its treatment of its workers. Gap, Inc. had grown into a conglomerate, with product lines far afield from its original blue jeans and pocket T-shirts. As the new century arrived, however, the dual impact of Generation Y's collective dissing of the Gap and the five-year campaign by Global Exchange were affecting the bottom line.

In the frantic aftermath of Robert Fisher's abrupt resignation, the first collection of the new century fell with a thud. Bloomberg News reported on April 5, 2000, that the Gap's sales in March were off by 11 percent, sending the company's stock into a dive. A month later the *New York Times* reported that "[p]erhaps the biggest disappointment was Gap, Inc. which has been uncharacteristically off the mark with its fashions [*sic*] lately," noting that sales growth was about half of what Wall Street had expected.[1]

But it is more than missing the mark in a given season. It is about two other things. Foremost, it is about a fundamental shift in the relationship between a brand, the brand's managers and the consumer. When middle-aged men like Jim Hightower can ridicule the naked hypocrisy that Youth Culture, in its idealism, instinctively zeros in upon, then there is backlash mounting. "The Gap is uncool," a twenty-year-old protester told me, "because the Gap is the establishment. In the quest for social justice on a global scale, Mickey Drexler is the enemy and Donald Fisher is 'the Man.' "

Generation Y, which, because of the invincibility that all youth everywhere see in themselves, equates its elders with decay. Physical decay is often associated by youths with *moral* decay. Younger generations easily fault their elders for the world's problems. "What a drag it is getting old," the Rolling Stones sang of the human condition. It also applies to corporate brands.

The value of the Gap as a brand was diminished further because it was targeted by Generation Y social activists. For a generation of Americans that some say is a testosterone high, such a characterization cannot be suffered silently. Donald Fisher and Mickey Drexler were mistaken to believe that Generation Y was as passive as Generation X had been. The Generation X teenagers were, by comparison, innocent and simple.

Generation Y, by comparison, was the first wave of teenagers who were coming of age with the Internet and MTV. They were sophisticated in ways no one in corporate America understood fully: Generation Y-ers were the ones who, just for the fun it, were capable of unleashing computer viruses upon the world, sending entire companies, government agencies and private networks crashing around the world. This is the kind of individual and communal intensity that characterizes active resistance against the Gap by members of Generation Y. That Leila Salazar, in an inspired campaign of subterfuge, could harness the moral outrage of an entire generation and impact the bottom line of the largest clothing retailer in the world proves the economic power 70 million Americans of Generation Y held over the Gap.

"Ralph Lauren and Tommy Hilfiger exploit workers in Saipan as well," one analyst for Citicorp Investments said, echoing the fact that investors were now taking notice of how Generation Y's repudiation of the Gap was affecting the company's bottom line. "It's the Gap that bears the brunt of the criticism because it's the Gap which has been targeted by activists."

Global Exchange's decision to target the Gap has been successful for two reasons. Foremost is that both Global Exchange and Gap, Inc. are based in San Francisco, thereby making Global Exchange's efforts an attempt to right wrongs in its own backyard—even if the wrongs are committed thousands of miles away. The second reason is that, through the democratic grass-roots nature of its campaign, Global Exchange has found resonance with members of Generation Y, who welcome its participation in other, broader efforts. The Seattle protests against the World Trade Organization in the fall of 1999 and the Washington, D.C., protests against the World Bank in the spring of 2000 included workshops and meetings on the Gap. At the end of each of those protests, the Gap found itself with activists returning to their hometowns across America with an anti-Gap message to spread to others.

Working with other human and labor organizations, for instance, Global Exchange has made significant strides to advance all their positions. Leila Salazar reports on how Global Exchange settled a suit against apparel manufacturers doing business in Saipan:

On March 29, 2000 our attorneys announced that eight more companies settled the Saipan lawsuit. The companies which settled [the] lawsuit are Calvin Klein, Tommy Hilfiger, Sears, Liz Claiborne, Oshkosh B'Gosh, Jones Apparel, The May Company, and Warnaco. Calvin and Liz were not named in the original suit. This means that out of the 18 retailers and manufacturers named in the original suit, only 4 remain.[2] Since Gap, Inc. is the largest retailer and manufacturer on the island and still continues to deny "allegations" that they have sweatshops on Saipan and that our actions are affecting their sales, we will continue to put pressure on Gap, Inc. until they settle the suit and agree to pay all of their workers a living wage. . . . *Business Week* reporter Louise Lee wrote throughout the year 2000 that Gap sales continued to decline, disenchanted Gap investors continued to sell their shares thereby driving stock prices down and key Gap, Inc. executives continued to leave the company. We fight them in the courts and we fight them in the streets. We are engaged in a program of constructive engagement, not a boycott, which is why we are winning.[3]

The Gap responded to the controversy over its labels by posting on its Web site (*www.gapinc.com/about*) the following explanation:

There are rumors that Gap Inc. has misled consumers by labeling clothing from Saipan as "Made in the USA." In fact, the federal government requires that the accurate country of origin be reflected on all labels of apparel sold in the United States. Given that the Northern Marianas Islands (Saipan) is a U.S. territory, Gap Inc.—like all other retailers—is required by law to include "USA" on the labels of all goods produced in Saipan and sold in the United States.

To avoid confusing consumers who may not know that Saipan is a U.S. territory, Gap Inc.'s long-standing policy is to label all clothing produced for the company in Saipan as "Made in the Northern Marianas Islands (USA)."

Activists were not entirely convinced and pressed forward, organizing rallies and demonstrations as the twenty-first century began. But there was progress to report. Leila Salazar of Global Exchange, for instance, stated that Gap had made an effort to improve the labor practices overseas in the factories where its clothing is manufactured.

"We, at Global Exchange, feel that this is a great step in understanding our differences and knowing where both sides are coming from," she said in an e-mail communication to all the people in her network at the end of 2000. "We don't know what will come of our discussions [to ensure compliance], but we hope to continue these types of discussions in the future."

"Sales at the Gap's core business are in a catastrophic decline," a New York retail analyst concluded in May 2000, predicting a "dismal" summer for the Gap's core business. It was. The vulnerability of the Gap as a brand also became painfully evident when Donald Fisher stepped down as CEO of Gap, Inc. In his mistaken belief that his particular genius could carry on without him, when Mickey Drexler took over Donald Fisher's responsibilities in 1995, Donald Fisher withdrew more and more from the day-to-day operations of the business. Thirty-six months after his decision—perhaps because of his mistaken belief that the proper role of septuagenarians is to retire from work—it was undeniable that the Gap was in trouble.

The splendid formula for success he fine-tuned in the seventies—and which gave rise to stunning explosive growth in the eighties—had apparently been forgotten. His intuitive sense was lost in a dizzying—and distracting—avalanche of projects and products, marketing strategies and merchandising campaigns. Gap, Inc. had lost its focus. In 1998 alone, for instance, Old Navy cosmetics, Gap Body Shops, Gap-to-Go (delivering jeans like take-out pizza), and Banana Republic's credit card were introduced. And all the while, the Gap's core business was suffering in unprecedented ways. Donald Fisher, the cool cat, was now, to the Gap's detriment, an aloof one—and the Gap brand suffered.

Mickey Drexler's strength has been in focusing on developing a clear, simple image for the Gap, supervising a national expansion program and securing foreign manufacturers to produce its product lines competitively. These are different talents than those required to manage diversified product lines for differentiated corporate brands. It's one thing to manage factories making blue jeans in Southeast Asia or Latin America. It's another to commission tableware, Christmas ornaments and colognes.

In the mid-eighties both Donald Fisher and Mickey Drexler recognized the limits of their management team. This is why, rather than enduring a costly learning curve, Pottery Barn was sold off. This is also the reason why when good ideas became bad business, such as Hemisphere and Gap Shoes, they were shut down before they became drains on corporate resources. These lessons were forgotten as the nineties ended. What is the home division of Banana Republic if not an attempt to compete with the upscale lines found at Pottery Barn? What are colognes, shoes and leather desk accessories if not an attempt to provide the exclusive spirit of Hemisphere to Gap, Inc.'s affluent customers?

There were problems of a structural nature within the organization as well. The Coca-Cola Company is not about selling sugared water; it is about engineering logistics to deliver refreshments to consumers the world over. With Donald Fisher's relinquishing his duties and involvement in the company's day-to-day operations, the discipline and genius he had brought to the endeavor began to disappear. He became more concerned with civic matters—from being the chairman of the Presidio Trust to being consumed by controversies over the logging of redwoods, to lobbying San Francisco city government for more downtown parking garages, to curating his outstanding collection of modern art. Donald Fisher's absence was felt with increasing urgency as Gap, Inc. lost its focus—and its edge. Throughout 1999, sales continued to be sluggish at the core division but this was readily dismissed by Gap executives as "mistakes" concerning fashion.

These weren't fashion "mistakes," but rather they were problems associated with weak brands. Robert Fisher had blundered in the 1998–99—as Mickey Drexler had in 1993–95—into thinking an experiment in fashion would be an antidote for the relentless cannibalism Old Navy had unleashed. The lesson, ignored by the Gap at its own peril, is that any effort to embark on "fashion" results in a self-defeating marketing tautology: the Gap has succeeded by being antifashion, so it cannot package itself as being about fashion. The public humiliation Robert Fisher suffered when he resigned less than two weeks after Old Navy opened its flagship store in downtown San Francisco was a measure of just how dismal sales at the Gap had become.

"That entire division is becoming undone completely," one industry watcher remarked. "I don't know if there is anything that can be done to make Gap hot again."

In November 1999 Mickey Drexler took over the Gap stores precisely to work his magic. But in a move that defied both explanation and reason, Mickey Drexler sought salvation in—of all things—fashion! The Gap, ignoring the lessons of its failed forays into fashion in the nineties, launched yet another fashion line in the spring of 2000. Actually stunned by Oldsmobile's scathing ridicule during the Super Bowl, the Gap had not pulled much of its television advertising off the air. Consumers were confused by

Oldsmobile's send-ups of the Gap and the Gap's own commercials, which came across as sillier with every airing.

The Gap sought to introduce its first post-Fisher fashion during the Oscars at the end of March. This would not only relaunch the Gap as a brand throughout the world but would also project Mickey Drexler's vision with clear authority. The anticipation built in the weeks before Oscar night. As much speculation and buzz surrounded the unveiling of the Gap advertisements as did guesses of who would be winning Oscars that night. But what happened during the Oscars was stunning.

The world had changed dramatically. Generation Y's repudiation of the Gap's antifashion philosophy was complete. The Gap chose to use stylized renditions of dances from the sixties musical *West Side Story* to introduce its new line of jeans and khakis. The Gap's commercial exploded onto the television screen with Technicolor intensity, an accelerated tempo and stunning choreography. It was over the top—to the detriment of the clothes. The bright colors clashed and the frenzied dancing was disorienting. The blasted denims for men and the capri pants for women were lost in a kaleidoscope of colors and movement. In fact, there was so much dancing, it was not clear precisely what the *products* were. The dancers' outfits were so ordinary that many viewers mistakenly believed the commercials were not the Gap's— and it was only *after* the Gap logo flashed across the screen at the end of each commercial that the sponsor was made clear.

"What was that all about?" one bewildered woman in her thirties rhetorically asked in the "comments" portion of a questionnaire filled out after watching the Oscars. "Is the Gap sponsoring a revival of *West Side Story* on Broadway? I don't get it."

Most members of Generation Y didn't get it either. It was at the Oscars, in fact, that it became clear how completely out of touch the Gap had become. The so-called fashion championed by Mickey Drexler was derived from the "look" popularized by Audrey Hepburn as interpreted by Hubert de Givenchy in the sixties. The Gap, in essence, was offering thirty-year-old knockoffs as its vision for the twenty-first century.

It is in this conflict that the greatest dilemma the Gap confronts is found. Whereas in the past the Gap had offered vital reinterpretations of its "classic basics"—the pillars upon which its antifashion philosophy was based— it now offered yawns. The mood of the times was captured perfectly by Nirvana's nihilistic song, "Smells Like Teen Spirit." This ennui manifested itself as apathy towards the Gap as a brand. The Gap's clothes, mockingly, in fact became nothing less than the "Salieri Collection." This was a reference to Peter Shaffer's play, *Amadeus*, in which composer Antonio Salieri, whose talents are eclipsed by those of his rival Wolfgang Amadeus Mozart, declares himself the Patron Saint of Mediocrities and by comparison a failure. Thus whenever the Gap attempts to introduce a collection that breaks through a well-constructed ceiling of mediocrity, it too fails miserably. Since 1995, the Gap had become big, bland and boring, thus reduced to a sad parody of its former brilliance.

Consider for a moment that Natalie Wood, who rose to fame portraying Maria in *West Side Story, drowned* before most members of Generation Y were *born*. Then consider how naïve the styles embodied by Jacqueline Kennedy appear to the sophisticated and jaded members of Generation Y. When Mickey Drexler first introduced a "fashion" line at the Gap in 1987, it bombed. Another attempt, made in 1991, was disastrous. The "fashion" items introduced four years later in 1995 were also a dreadful disappointment. What made anyone think that the blasted denim and capri pants launched in the 2000 would fare any better?

FAST ASSOCIATION WITH HOMOSEXUALITY THAT ALIENATES STRAIGHT MALES BETWEEN THE AGES OF EIGHTEEN AND TWENTY-FIVE

The gay aesthetics developed by Banana Republic proved a successful strategy for developing the lucrative urban professional niche market, but what plays well in New York and San Francisco cannot be applied across the country. Nor can it be applied across all demographics. The most highly coveted demographics in America are heterosexual males between the ages of eighteen and twenty-five. These are consumers whose disposable income slips through their fingers effortlessly, spent on purchases that are impulsive, careless and instantly gratifying.

If Banana Republic has apparently cornered the urban gay market, then the genius of J. Crew and Abercrombie & Fitch is the splendid way they have co-opted the Gap's male *heterosexual* youth. Both J. Crew and Abercrombie & Fitch have, in fact, done a remarkable job of segmenting this consumer. J. Crew has made significant inroads among college-age young men and women. Around campuses throughout the United States and Canada, J. Crew is one of the favorite clothiers, and loyalty to it among consumers extends into their early twenties. This merchant's association with collegiate life is so strong, in fact, that J. Crew has had its catalog spoofed in the spirit of the satire pioneered by *National Lampoon* in the seventies. *J. Crewd* by Justin Racz is a well-humored send-up of the J. Crew company, a mock catalog purporting to sell ridiculous things such as the "unabomber jacket" and making a fashion statement with its "redefining vest, sleeveless." Satire by college students reveals a definite affection, respect—and affinity—for a retailer. This is the process by which a brand becomes an intimate part of their lives.

Abercrombie & Fitch, on the other hand, is a hit among high school–age young men. By resorting to the irrationality and passion of sports, specifically high school sports, Abercrombie & Fitch has successfully exploited the fact that the Banana Republic's apparent embrace of gay aesthetics has alienated an entire generation of heterosexual young men who are coming of age. As a merchandising strategy, the testosterone-rich and life-affirming imagery of Abercrombie & Fitch and J. Crew is astonishing.

Then again, this is not a new phenomenon, for consider Thorstein Veblen, writing—in 1899—of the emotional nature of sports and sporting:

> There is a feeling—usually vague and not commonly avowed in so many words by the apologist himself, but ordinarily perceptible in the manner of his discourse—that these sports, as well as the general range of predaceous impulses and habits of thought which underlie the sporting character, do not altogether commend themselves to common sense.[4]

Emotions need not make any more sense than consumer decisions, however. Together with traditional retailers that have established firm loyalties among the upwardly mobile middle classes, Land's End and L.L. Bean, both J. Crew and Abercrombie & Fitch are now firmly entrenched in the lives of the same age group that was attracted to the Gap in the eighties.

The image of the Gap's apparent homosexuality versus J. Crew's and Abercrombie & Fitch's heterosexuality need not be based in fact, but only in how these brands are *perceived*. This is a natural outgrowth of what Edward Bernays pioneered as the father of spin. "Advertisers had always pressed consumers to pick one product over another, and press agents had shilled stories for their clients," Larry Tye reports, "but now Bernays and a band of colleagues were skillfully manipulating symbols and trends in ways that affected what average Americans ate for breakfast, what sorts of homes they bought, and what colors they chose."[5] What mattered, in essence, was how perceptions, rational or otherwise, could be best skillfully *manipulated* and then marketed and packaged to create branding. Maggie Gross had excelled at inventing a brand image for Gap, Inc., but without her the brand itself lost its focus. Retailers like J. Crew, Abercrombie & Fitch and even Brooks Brothers began to fill in the void.

A measure of how far gay aesthetics are *perceived* to have penetrated the Gap could be seen in something as simple as the advertising imagery used. In Abercrombie & Fitch's enormous Spring Break 2000 catalog, for instance, littered throughout the clothes are articles aimed at Generation Y. In one such article, titled, "Sailor Boy," the first-person account includes the following:

> I was surfing in the steepest waves I had ever experienced, and I can recall grasping the boat as it took off like a rocket. . . . Instantly the adrenaline rushed through my veins, and I felt more alive than ever before. I discovered this is what I lived for. I've asked myself a thousand times why that is. Maybe it's to fulfill the dream of that little boy who wanted to grow up and win a gold medal, or maybe it's just the rush of the race.[6]

It is clear that Abercrombie & Fitch strikes a chord with youth, its search for adventure in the world at large and its search for identity through self-discovery. Abercrombie & Fitch presents itself in a straightforward manner in which boys are boys and girls are girls and everyone is living a life-affirming, heterosexual lifestyle. Compare that with the vacuous she-nanigans that engulfed the production of the Gap's *West Side Story* commercials. The colors, choreography and obsessive fussed-over fabulosity employed was monumental.

It reached such a "sissy" level that, at one point, reportedly, a group of the dancers were singing the words of one of the songs: "I feel pretty/Oh, so pretty/I feel pretty, and witty and bright/And I pity/Any girl who isn't me tonight." This was the verse being sung by the *boys*. Such Banana-Republicanism suffused the image of the ad, evidence that, somewhere in all that shuffle of constant "repositionings," the company was in danger of losing touch with the overwhelming majority of heterosexual Youth Culture.

Banana Republic projects what holds true in San Francisco and New York onto the rest of the country. The emergence of so-called gay aesthetics as a cultural and marketing phenomenon first occurred in the seventies in San Francisco. Tracing this history Richard Rodriguez writes:

> It was no coincidence that homosexuals migrated to San Francisco in the 1970s, for the city was famed as a playful place, more Catholic than Protestant in its eschatological intuition. . . . The Castro [neighborhood] was an entire district. The Castro had Victorian houses and churches, bookstores and restaurants, gyms, dry cleaners, supermarkets and an elected member of the [city government's] Board of Supervisors. The Castro supported baths and bars, but there was nothing furtive about them. . . . The light of day discovered a new confidence, a new politics. Also a new look—a noncosmopolitan, Burt Reynolds, butch-kid style: beer, ball games, Levi's, short hair, muscles.
>
> Gay men who lived elsewhere in the city . . . often spoke with derision of "Castro clones," describing the look, or scorned what they called the ghettoization of homosexuality.[7]

In the seventies, the gay "look" was "butch." In the eighties, however, the emergence of AIDS resulted in an opportunity for homosexuality to break out of its ghetto: red ribbons became one way for many to express their sexual orientation in a politically correct manner. Without having to say so, suddenly, men throughout the United States—flight attendants, waiters, florists, hairdressers at first, then realtors, government bureaucrats, lawyers, businessmen and executives began to wear red ribbons—making gays more visible.

After Elizabeth Taylor founded the American Foundation for AIDS Research, or AmFAR, everywhere red ribbons became, in fact, *de rigueur* accessories of political correctness—and it gave gays a greater confidence to make their presence known on the public stage of civic life. When others began to wear the red ribbons, apart from empathizing with those afflicted with AIDS, it became a statement of solidarity with the gay rights movement. I remember a tailor who had fitted me for trousers at Nordstrom for several years in the early eighties who suddenly began to wear a red ribbon on his lapel at the end of the eighties. What was noteworthy, however, was how he himself changed in his demeanor and comportment. Whereas before he would say, "I think this shirt and this tie would look good on you, sir," suddenly, he began to say things like, "I think this shirt and tie will look fabulous on you. Absolutely fabulous." This was not the case with salesmen at Brooks Brothers or Paul Stuart.

The closeted salesmen at clothing stores throughout America, in a sense, came out. AIDS, too, forced many designers to admit publicly their homosexuality, from Perry Ellis to Halston. In the twenty years since the Castro became the "Gay Mecca" there was a transformation in the "look" of the Castro clone. The "butch" style gave way to the "twinkie" look—clothes for men who, as boys, were called "sissies" or "mama's boys." The AIDS crisis made it possible for individuals to be more open and honest about their lives, which is an understandably healthy thing. Gays had long been "loathed" and "despised" as "deviants."[8]

The question for Banana Republic, however, was how to make gay "visibility" translate into higher *sales*. Since the ouster of Mel and Patricia Ziegler at Banana Republic, first under Tasha Polizzi and then under Jeanne Jackson, Banana Republic introduced collections of clothes that resembled the aesthetics of the homosexual "twinkie" stereotype—clothes that were fussed over, looked slightly effeminate and had a certain look appropriate for an urban (office worker) environment. Attention to fabrics, buttons, stitching and style worked together to give a coherent "look."

It is important to distinguish between *tailoring* and gay aesthetics. An article of clothing can be constructed from fine materials, be exquisitely cut, perfectly fitted and look masculine. Think of Cary Grant or the Duke of Windsor. What was emerging at Banana Republic was something else altogether. Now think of the sleek and feminine clothes of Audrey Hepburn: Banana Republic clothes for men resemble the delicate cuts and forms she popularized. Just as the "butch" Castro clone emerged as an image in the seventies, in the nineties, a "twinkie" clone evolved in successive collections from Banana Republic.

Gap officials recognized that Banana Republic was "different" and were weary of having this particular kind of fabulosity affect the Gap's core business. By the nineties, it could no longer be denied that, as was the case throughout society at large, the "twinkie" look was spreading throughout mainstream culture. Consider the Caesar haircuts and clothes on the male cast members of *Friends* and *Beverly Hills 90210*. The overly groomed hair, the increasingly fussed clothing and the frequent wardrobe changes reflected the new gay look in mainstream culture.[9]

The emerging gay subtext of the Gap's image was obvious to the most casual of observers. Indeed, in an episode titled "Coffee and Commitment" that originally aired on January 4, 2001, Will Truman, the gay attorney portrayed by Eric McCormack on the popular *Will & Grace* NBC sitcom, could nonchalantly say he would be happy to attend the same-sex commitment ceremony of two gay friends with any one of "the Gap dancers."

In the seventies, as Richard Rodriguez argues, the gay look was *noncosmopolitan* (Banana Republic Safari), but in the nineties, it had become very *cosmopolitan* (Banana Republic Metro Urban). In the intervening two decades, as gays in San Francisco established themselves as a powerful political voting bloc, their influence in the city's civic life became more noticeable. In the same way that, say, the Irish dominate the civic life of Boston and Cubans do in Miami, it was the gay and lesbian community that established itself as a highly visible constituency in San Francisco. For Gap, Inc., a pillar of the San Francisco business community, the company's open and tolerant work environment nurtured its corporate employees' creativity—and influence. It won praise and was held as an exemplary corporate citizen for the way it treated everyone in its organization with one exception: its store clerks.

"I love working for Old Navy," said Richard Jennings, a gay African American who works in design at the corporate offices. "This is a wonderful company to work for. It just is a great place where I'm respected. It's great."

Kudos from an individual who, by virtue of being both a racial and sexual minority, faces double the discrimination speaks volumes about the kind of tolerant, nonjudgmental and welcoming corporate culture Gap, Inc. has nurtured over the past three decades. As such, Banana Republic's "repositioned" line of clothes boasted stores and a catalog filled with "urban" and "metro" clothes that paralleled and was ideally suited for the changes in contemporary gay life in the big city.

Banana Republic did not, however, have a monopoly on the perceived association with homosexuality. As 2001 began, questions were raised about the gay elements that were slowly being introduced into the advertising for the Old Navy brand. Consider, for instance, the perplexing appearance of Megan Mullally, the actress who portrays fag-hag Karen Walker on the popular television show *Will & Grace*. Featured in commercials for Old Navy at the end of 2000, she was surrounded by four effeminate young men who danced and pranced about, presumably in an advertisement for men's sleepwear that ended with the campy tag-line, "These bottoms are the tops!"

No doubt they were, but what heterosexual America may not have realized, however, was that in contemporary homosexual vernacular, or SQE, that statement constitutes a compliment dominant gay men pay to their passive partners at the conclusion of anal intercourse. The gay inside joke made Old Navy a laughing stock within the gay community from coast to

coast—and those responsible for creating the commercial must have delighted at their mischievous cleverness—but at what cost?

Doesn't an antic such as this erode the value of the Old Navy brand? Isn't
shareholder value diminished when a company's advertising ridicules its
own brand? What was the purpose of Old Navy showcasing a gay double
entendre in its Christmas 2000 campaign on national television during a
time when heterosexual young men already had serious doubts about the
masculinity projected by the Gap's brands?

"We believe Gap is a troubled and struggling company, and think it is
only natural that investors . . . would gravitate towards healthy vehicles,
rather than to the shares of a problem-plagued company," Donald Trot, an
analyst at Jefferies, stated on January 26, 2001, affirming a "hold" rating on
Gap's stock. Not surprisingly, that same month, *Vanity Fair* declared that
"casual" clothing as a trend for the new year was definitely out.

Gap, Inc. does not break down its employees by sexual preference.[10] If
one assumes that homosexuality is randomly distributed throughout all
human societies and if one further assumes that around 10 percent of any
human population group consists of homosexuals, then, in the absence of
discrimination, one would expect to find that approximately this same percentage of people are homosexual in any given company. For Gap, Inc.—as
any other company anywhere in the world that does not discriminate on
the basis of sexual orientation—one can presume that one in ten employees
is homosexual. If one finds a higher percentage, then other factors must be
at work. To determine whether or not this is the case requires a little deduc-
tive reasoning. Gap, Inc.'s world headquarters are located at One Harrison
Street in San Francisco. Gap, Inc. also occupies nearby office buildings. To
ascertain, therefore, the number of homosexuals who work at Gap, Inc. is as
simple a matter as visiting the nearby health clubs.

In short order it is easy to find young men and women, faithful followers
of the northern California religion of salvation through working out regu-
larly, everywhere. There are young men lifting weights, young women at
treadmills, everyone at the power aerobics. But through casual observation
of the sexual politics of health clubs—who is checking out whom—it becomes clear. As one (single) young woman at the health club in the lobby of
Old Navy's offices phrased it with resignation in her voice, "all the girls are
looking at the guys, but all the guys are looking at each other."[11]

While one cannot determine one's sexual orientation by appearances,
these are the perceptions of the young people who work near Gap, Inc.'s
headquarters. Nowhere was the heterosexual repudiation of the androgy-
nous-gay aesthetics offered by the Gap more evident than in the appearance of Charlize Theron at the Oscars. Her presence was nothing less than
thunderous. It was as if Venus had risen from the sea, a vision of beauty that
defied superlatives. The way she looked that night as she walked to the po-
dium in a Vera Wang gown was arresting. Her elegance, style and glamour,

when juxtaposed to the ordinariness of the young women working up their sweaty essence as they cavorted in those aerobic Gap commercials, was light years ahead in evolutionary terms.

Whereas the young women in the Gap's advertisements were nothing less than ordinary, Charlize Theron's essence was one of sublime femininity and physical beauty. The world had come a long way from the 1996 Oscars when Sharon Stone wore a Gap mock turtleneck. Charlize Theron's presence was a stark reminder of the power of dress in civilized society, which was a rebuke to the androgynous youths who filled the Gap's commercials.

"Look at these boys," an African-American young woman who had become a teenager in 1996 commented when shown the Gap advertisement that appeared in the April 2000 issue of *Vanity Fair*. "The way they are holding their wrists is *so* queer! You just know the boys want to be dancing with the *other* boys! This is for *gays*, that's all I can say. It's just like Banana Republic—clothes for gay boys. *Gays, gays, gays.* I mean, you can live your life anyway you want to—but some things are *wrong*."[12]

If this is a terse pronouncement from a member of Generation Y, then it is an opinion formed, in part, because of the inexperience of youth. This opinion, however informed, is valid for it affects consumer spending. Perception in merchandising is everything. If Generation Y is turned off, this translates in lost sales. The *West Side Story* advertising campaign was short-lived. Moral opinions aside, the point could be summed up by observing that if Mickey Drexler wandered through the Gap in 1996 and "heroin chic" came to mind, it is possible for consumers to wander through Banana Republic in 2001 and think, in SQE terms, "fag central."

To appreciate how far creeping homosexuality had crept into Gap, Inc.'s brands, consider how the characters on *Will & Grace*, the only network sitcom featuring gay characters, embraced each Gap brand. Subtle nuances of Megan Mullally's campy double entendres about gay sex acts and Eric McCormack's lust for the Gap dancers were one thing.

But in an episode titled "Love Plus One," which first aired on November 9, 2000, Sean Hayes's character, Jack McFarland, takes a part-time job at Banana Republic. Jack, as an employee of Banana Republic, when not enamored by and attempting to hit on Matthew, a gay customer over whom he is smitten, amuses himself by lisping into his headphone and sashaying to and fro throughout the store in a hilarious satire of the way gay men behave in Banana Republic stores. (Jack McFarland prancing around Banana Republic evokes the sublime absurdity of Lucy Ricardo stomping in a vat full of grapes.) It turns out, however, that Banana Republican Matthew ignores Jack altogether and would rather turn a trick with Will Truman—to Jack's chagrin.

Reflecting the perceptions and values of American society, *Will & Grace* thus portrays Banana Republic as a place where gay men go to cruise and be cruised, and where the sexual tension is so high it results in friends becoming jealous of each other over the attention of a potential fling. Almost as an afterthought, Banana Republic is also a place that has clothes for sale.

What makes the obvious importance of Gap, Inc.'s brands in the lives of gays more blatant, moreover, is how the characters are insidious send-ups of gay stereotypes consistent with SQE usage. Will Truman is the aspiring gym-bunny who, for lack of discipline and steroids, is fast becoming a troll. Jack McFarland is a quintessential twinkie, which is to say, a common twink. Grace Adler and Karen Walker are maladjusted heterosexual women whose insecurities and low self-esteem make it impossible for them to sustain healthy relationships with straight men, forcing them to find comfort in the company of gay men—with whom they form friendships that are as sexually non-threatening as they are infantile. "If I knew why straight guys did anything," Grace Adler says in an angered moment of compelling clarity confessing the fundamental unhappiness in her life, "why would I be hanging out with you two *homos?*"

The Gap, Banana Republic, and Old Navy are the only brands in corporate America that enjoy recurring, and central, roles in how the lives of gays are portrayed on network television, an alienating fact that is not lost on young heterosexual American men. In fact, that Generation Y is responsible for $200 billion in consumer spending in the United States means that their perceptions, however misguided or ill-informed, have an impact at the Gap's cash register, day in and day out.

IDENTIFICATION WITH SOCIAL INJUSTICES AND PORNOGRAPHY

The world is moving faster and faster and ever faster. The familiar brands embraced by Generation Y—FUBU, Phat Farm, Sean Jean—were *the* niche labels of the nineties. But as the present decade began, however, second-generation Generation Y niche labels, with extreme names, began to emerge from New York's SoHo stores such as Active Ware, Yellow Rat Bastard and Pulse. These newer labels, in a curious way, pushed the envelope by building on merchandising tactics the Gap had pioneered.

It cannot be denied that the Gap had anticipated the future brilliantly. The Gap was familiar and comfortable, but it wasn't a brand that held currency with America's Youth Culture in the year 2001. It wasn't cool any longer. Donald Fisher, by revolutionizing American merchandising in the last quarter of the twentieth century, showed us the future of materialism in advanced capitalist economies. But it would be others who held power over the desires of Generation Y. The relentless campaign against the Gap spearheaded by Global Exchange fuels the Gap-lash.

One has to consider the impact of consumerism and commercial desire. Today this is a consequence of living in a consumer market in which MTV has taken over the cultural role of arbiter of taste from individuals such as Diana Vreeland and Thomas Hoving. Instead of refinement, consumers embrace immediacy, which is often coarse and common. I witnessed Mrs. Vreeland tearing the Gap's ads out of fashion magazines, offering the terse explanation, "This doesn't belong in here." And when pressed for a clarification, Mrs. Vreeland, who was born in France, replied, "Americans have taken the *idea* of egalitarianism too far. With this [the Gap] spreading everywhere, well, they might as well omit the word 'discernment' from dictionaries henceforth!"

The arbiters of taste of yesteryear have thus been replaced with mass merchandisers of mass tastelessness. This is what the baby boomers had done to the Matures, of course. It is what every generation has done since World War II. The difference, however, is that Generation Y has tremendous economic power. That Generation Y-ers equate consumerism with immorality challenges the premise of the market economy. No other generation has had a "Buy Nothing Day," for instance. And while Youth Culture repudiated the Vietnam War in the sixties when the Gap first opened its doors, it now lashes out against the globalization of trade by denouncing the World Bank, the International Monetary Fund, the World Trade Organization—and by vandalizing the Gap in downtown Seattle. This raises troubling questions about the violent turn in the nature of civic discourse.

Generation Y has a peculiar way of looking at the world. To a generation that has been raised with overt sexuality in contemporary culture, rapid-fire technological advances and an acceleration of lifestyle trends, it is charmingly prudish. While vulgarity in song lyrics, exhibitionism in advertising and coarse attitudes toward human sexuality abound, behind a seemingly jaded facade lie fragile sensibilities and sensitivities. On a political level, the astounding impact Global Exchange is having on galvanizing Generation Y against the Gap speaks of a sophistication where empathy for others translates into action. On a cultural level, despite the vulgarity and visual intrusiveness of MTV, there is a rejection of pornography. The box office failure of *Fight Club*, starring Brad Pitt and Edward Norton, suggests a certain fatigue. The reason this is so resides in the expanding understanding of "pornography" among members of Generation Y. In a time when sexuality is everywhere in the media, it no longer has *shock* or *pornographic* value per se. The idea that pornography now incorporates offenses beyond sexuality is accepted. The third definition of "pornography" in *Merriam-Webster's Collegiate Dictionary*, for instance, reads, "the depiction of acts in a sensational manner so as to arouse a quick emotional reaction." The example given is "the *pornography* of violence."

Excessive consumerism is also, on occasion, linked to pornography. That Gap, Inc.'s merchandising strategy is reported as "pornography" in this discussion is neither flippant nor malicious. It is done to reflect the one word that members of Generation Y themselves used over and over again.

More than "obscene," the word "pornography" was the adjective of choice when describing the angst they felt over the Gap's materialism.[13] Karl Marx, of course, was the first to equate capitalist materialism with immorality in the nineteenth century. Charles Dickens was another. The leading voice on the international scene at the end of the twentieth century denouncing this as "degeneracy" is Fidel Castro. There is irony in the fact that John Paul II, communism's most outspoken nemesis, also warns the former nations of the Eastern bloc that excessive materialism is immoral and pornographic.

The Vatican, alarmed at the wretched excesses and social inequities in former Communist countries making the transition to free market economies, warns of "economic violence." If reforms unleash "unchecked materialism," then this deprives humans of "dignity and spirituality." The danger for these nations in transition is the evil of "social pornography." This, in turn, stands in opposition to the doctrine of the "faithful" and historical "Christian values."[14]

This view is enthusiastically embraced by civic-minded members of Generation Y. What accounts for this passion? Corporate America has given Generation Y-ers material excess in their material world, a world that is filled with creature comforts like no other generation of young people have ever enjoyed. In fact, the only area of their lives where young people are wanting is in their spiritual lives. This is one compelling reason why taking an anti-Gap stance, for youths, approximates the experience of religious redemption. What is construed as a spiritual isolation becomes social alienation: the false comfort of consumption for consumption's sake takes on a pornographic edge.[15]

Thus excessive violence (as in *Fight Club*) and excessive consumerism (embarrassment of riches at the end of the nineties) are now equated with "pornography." Generation Y eagerly embraces this broadening of the idea of "pornography" to include social and political causes. In fact, this expanded understanding of pornography is the moral authority upon which Global Exchange can mobilize so many members of Generation Y. The cultural ambiance of San Francisco—what Richard Rodriguez describes as this city's Catholic "eschatological intuition"—fits perfectly with Global Exchange's program. The protests organized by Global Exchange, after all, are like "pilgrimages of the outraged," and their festive mood resembles Catholic processions of the faithful bearing witness. It is in the tradition of San Francisco as a community to encourage the public display of private convictions, whether it is the Summer of Love's celebration alternative morality or Global Exchange's repudiation of Gap, Inc.'s materialism. The Gap's ubiquity is a constant reminder of wretched consumption at home and of the systematic exploitation of worker rights abroad. To the Gap's critics this is nothing less than "pornographic."

In this emerging worldview of the twenty-first century wherein excessive consumerism is equated with pornography, civic-minded members of Generation Y might as well equate the dark blue squares with the white "G" "A" "P" letters with "X" "X" "X." What is often overlooked is that, in the political beliefs of youths, the fight against "globalization" is closely associated with a stand against excessive consumerism. The very idea that standards of living are measures of materialistic consumption offends the sensibilities of Generation Y. Moral ambivalence should not stand in the way of social activism. Thus Generation Y repudiates both the values presented by *Fight Club* and the Gap. The Gap-lash of the nineties became porn-fatigue and Gap-fatigue in the first decade of the twenty-first century.

Don and Mickey's "excellent adventure in retailing" has stalled in no uncertain terms. This comes from a failure to accept that the Gap is not a mature company. The subtext of implied drug abuse in the "zombie chic" advertising raises eyebrows. Its director of advertising is photographed, barefoot, sitting on the floor, and flippantly making the cavalier statement that the company doesn't think things through too hard. Mickey Drexler pontificates on the Zen-like desire to have the Gap evolve into the center of our lives in much the way milk and eggs are at the core of one's harmonic "experience" in a supermarket. Such vacuous ambitions send shivers through the collective spines of Wall Street investors and individual shareholders alike.

The worldview championed by the Gap over the past three decades is one that is openly ridiculed by social observers. David Brooks, writing of America's new elite, the bourgeois bohemians—or Bobos, for short—notes:

The key is to be youthful, daring, and avant-garde, to personify change. The center of gravity of the American business culture has moved westward and youthward. Impressive formality has been replaced by open-minded daring. Corporate America has gone more casual. Microsoft executives appear on the cover of *Fortune* with beanie propeller hats on their heads. Others are photographed looking like mellowing rock stars, wearing expensive collarless linen shirts or multi-colored sweaters or rag-wool socks under funky but expensive sandals. Often they'll be shown in jeans, standing proudly in the main hallway of a Rocky Mountain log mansion. You'd never find a bunch of people in blue suits, white shirts, and red ties in a software company. These wild things will be wearing clunky boots, ripped jeans, tattered university sweaters, and those tiny European glasses that give you as much peripheral vision as an astigmatic worm. . . . In this new era you've got to use the phrase "We're moving from an age in which . . ." a lot. After all, we are moving from a power society to a knowledge society, from a linear society to a postlinear society, from a hierarchical society to a networked society, from a skim milk society to a 2–percent-fat milk society.[16]

That the Gap's impact on society—alienating youth, enabling Bobos—is now satirized and subjected to old-fashioned ridicule has alarmed investors who, for the first time, openly question the firm's "direction," meaning future profitability.[17] These concerns are real, but the challenges are not insurmountable. There are concrete steps that Gap, Inc. can take, not to *reposition* itself, but to redirect itself. The task at hand is to focus on its core business and streamline its vision. The Gap sells everyday clothes, the kind of enterprise that can be profitable and discreet, the way successful manufacturers of utilitarian, everyday products are.

A certain caution is in order, however. In the summer of 2000, it was disconcerting to hear people in San Francisco and New York state, incessantly, the words "reposition" and the "Gap." Whereas in the past the word "reposition" had alluded to a managerial style based on a dialectic—take what we have, incorporate what we have learned, offer a synthesis that becomes the current standard—by the time the twenty-first century had arrived, "reposition" evoked a certain desperation that is normally called "reorganization" in bankruptcy proceedings.

The urgent mission of which Gap, Inc. cannot lose sight is the need to revive its core business. David Brooks, for one, is skeptical of the ability of stores like the Gap to arrest the decline precipitated by its silliness. He argues that "[t]he Bobos have invaded the business world, and they have brought their countercultural mental framework with them to the old conference rooms of the bourgeoisie. It's no accident that the Bay Area, the center of the Summer of Love, is now also the home for a disproportionate number of educated-class retailers, like the Gap."[18] Be that as it may, for the Gap and as a brand, a comprehensive strategic program to reposition its core business must include the following four steps.

FOCUS ON THE GAP AS A BRAND

Old Navy's success pointed out the Gap's failure as a premium brand. The notion of the Gap as a brand similar to "generic" products like supermarket staples, such as milk and eggs, must be discarded. "Gaps" will never be sold by the stack. The Gap is in the business of casual and leisure clothing that defies fashion by transcending fashion trends. To accomplish this, Gap, Inc. should disband its line of accessories. "Relationship marketing" is nothing less than the merchandising of distractions that confuse consumers, take up considerable corporate resources and clutter up the stores. Whether it is the Gap selling soap or Starbucks selling picture frames, effort can be directed in more constructive ways for growing the core business. The Gap should immediately shut down its scents, fragrances and home accessories lines.

The development of the Gap as a brand might require the consolidation of Gap, Gap Kids, Baby Gap, and Gap Body Shops under one roof. The strategy of clustering the stores has led not only to internal cannibalization among the brands but a cheapening of the Gap as a brand. By being everywhere, it becomes invisible, as people succumb to "Gap-fatigue." The

Gap's brand, in major urban centers around the country, has receded from the public's consciousness by virtue of its becoming visual "white noise." The Gap stores should be redesigned and consolidated to sell all divisions' products under one roof. The Gap is now confronting the same challenges that faced Miller's Outpost in the mid-eighties. By failing to articulate clearly its brand with one voice, Miller's Outpost became defined in consumers' minds as a store that attempted to impose a regional dress as a national uniform. The success of Banana Republic has, in fundamental ways, confused consumers about what the Gap represents as a brand. The Gap must welcome potential solutions to the problems its brand faces among young heterosexual males.

This is not an easy task, but it is not an impossible one, either. "It isn't really how long a brand's been around that determines if it's hot," German Medina of the Yellow Rat Bastard store in New York explained. "It's about having the right stuff that connects with the street. Sometimes it takes years before you can get it right. Sometimes you lose it but get it back. Sometimes you lose it and it never comes back. Sometimes you never had it in the first place. It's hard to keep it once you're in every mall. The Gap lost it around five or six years ago [in 1996]. Will they ever be cool again? It all depends. But I doubt it. Maybe in twenty years there will be a 'retro-Gap' fad, but the clothes are so boring and unimaginative, I can't see that, unless a fashion fluke comes along, like what happened with Hush Puppies for about a two-year period recently. At this point, Levi's® is cooler than the Gap."

Yellow Rat Bastard, a cutting-edge store selling sartorial clothes to the flyest (read: coolest) members of Generation Y who want to release their Inner Hipsters (read: become trend-setting Alpha Consumers), dominates the Youth Culture scene in New York in 2001. Indeed, it's the kind of store that publishes a catalog that includes clothes and essays on street art (graffiti), reviews underground bands, has interviews with notables and rates adult videos aimed at Generation Y-ers. It is an authentic turn-of-the-century enterprise.

"Look at Playboy," German Medina continued by way of explanation. "They were out of the scene for so, so long, but now with their new casual shirts, it is one of the hottest items to hit the streets in the last two years. We're even selling them to clients in London, Berlin and Tokyo." The Playboy shirt, modeled after the Hawaiian shirt (except that it displays a composite of multiple covers of the *Playboy* issues instead of tropical flora, similar to shirts with samurai warriors, Japanese calligraphy or anime characters), speaks of the cyclical nature of what becomes cool decade after decade. That Playboy can make a comeback and reconnect, after being dissed as something as hopeless and uncool as the seventies television show *Three's Company*, is itself intriguing for another reason: it demonstrates how established businesses need new blood to remain youthful. When the image of the Gap as a brand was raised to these purveyors of hipness, German Medina and his colleagues, Hazem Shiridi and Aldo Herrera, laughed out loud. "The Gap's been uncool for at least six years. Maybe longer," one of the young men offered, the others nodding in agreement.[19] "It comes down to guys wanting to look like men, not sissies," Hazem Shiridi argued.

The idea of a brand's place in the life of consumers is also changing as markets become increasingly segmented. For Generation Y-ers who are ravers, for instance, the preferred brands are Lithium and UFO. For those who are into hip-hop, it's Triple Five Soul and Ecko. Crossover brands such as Serial Killer are a more difficult achievement about which few brands can boast. Critics point out that these brands, which embrace indecency, are what made it possible for a notorious brand like Playboy to make a comeback. "That Playboy can reconnect with Youth Culture is a result of the emerging social acceptance of 'porn chic' in the twenty-first century," one fashion maven noted, adding that her own children sought these labels exclusively.

The further coarsening of American contemporary culture is, in fact, the defining trend sweeping throughout the United States. It is a phenomenon of seismic consequence worldwide, roughly analogous to the cultural impact the youth movement in 1968 had on the Western world. Consider, for instance, that "girlie" fashion advice columns—female Generation Y-ers often refer to themselves as girls—include first-person narratives on how young women can, and should, achieve equality with men by, of all things, urinating in public. "I talked this pissing in public obsession up with many friends," Jessica Smith writes in this new interpretation of feminism about which Gloria Steinam is silent. "I'm an open-minded girl so that very evening after some cocktails I took it to the streets. I was in a crowded bar where the line is always long, so I went outside and found a semiprivate, little corner area. I dropped my drawers to a point, did the sickly leaning practice that girls have to do even with some toilets [and] after some deep breaths and concentration I let it rip."[20]

The boys are not far behind when it comes to a brouhaha over pushing the envelope. Consider for a moment Marc Ecko, a ruggedly handsome and successful twenty-something designer with his own line of hot clothes, who, in 2000, entered into contracts with both Playboy Enterprises, the National Football League, and Brooks Brothers. When Marc Ecko is interviewed he, for the fun of it, makes cavalier pronouncements. Designing clothes is an experience similar to wearing boxer shorts one learns, with Ecko explaining that his personal philosophy on clothing is that "[i]t's all about being all over the place . . . feeling what you want to feel for the moment."

Marc Ecko thus summarizes the *zeitgeist* of Generation Y by arguing that, in the sociopolitical context of the realities of the twenty-first century, his clothes reflect a culture in which "attention deficit disorder is like the common cold." This is presumably why he described—pharmaceutically—his last collection in 2000 as "the theme is . . . Ritalin." This resonance is why his clothes are everywhere Youth Culture wants to be. And the look for his new brand introduced in 2001—"the Physical Science," or "Phys. Sci." for short—was summed up succinctly as "Prada Sport meets the NFL." This is the visual immediacy of MTV and the Internet channeling through the minds and bodies of youths. Then he rhetorically asks, by way of concluding, "Feel me?"

It's like, whatever . . .

The linguistic subversion of Generation Y—where "feeling someone up" is presented as an integral part of the corporate branding process—creates a parallel idiom that defines who's in and who's out. These are, therefore, the disjointed challenges that confront the Gap as it redefines its own brand. It is in this cultural context that Gap, Inc. becomes archaic—and irrelevant to the moment—as an extinct dinosaur. If the Gap is therefore to achieve the kind of success Playboy, by enlisting leading talents of this new generation of youths, has managed to pull off in a stunning *coup de grâce*, substantial strides on that evolutionary scale are in order.

The Gap brand faces no alternative but to refocus itself. Its clothes have to get "it" right, whatever the "it" is that brands like UFO and Kikgirl have. Whatever "it" may in fact be, it is what Marc Ecko possesses with an exuberant confidence. How can the Gap compete with that? Is Donald Fisher going to hold a news conference to announce that their new line, like Marc Ecko's, is inspired by pharmaceuticals?

This, however, is the cultural vernacular of youths and these are the branding strategies that have captured the imagination of Youth Culture in the first decade of the new century. The energy of youth escapes the Gap. William Shakespeare reminded us of this in *Hamlet*, where he wrote, "Be wary then, best safety lies in fear: / Youth to itself rebels, though none else near." The lack of creativity at the Gap is undeniable. Its antifashion philosophy has run its course. Mickey Drexler's merchandising ideas have, after fifteen years, become spent. The contrast was nowhere more evident than in the names generating—or not generating—a buzz in the scene. Whereas Marc Ecko's clothes and marketing can be described as self-referential post-modernist, the Gap's line under Ken Pilot can be summed up in one word: *laundry*.

To arrest the declining sales that intensified at the Gap's core business throughout the year 2000 and which loomed ominously as 2001 arrived—characterized by the ubiquitous "sale" signs encroaching on ever greater floor space—decisive steps are required. The year 2000 proved to be, as Heidi Kunz stated, one of sustained "confusion." Its confusion, both in terms of its marketing strategy and sexual identity, can only be arrested if it focuses on its core business. Specifically, the Gap must do the following.

DIFFERENTIATE BETWEEN THE GAP AND OLD NAVY

Gap should consolidate its position to compete with solid brands that hold appeal among young people, and Old Navy should see its mix become more downstream, competing more directly against Wal-Mart, K-Mart and Target. Old Navy must further downscale to stop cannibalizing the Gap's core business. The Old Navy brand must become a populist clothing brand, populist in the great American tradition of democratic values. Gap must be refocused to establish itself firmly as a middle-class product that offers values without affecting a "fashion" stance. In Mickey Drexler's analogy, after all, milk is milk and eggs are eggs without designer aspirations. In other words, if Old Navy is for the people, then Gap is a staple. With such brand differentiation, the Gap will be able to hold its own in suburban centers and Old Navy will become a mandatory weekend stop in urban centers, while each benefits from crossover sales. The challenge for Gap, then, is to rebuild its core business by differentiating between the brands of Gap and Old Navy. There will be continued resistance among consumers to distinguish between the brands on terms other than price point. This is a medium-term endeavor that must be carefully planned and fully executed in order to establish Gap firmly in the middle class and the Old Navy as a truly popular brand that cuts across the demographics of the nation.

The Gap must now use advertising to advance the brand and differentiate itself from the competition. Gap advertising in the year 2000 confused consumers and made it possible for other retailers, like Abercrombie & Fitch, to capitalize on its all-American, heterosexual imagery and context. That the demographically most lucrative consumers have moved away from the Gap represents a continuing erosion of its core business. It isn't that the Gap's advertising campaigns alienate consumers as much as they reflect a perceived lack of value. When Old Navy and the Gap each launched lines of vests, Generation Y-ers went to both stores, compared quality and prices, and then shopped at Old Navy. What was clear was that both stores had essentially the same products, but the Old Navy's was 40 percent less.

It is clear that, as historian Gertrude Himmelfarb argues, there are two cultures in America. She describes the cause of this tearing asunder of the American culture, with unintended irony, as an "ethics gap"—an ethics gap where

the cultural divide helps explain the peculiar, almost schizoid nature of our present condition: the evidence of moral disarray on the one hand and of a religious-*cum*-moral revival on the other. This disjunction is apparent in small matters and large—in the fact, for example, that both gangsta rap and gospel rock are among today's fastest-growing forms of music; or that while raunchy talk shows are common on television, moralistic ones are on the radio; or that while a good many people were tolerant of President Clinton's sexual infidelities, many others purchased enough copies of William Bennett's *Death of Outrage* (most of whom presumably share his outrage) to have kept it on the best-seller list for months.

This polarization . . . has larger ramifications, affecting beliefs, attitudes, values, and practices on a host of subjects ranging from private morality to public policy, from popular culture to high culture, from crime to education, welfare, and the family. In some respects, it is even more divisive than the class polarization that Karl Marx saw as the crucial fact of life under capitalism.[21]

Then again, "polarization" to merchandisers is a value-neutral word for "differentiation" within a segmented market—the Gap brand for one culture, the Old Navy brand for another. To Generation Y-ers this gap between cultures demonstrated that not only was the Gap a "rip-off" but that, curiously, the Gap was knocking off Old Navy's styles. The reasoning among youths was simply that, since everyone was buying and wearing Old Navy vests, then they must have launched their line first, with the Gap's "Everybody in vests" campaign being a hurried effort to "catch up" with Old Navy. This is how youths think and see the world around them. Gap, Inc. must clearly differentiate between the Gap and Old Navy brands. It is too late for the Gap to win over Generation Y, but it can work to position itself so that when the next generation of consumers come of age—beginning in 2014—it will continue to wear Gap clothes. One approach is to nurture strong brand loyalty among the infants and young children dressed in Baby Gap and Gap Kids. The success of these divisions among baby boomer parents offers Gap, Inc. a competitive advantage.

IDENTIFY CLOSELY WITH THE HETEROSEXUAL MAJORITY OF CONSUMERS

The realization that Banana Republic would be associated in the minds of many consumers with gay aesthetics first hit home when the Gap had to do damage control after Tasha Polizzi's failed homoerotic advertising was pulled. But as the numbers continued to come in, Mickey Drexler adopted the marketing strategy that Banana Republic had used, perhaps in an attempt to boost sales at the Gap's core business, at least in the short term. To understand the economic and social impact of what happens when a company becomes too closely associated with gay aesthetics, consider the fate of the Kenneth Cole brand.

Through the campiness of its advertising and the wit portrayed by the Kenneth Cole brand, it has been enthusiastically received by the gay community. Thus, if "homosexuality" is reduced to a market niche, it can become difficult to go mainstream. Herein lies the irony of a generational shift in how aesthetics are perceived. Mickey Drexler, not unlike most heterosexual businessmen, perhaps confuses *gay* aesthetics with *Youth* Culture. To be sure, homosexuals obsess about staying young, but that doesn't mean they *are* young. One can work out at the gym and take vitamins and have cosmetic surgery and look two decades younger than one's age, but that doesn't mean that a forty-year-old man connects with the life and culture experience of a twenty year old. Homosexuals at Gap, Inc., for the most part are, in fact, Generation X-ers, and their worldview reflects the worldview of that particular generation. Instead of acquiring the hipness—knowing what was "phat" and "fly" in Generation Y vocabulary—Gap, Inc. succeeded only in being, quite by accident, associated with gay fashion sensibilities.

In essence, Gap clothes began to reflect the kind of evolution that had previously unfolded at Banana Republic: Gap, Inc.'s employees were designing the kinds of clothes *they* themselves wanted for the kind of lifestyle *they* wanted to live. (Think of the ridiculous sight of young men wearing capri pants in New York and Los Angeles in the summer of 2000.) The problem with this, of course, is that the remaining 90 percent of the American population is not interested in clothes that are appropriate for the gay lifestyle—as decried by Michelangelo Signorile: to shoot up steroids, to buff up at the gym, to hop on a plane to a "circuit" party, to get high on recreational drugs, or to get drunk out of their minds and end up engaging in private or public sex, finally collapsing before the sun rises the next morning.[22]

This was the aura projected by Banana Republic at the end of the nineties, an image masterfully exploited by J. Crew and Abercrombie & Fitch to their own advantage. The Gap's homosexual "vibes" turned off adolescent males as the nineties ended and resulted in hundreds of thousands of highly coveted consumers spending at the Gap's competition. Consider something as innocuous as the music played in the Gap stores. Compiled by corporate offices in San Francisco and distributed to the stores around the world, the in-house music reflected an increasingly gay disco sound that surprised consumers.

In the second half of 2000, for instance, while visiting the Gap store in Dadeland Mall, deep in the heart of Miami's suburban neighborhoods, the Pet Shop Boys, a cult British band whose campy songs are anthems within the gay community, was playing.[23] The Gap employees were moving their bodies in rhythm to the words of a song that includes phrases such as "I feel like taking all my clothes off," while a few shoppers looked up, with surprised expressions on their faces. If the imagery evoked by the song was not terrifying enough—two skinny, clammy-white homosexual twinkies jumping up and down naked in a field of daisies—then the sight of Gap employees lip-syncing into their headsets was itself quite disconcerting enough.[24]

HETEROSEXUALITY TO THE GAP! HETEROSEXUALITY TO THE GAP! COME IN, GAP!

This is all the more reason for Gap, Inc. to divest itself of Banana Republic. With a strong balance sheet and definite branding within its niche market, Banana Republic can be sold to another company or investors who have long nurtured the emergence of gay aesthetics into the mainstream.

The proceeds from the sale of Banana Republic would allow the necessary funds to pour into the core business—or launch complementary divisions.

KEEP UP WITH THE BABY BOOMERS LIFE CYCLE

The Gap has found its most loyal following among the baby boomers. It makes sense to build on that relationship. As the baby boomers become older, the Gap would do well to meet the unique needs of this market segment. Old Navy was on target with its attempt to reach out to busy families on budgets. There's nothing wrong with shopping being "fun again," as Old Navy strove to demonstrate, provided it is also profitable. Within five years, it became clear that if the Gap had hoped volume would compensate for razor-thin margins at Old Navy, then its expectations were not met.

The Gap risks its hard-earned credibility by blurring the distinctions between its brands, and it risks losing its customers to well-established competitors who continue to eat away at its core constituency. Land's End, L.L. Bean and the reinvigorated Brooks Brothers are the retailers that have profited handsomely from the miscalculations at the Gap. There is, of course, a certain sadness in the disarray engulfing the Gap, a disarray that is heightened by the Gap's stubborn refusal to address legitimate concerns of the buying public. The Gap's refusal to join other clothiers in negotiating with consumer advocates concerned about the working conditions of the men, women and children who are employed in factories around the world smacks of grandiose machismo, a characterization in line with certain incidents in which women executives were made scapegoats throughout its corporate history.

The most effective way for Gap, Inc. to respond to the growing calls for it to act responsibly is, quite simply, to silence its critics by getting it together and integrating vertically. Since 1976 Donald Fisher has articulated his desire to integrate fully and completely all of Gap, Inc.'s operations. Mickey Drexler was hired in 1983 precisely to implement this vision. The single thing left is for Gap, Inc. to *own* and *operate* the factories, here and abroad, that manufacture its clothes. That the Gap refuses to do so can reasonably be interpreted as a disingenuous attempt to continue to exploit powerless workers who have little legal recourse to improve their lives. When Gap responds to critics by relocating its sourcing operations from one end of the country to another, this is seen by activists as a desperate attempt to run away from its critics—and its social responsibility.

Of greater concern, moreover, is that this needless controversy only serves to undermine and erode the Gap's credibility and its image among the public. Baby boomers and Generation X-ers are educated men and women concerned that members of corporate America conduct themselves as responsible members of society. As critics, most notably Global Exchange, raise their voices and point out tirelessly that the Gap acts in a "reprehensible" way, the Gap forgets that baby boomers and Generation X-ers are listening. The Gap already lost Generation Y. It is at risk of losing touch with these other generations.

It would be a mistake for Gap not to resolve once and for all the sweat-shop issue, which is a tiresome obstacle that clouds its future. Then it could properly focus on how to best cultivate its relationship with baby boomers in particular. In the same manner that Gap, Inc. was right on the mark in ex-panding to serve the needs of baby boomers when this generation became parents by ingeniously launching Baby Gap and Gap Kids, the first decade of the twenty-first century is the opportune moment for the Gap to launch a new division aimed at those millions of consumers whose children are now adults and they themselves are approaching, if not entering, their retire-ment years.

"Gap Silver" could very well be designed for the generation of Ameri-cans who are living longer, remaining more active and have passed retire-ment age. The next two decades are going to witness the emergence of a large, healthy, active, engaged and financially comfortable generation of older Americans. With disposable income levels never before seen in the nation's history, these consumers are determined to be proactive in their health maintenance and care. The Gap's brand could be expanded as the mainstay clothier to this empowered generation of Americans.

Advances in medical science and healthier lifestyles converge to create an ideal market for expanding further the Gap's antifashion philosophy of comfortable and casual clothes. It is absurd not to design clothes for the body shapes of older consumers who remain active, playing golf, riding bi-cycles, engaging in sports and adventure travel well into their seventies and eighties. "Write the words and make believe," sounded over the air-waves on MTV and radio throughout the hot and long summer of 2000, "there is truth in the space between."[25] That there is a dearth of clothes de-signed for this segment of the population exclusively is instructive of how the obsessive quest for youth blinds corporate America to the dignity and vitality with which older Americans are now living their lives.

For the Gap to divert its efforts into a misguided attempt to appropriate Youth Culture—when, by virtue of having become the largest retailer in the nation, it is now the standard against which adolescents searching for their individual and generational identity must rebel—is a misguided market-ing strategy. The Gap is at a point in its history where it can avoid the mis-take Miller's Outpost made in 1980. Donald Fisher learned from Fred Pressman's mistake at Barneys and astutely hired individuals because of their talents and capabilities. The Gap must learn from Miller's Outpost's errors. This is the kind of vision required to get the Gap to see its proper place in the lives of its core customers.

When the world is at one's feet, one needs to go nowhere. The world knocks at one's door.

204   Into—and Out of—The GAP

I remember as a child the man who would come once every so often to cut my hair. He would set up a horse for me to sit on, the kind of fanciful horse one rode at the circus carousels. I'd sit there, pretending to gallop off somewhere while he trimmed my hair. I also remember the gentleman who arrived with trousers and shirts and suits. And I would have to stand very still on an ottoman while he fussed with pins and chalks, making sure that the adjustments were made just so and that I was perfectly still, lest I get pricked by a needle.

The kind grooming and quality of clothes of yesteryear were both transformed by the Gap's antifashion philosophy. The introduction—and wide social acceptance—of sizes that came in S, M, L and XL shaped how Americans dressed. This naive acceptance of the ordinary had tremendous social consequence. The economic wherewithal to translate social egalitarianism into a culture, after all, is not just the ascendance of lowbrow into highbrow in American society. It is the triumph of the common. It is the equating of culture, by which one means civility, to a certain complete and appalling disregard for *discernment*. Consider that corporate America encourages managers to attend the seminars, run by high-priced consultants, to teach their employees how to navigate a properly set table and the fundamentals of everyday courtesy.[26] American businesses are struggling to incorporate employees in their twenties and thirties who were raised without an education in personal grooming, social etiquette and how to dress. This knowledge represents a competitive advantage in both international business and social settings.[27]

What was once a part of one's proper upbringing, now requires enlisting professionals, a pathetic commentary on American society. In the same way that professional consultants decipher table settings, psychologists now step up and offer the startling finding that how people dress affects how others view them.[28]

In such a society, there is a loss of moral authority and discerning taste. Whereas in the past arbiters of taste and refinement, whether Diana Vreeland or Thomas Hoving, prevailed, in the world as merchandised by Gap, Inc., these have been replaced by the likes of Tina Brown and David Geffen, purveyors of the vulgar and the common, mass-produced and efficiently packaged for the instant gratification and consumption by the multitudes. The idea that quality delineates between that which is worth*while* and that which is worth*less* is scoffed at as antidemocratic and unceremoniously dismissed as "irrelevant." The Microsoft executives who were photographed wearing beanie hats with propellers did not help their credibility, and this was one reason why they ended up pleading their case before the Supreme Court, where a certain decorum prevails. In this irrelevance, then, the Gap thrived spectacularly. But the world has changed once more from what it was in the afterglow of that spent Summer of Love. It is an amazing thing when one thinks about it, really. Every night one goes to sleep and then, upon waking, one finds the world has completed its revolution on its axis and one is back where one began the previous day.

America had definitely fallen out of the Gap by 2001. "We've made our own mistakes, but the retail environment also has changed dramatically in the past year," Mickey Drexler said as 2001 began and the dismal year 2000 was assessed by investment analysts. "In response, we'll be managing costs and inventory more tightly. But our emphasis is on creating fresh, distinctive product across our brands to drive customer demand."

While overall sales increased 14 percent in 2000, this was accomplished only by opening more and more stores. A more accurate portrait of the Gap's performance lay in the announcement that the Gap's same-store sales for December 2000 declined by 6 percent, compared to a 5 percent increase in December 1999. Indeed, after a disappointing 1999—which saw Robert Fisher step down—2000 proved to be nothing short of appalling. The comparable sales by brand for December 2000 said it all:

Gap Domestic: negative low single digit versus negative low single digit in 1999;

Gap International: negative low single digit versus positive low twenties in 1999;

Banana Republic: negative low single digit versus positive high single digit in 1999; and

Old Navy: negative low teens versus positive high single digit in 1999.

"December [2000] was a disappointing month in what has been a difficult year," Mickey Drexler told analysts. "Our sales were driven primarily by price, not product, which significantly affected our margins."

This was evident in the stock's performance throughout 2000. Closing at 43⅛ on the first business day of the year, January 3, 2000, the Gap ended the year at 25½ on December 29, 2000, a decline of 40 percent. "After a year of poor sales and earnings," *Business Week* reported on January 8, 2001, "CEO Drexler is under increasing pressure to fix the Gap. Its three retail units are stumbling on everything from fashion to expansion." Urging the Gap to get "back on track," this business publication was first to imply that Gap, Inc. had suffered a derailment.

The new millennium commenced with yet another series of "repositionings" at the Gap, Banana Republic and Old Navy. But insofar as "consumer demand" referred to Generation Y, the Gap's moment had clearly passed. Indeed, the vision and energy it once had was appropriated by other companies that had successfully connected with the first wave of Generation Y in the nineties. As the second wave of that fly generation of Americans entered their teenage years in the first decade of the twenty-first century, the Gap was dissed and dismissed, worthy of scorn for its global exploitation of humanity around the globe, and for the kinds of clothes only the uncool would wear.

The success of the Gap's antifashion philosophy had suffused American culture with greater and greater currency as the seventies ended and the eighties began. The idea that casual classics would emerge as the signature American look for the last quarter of the twentieth century was broadcast to the entire world through cultural exports. It was also a strong image within the United States.

Recall Tom Cruise posing in Gap clothes in *Risky Business*, the film that made him a star in 1983. Now fast-forward seventeen years. Tom Cruise, interviewed in the April 2000 issue of *Talk* magazine, is still wearing a white T-shirt and a pair of blue jeans. But his clothes reflect the aesthetics and sensibilities of the sophisticated and savvy members of Generation Y. Tom Cruise is photographed wearing a Marc Jacobs blue long-sleeve T-shirt over an Abercrombie & Fitch white short-sleeve T-shirt and a pair of jeans from Tommy Jeans. Two months later Tom Cruise appears on the cover of *Vanity Fair*, still dressed in jeans and a T-shirt, but this time both are by Helmut Lang, ending forevermore the monopoly of the Gap's pocket T-shirt.

The Age of the Gap, heralded by Tom Cruise in 1983 was thus ended by him in 2000. Generation Y instinctively understood that, as far as coolness is concerned it is the messenger as much as the message that counts. Tom Cruise is cool and the message is that the Gap is no longer cool. While the Gap was oblivious to it, Youth Culture did an about-face and turned its back.

For youths at the end of the year 2000, what captured the imagination of Generation Y had emerged from the streets of New York. Style and freedom, so long denied them by the conformity of the Gap's "Everybody the same" clothing, was found in other labels. Indeed, the brands worn by the hippest of the hip and the flyest of the fly among Generation Y, the *true* "promised brands," had nothing to do with the Gap. These new brands may have been inspired by the Gap's nihilism and its vacuous antifashion philosophy but they were lightyears ahead in how they were perceived. The Gap, to its horror, realized that it had engendered a generation of jaded consumers who now repudiated everything the Gap represented. Generation Y was beyond the Gap. And this was evident in the names of the brands that Generation Y embraced: Triple Five Soul, Lithium, Serial Killer and—of course—Porn Star.

A GAP CHRONOLOGY

1969   The first Gap store opens in San Francisco.

1970   The Gap opens its second store.

1973   The Gap's growth, fueled by sales of Levi's®, reaches 100 stores.

1976   The Gap launches its I.P.O.

The Gap acquires You & You, a national chain of 30 stores.

The Gap surpasses 200 stores.

1978   The Federal Trade Commission's Consent Order spells out that Levi's can no longer dictate retail prices.

The Gap experiences competition as other retailers begin to discount Levi's®.

Donald Fisher resolves to integrate the Gap "vertically" in order to eliminate middlemen and to control all aspects of the business.

1980   The Gap's private label business becomes more important to the Gap's bottom line as margins from the sales of Levi's vanish.

Miller's Outpost, the Gap's chief competitor, decides not to introduce khakis, focusing on the urban cowboy fad based on regional Western clothes, alienating mainstream consumers.

1983   Mickey Drexler is named president of Gap division

Banana Republic is acquired.

Risky Business christens Gap as the cool look for suburban teenagers.

1984   Mickey Drexler drops all private labels, except Gap.

"Vertical integration" of Gap, Inc. accelerates as in-house teams design collections.

The pocket T-shirt is introduced.

Gap acquires Pottery Barn.

1985   A line of "classic" basics is introduced.

The Gap sells only Levi's® and Gap brands.

1986   Gap Kids is launched.

Maggie Gross introduces a new, updated logo.

1987   Mickey Drexler is named president of Gap, Inc.

First store abroad opens in London.

Gap sells Pottery Barn.

Mickey Drexler launches high-end store, Hemisphere.

The Gap slashes prices for the first time since 1978 as competition intensifies.

1988   Mel and Patricia Ziegler are forced out at Banana Republic.

Tasha Polizzi's line at Banana Republic is a disaster.

Maggie Gross's "Individuals of style" campaign makes Gap hot.

1989   The Gap's pocket T-shirt becomes the fashion statement of the second half of the eighties.

Hemisphere is closed down.

1990   Baby Gap is launched.

Maggie Gross develops a "uniform" look to streamline "branding" of the Gap.

1991   The Gap drops Levi's® altogether.

1992   The Gap's basic line is widely adopted by competitors; sales plummet.

The Gap is forced to slash prices for the first time in the nineties.

Gap Shoes is launched.

1993   Maggie Gross's "Who wore khakis?" is launched.

Mickey Drexler launches a fashion line at the Gap that bombs.

Gap is mocked on *Saturday Night Live*; the Gap replaces McDonald's as Generation Y's metaphor for a dead-end job in corporate America.

1994   Old Navy is launched.

Gap Scents is introduced.

Gap Shoes is closed down.

1995   Mickey Drexler is named CEO of Gap, Inc.

Donald Fisher retains the title of chairman of board of Gap, Inc.

Jeanne Jackson "repositions" Banana Republic.

Banana Republic Body Care is introduced.

Global Exchange targets Gap to protest labor abuses abroad.

"Gap-lash" impacts sales; first year in which the Gap experiences no growth.

1996   Mickey Drexler "repositions" the Gap, dropping all "fashion" items.

Maggie Gross is fired; all current advertising is suspended.

Banana Republic's catering to urban gays is a success.

Banana Republic launches its home line.

1997   Old Navy surpasses $1 billion in sales.

The Gap returns to television advertising with LL Cool J.

"Repositioned" Gap and Banana Republic are both hot.

Liza Schultz is named one of *Time* magazine's most influential Americans.

Gap fragrance "Blue No. 655" is launched.

1998   "Khakis swing," "Khakis rock," and "Khakis groove" ads are spectacular success.

Banana Republic catalog returns.

Sharon Stone wears Gap to present an Oscar.

Old Navy launches cosmetics line.

Gap Body Shops introduced.

Gap-to-Go delivers clothes like take-out pizza.

Banana Republic launches credit card.

1999   "Zombie chic" ads turn off consumers.

Old Navy, under the direction of Jenny Ming, surpasses the Gap in sales; Old Navy continues to cannibalize the Gap's core business.

Robert Fisher resigns as president of Gap division; no Fisher is now involved in the day-to-day operations at Gap, Inc.

Global Exchange's anti-Gap campaign picks up momentum at the protests against the World Trade Organization in Seattle.

Workers at sweatshops that manufacture Gap clothing tour the United States.

2000   Oldsmobile advertisements mock the Gap during the Super Bowl.

Tom Cruise appears on the cover of *Vanity Fair* and *Talk* wearing jeans and T-shirts—but not from the Gap.

The Gap launches its *West Side Story* advertising on Oscars night.

Capri line is quickly copied by competitors at lower prices.

Sales at Gap plunge in first quarter, sending share prices plummeting.

Ken Pilot is named president of Gap Division.

Jeanne Jackson resigns as president of Banana Republic.

Banana Republic expands discounts for the employees of Fortune 500 companies.

Global Exchange intensifies its protests, emboldened by demonstrations held in Washington, D.C., against the World Bank and the International Monetary Fund.

Same-store sales at Old Navy fail to meet expectations in the first half of 2000.

"Markdown Madness," with discounts exceeding 50 percent are introduced at Old Navy; analysts dismiss this as evidence of an attempt to price for cash flow.

Corporate America begins to encourage employees to dress "professionally," cutting back on casual days.

Saturday Night Live airs scathing ridicule of the Gap's *West Side Story* advertisements and launches "Gap Fat: When You're XXXL" satire.

Gap initiates first major launch of Gap Body Shops.

Old Navy stumbles as sales at the Gap's core business continue to weaken; stock loses more than half its value as the year progresses.

In the second half of the year, leading executives leave the company by "mutual agreement."

Gap, Inc. hires Modernista to create high-visibility ads for the Christmas 2000 campaign.

Old Navy announced an $89 million investment for its first foreign store in Toronto, Canada, scheduled to open in the second half of 2001.

Will & Grace, the ABC sitcom, associates the Gap, Banana Republic and Old Navy brands with contemporary American gay lives and "outs" Banana Republic as a store for gays.

In a sign of desperation, Gap and Old Navy revive the failed Capri look for 2001, this time as a "boot cut" Capri.

L Reports, which tracks the attitudes of trend-setting "Alpha Consumers" announces in 2001 that 18 to 30-year-olds are turned off by the "Gap Empire."

Gap sales approach $14 billion at its 3,700 stores worldwide.

Notes

PREFACE

1. Julie Henderson Kanberg, vice president, associate general counsel for Gap, Inc. sent a letter dated July 27, 2000, in which she acknowledged receipt of certain chapters. She wrote that the discussion "presents what appears to be a single or minority view as the universal truth." This was followed with the assertion that "we have not undertaken to review [the chapters submitted] for factual accuracy. To ask us to do so would be to impose a considerable burden on a number of people within this organization, a burden that is neither fairly nor appropriately placed on us." In a subsequent letter dated November 6, 2000, she requested that "[t]o be fair to our company and your readers, . . . [do] indicate that the Gap Inc. expressly declined to review the chapters provided for factual accuracy." Other parties contacted for this book agreed to review the material.

INTRODUCTION

1. The Banana Republic flagship store at Grant Avenue and Sutter Street, ironically, is located in the same location where Hemisphere, a spectacular disaster as the Gap's first attempt at the high-end market, once stood. In the fall of 1998 I went to the Banana Republic flagship store and purchased two suede shirts, one each in black and beige. I remarked to the sales associate that those shirts were what one would have expected to find at Hemisphere. "What's that?" he asked. Before I could explain, his co-worker interjected, "That's the in-flight magazine for United Airlines. My ex-boyfriend was an airline-princess."

2. The Teenage Research Unlimited study reported that whereas 12 percent of those in Generation Y thought the Gap was "cool" in 1995, only 8 percent thought so in 1999.

3. Abercrombie & Fitch tied Old Navy in terms of coolness among Generation Y-ers, both receiving a ranking of 8 percent in the Teenage Research Unlimited study.

4. In 1999 and 2000, LFO, Blink 182, LEN, Eminem, Korn, Limp Bizkit, Filter, Smash Mouth, Vertical Horizon, Slipknot and Third Eye Blind were some of the happening groups that captured the imagination of Generation Y—and that cultivated anti-antifashion images.

5. The term "gayness" refers to the ascension of homosexual aesthetics in mainstream culture, the epitome of which are the ubiquitous Caesar haircuts popularized in the nineties.

6. The relationship between Baby Gap, Gap Kids and Gap as consumer brands was characterized as one of "mutuality" by Teri Agins of the *Wall Street Journal*—and the product of the Gap's brand manager, Maggie Gross, as we shall see in chapter 5.

7. In 1999 Madonna turned forty. And in the fall of 2000 when Madonna introduced her new look on the video for "Music," while she looked gorgeous, the "look" was nonetheless derivative and satirical. Madonna's send-up resembled Jennifer Lopez cross-dressing in her boyfriend's (Sean "Puffy" Combs) clothes. Her jewelry was consistent with the gold fad launched by the film, *Gladiator*, starring Russell Crowe.

8. *Pop-Up Video* is a send-up of old music videos on VH1, MTV's rival network. Whereas MTV and Generation Y grew up together, VH1 has greater appeal among Generation X-ers and baby boomers.

9. Levi's® had stumbled in its efforts to revitalize its brand at the end of the nineties. Three campaigns—"Opt. for the original," "Calvin wore them" and "Our models can beat up your models"—fared poorly in both print and broadcast media.

10. "Casual Friday" was pioneered by Alcoa in Pittsburgh in 1991. But it was IBM, which, in 1995, went casual every day of the week, helping transform America into a nation of slobs.

11. In the corporate world, ironically, "casual casualties" were found in places like the Ivy League clubs, where short-sleeve tattersalls, Nike Airs® and wrinkled khakis were inexplicably in vogue.

12. Kurt Cobain's suicide and Kate Moss's rumored anorexia did much to limit the appeal of both fashion looks.

13. To *dis* is slang for to disrespect: "You dissed me every chance you got."

14. This protester had obviously seen *Austin Powers: The Spy Who Shagged Me*. Dr. Evil, explaining on the *Jerry Springer Show* why he abandoned his son, states that his young son just wasn't evil enough. "You are the Diet Coke of evil. Just one calorie," our villain offers.

15. The next generation—those born on or after January 1, 2001, are expected to be called "Generation D," for they will be the first generation born in the digital age.

16. Thorstein Veblen, *The Theory of the Leisure Class*, pages 168–169.

17. Alison Lurie, *The Language of Clothes*, page 77.

18. Ibid., page 78.

19. *Bye-Bye Birdie* starred Janet Leigh, Dick Van Dyke, Ann-Margaret, Paul Lynde and Maureen Stapleton and remains a popular musical performed in high schools throughout the country.

20. John Seabrook writes for the *New Yorker* magazine on subjects that include MTV.

21. John Seabrook, *Nobrow*, pages 45–46.

22. Ibid., pages 59–60.

23. Ibid., pages 62–63.

CHAPTER 1

1. Splendid accounts are found in Tom Wolfe's *Radical Chic & Mau-Mauing the Flak Catchers* and *The Electric Kool-Aid Acid Test*.

2. The information from the service bureau also allowed the Gap to see what was missing—from either employee or customer theft. The analysis of when customers shopped, furthermore, allowed for more efficient schedules for staff.

3. Paco Underhill, *Why We Buy*, page 49.

4. Teri Agins, *The End of Fashion*, page 182.

5. "Who was that guy?" one of the Cuban-American kids asked. When I asked her why she wanted to know, she replied, "I don't know. He seemed so cool. I wish my dad were like him."

6. Teri Agins, *The End of Fashion*, pages 186–187.

7. Gap, Inc., by comparison, operated over 3,800 stores throughout the world.

8. "Ah, Paris. The Sights. The Food. The Gap?" by Constance Rosenblum, *New York Times*, July 12, 2000, page D9.

CHAPTER 2

1. Survey of 245 adults over the age of thirty-five taken in downtown San Francisco in July 1999.

2. James Gleick, *Faster*, page 10.

3. Joan Didion, *Miami*, page 52.

4. Gays have traditionally been excluded by banning "gentlemen bachelors" from consideration for membership or participation in certain clubs or functions.

5. Interestingly, when Donald Trump established Mar-a-Lago Club, that he openly welcomed Jews resulted in his being ostracized by certain elements within Palm Beach society for, as one phrased it, "the arrogance of that parvenu." Mar-a-Lago, incidentally, means sea to lake in Spanish. The Spanish settled most of early Florida.

6. The segregation between English- and Spanish-speaking America astounds in how delineated it has become: monolingual magazines, radio stations and television channels seldom provide any bilingual content, inexplicably assuming that no one in the United States is either bilingual or bi-cultural.

7. In the course of interviewing prominent San Franciscans in the spring of 2000, one gentleman dismissed Donald Fisher as "a fat, old, bald Jew," which presumably was acceptable, given that the speaker was a fat, old, bald Protestant.

8. Paco Underhill, *Why We Buy*, page 184.

9. Other retailers are emulating the Gap strategy more forcefully; Starbucks, for instance, sells CDs of the music played in their coffee shops, a clever marketing ploy.

10. "Ecstasy" is MDMA, an acronym for 3, 4-methylenedioxymethamphetamine, an illegal drug favored by young people who want to dance all night and into the early morning hours. "That's what the pocket's for," an eighteen year old who had been awake for thirty-six hours explained to me, while chewing on a straw to fight dry mouth, one of the side effects.

11. A "rave," which first entered mainstream popular culture lexicon in the eighties, refers to semi-clandestine warehouse parties, many participants of which can only sustain their energy levels all night long by using narcotics, "X" being one of the more popular choices.

12. Mary Boone, of the tony Fifth Avenue art gallery that bears her name, was reportedly wearing a Banana Republic outfit when she was arrested in September 1999 for distributing live 9-mm cartridges as souvenirs in connection with one of her art shows. "Does the First Amendment right to free speech include the right to the unfettered distribution of live ammunition?" a misguided art critic wondered. Perhaps, or perhaps not. (The matter was resolved to the satisfaction of both parties.) The all-time classic example of the notorious, shall we say, penetration of the Gap brand in all aspects of American life, however, remains the salacious story of a certain White House intern's Gap dress bearing President Bill Clinton's semen.

13. Teri Agins, *The End of Fashion*, page 185.

CHAPTER 3

1. Levi Strauss & Co. reached an agreement with the FTC that resulted in a Consent Order. Over the years the press has erroneously reported that it issued a ruling, in part because officials at the Gap and Levi Strauss & Co. have used both terms interchangeably. Allegations made against Levi Strauss & Co. were never proved. Regarding the sales problems that engulfed the company at the end of the nineties, Albert Moreno, senior vice president and general counsel for Levi Strauss & Co., stated, "Our sales declines in 1998 and 1999 are attributable to a number of business conditions and cyclical trends, including a global softening of basic denim jean sales in the late nineties, a shift in fashion trends that favored more fashion-forward products not traditionally associated with LS&CO., increased consumer interest in baggy 'urban' jean styles, and operational and delivery problems that resulted in missing a significant number of retail orders. We also did not always respond to these emerging fashion trends fast enough to capitalize on them, such as the baggy, urban jeans styles of the late nineties."

2. Personal communication, August 22, 2000.

3. Jeans were subsequently eroticized to the point where many critics voiced the concern that using under-aged models bordered on pedophilia.

4. Joshua Levine, *The Rise and Fall of the House of Barneys*, page 38.

5. Under the Carter administration it was Alfred Kahn who engineered the deregulation of the airline industry, which allowed individual carriers to set the fares they charged and permitted routes, landing rights and gate slots to be sold among the airlines as they saw best. The result was unprecedented growth in the

airline industry as more passengers flew on more routes to more places as never before.

6. In his interview with Nina Munk for "Gap Gets It," published in *Fortune*, August 3, 1998, Donald Fisher repeated the familiar story of why he hired Mickey Drexler.

7. Mickey Drexler himself is fond of recounting the natural working relationship he has with Donald Fisher.

8. Sales figures provided by Levi Strauss & Co. follow:

Year	Sales in Millions of Dollars
1978	1,682
1979	2,103
1980	2,815
1981	2,861
1982	2,579
1983	2,739
1984	2,507
1985	2,584
1986	2,767
1987	2,874
1988	3,116.7
1989	3,627.9
1990	4.247.0
1991	4,902.9
1992	5,570.3
1993	5,892.5
1994	6,074.3
1995	6,707.6
1996	7,136.3
1997	6,861.5
1998	5,930.6
1999	5,104.4

While the apparel market slows beginning in 1994, sales peak in 1996. The company reports that because of a "competitive jeans market," sales of basics decline. In subsequent years, because of "growth in designer jeans, VISS, private label and urban brands," coupled with sales declines at chain and department stores, Levi's enters a period of marked declines in sales worldwide. (Figures courtesy of Levi Strauss & Co.)

9. Zandl Group reported that among Generation Y-ers, only 11 percent percent identified Levi's as a favorite brand, which was down from 17 perent in 1999 and 36 percent in 1994. Similar declines in the Gap as a brand were recorded.

10. Levi's executives were still sensitive to and jealous of the Gap years after their rift. Consider Sean Dee, the marketing director for Levi's, who, a decade after the rupture with the Gap, discussed their fall of 2000 advertising campaign, "Make them your own," by saying, "We want to leverage our brand, because it isn't about everybody being *the same*."

11. At its peak, in 1996, sales reached $7.1 billion. The problems included a buyout engineered by Robert Haas, the scion of the family firm, who was besieged by family disputes and a collapsing market. When Peter Jacobi retired in January 1999, it took nine months to find a replacement, Philip Marineau. A marketing specialist at Pepsi, Mr. Marineau, it was hoped, would engineer a turnaround at Levi's the way John Scully, also from Pepsi, masterminded a turnaround at Apple Computer in the eighties.

12. Despite Philip Marineau's assurances to Alice Cuneo, a reporter for *Advertising Age*, in July 2000 many industry observers were not impressed. "Levi's Ties Recovery Plan to Fall Ad Spending Blitz," by Alice Cuneo, *Advertising Age*, July 2000 (vol. 71, issue 32), page 12.

13. "New Levi's CEO Unfurls Battle Plan as Sales Skid," by Carol Emert, *San Francisco Chronicle*, February 22, 2000.

CHAPTER 4

1. After the Zieglers were ousted, their critcism and sense of betrayal were documented in interviews with and leaks to the press. Gap, Inc. responded by prohibiting any of its employees from making any statement to the press. The Zieglers took a hiatus of several years before they launched the Republic of Tea in 1991, which they subsequently sold to a Midwestern beverage bottler three years later. Their "Third Republic," so to speak, ZoZa.com, an online retailer of Zen-inspired high-end apparel was launched in 2000. "We've built two very strong brands before, and we don't need parental supervision," Mel Ziegler, said to *Business Week*, a reference to the characterization of how he and Patricia Ziegler idolized Donald Fisher when Gap, Inc. first acquired Banana Republic.

2. A comprehensive discussion of how Jews in the garment industry, who were largely excluded from fashion design and upscale retailing, worked together is found in *The Rise and Fall of the House of Barneys: A Family Tale of Chutzpah, Glory and Greed* by Joshua Levine.

3. In San Francisco and New York, to be sure, prissy queens and Nell Monsters were jumping up and down, clapping their hands together in a joyous chorus of "That's fabulous! That's fabulous!" but the rest of the American public was not amused at all—and not buying any of it. In contemporary American homosexual vernacular, a "prissy queen" is a gay man with a snooty attitude (think of Noël Coward) and a "Nell Monster" is an insufferably catty and affected gay man (think of Oscar Wilde). Both terms are used in a value-neutral manner.

4. It is interesting to note that the "My chosen family" advertisements now enjoy a cult status among homosexuals; framed copies of the magazine ads are highly coveted possessions.

5. Teenage Research Unlimited's Coolest Brand Meter, for instance, reports that three times more teenage girls than teenage boys considered the Gap one of the "coolest" brands. For the Old Navy brand, the difference is not as great: only two and a half times as many teenage girls reported that brand as "coolest" compared with teenage boys. An analysis of the gender gap in self-reporting on the "coolest" brands is found at <www.teenresearch.com/syndicated/index report.html>

6. These figures are estimates based on contemporaneous analysts' figures.

CHAPTER 5

1. Or to be more accurate, "Shopping is fun again[SM]."

2. The word most often used was "stealing," but this is a hyperbole; employees are not slaves or chattel; they leave of their own volition. At worst, Gap can be accused of guerrilla recruiting, but not employee theft.

3. "Gap Gets It," by Nina Munk, *Fortune*, August 3, 1998.

CHAPTER 6

1. The contemporary homosexual look was showcased in catalogs of clothes from firms like International Male and the homoerotic art of Tom of Finland.

2. Alison Lurie, *The Language of Clothes*, pages 230–231.

3. Aca Joe was the retailer that specialized in casual clothes inspired by tropical beaches; it expanded rapidly in the mid-eighties. Its growth, however, was so fast and furious that it was unable to manage its inventory properly and it experienced severe difficulties. It was relaunched in 1999 by the Pacific Coast Apparel Company, which purchased the brand name.

4. Private communication, May 1998.

5. "Hip, Upscale Attitude Sweeps S.F.'s Gay Bars," by Dan Levy, *San Francisco Chronicle*, March 15, 1999.

6. In contemporary American gay vernacular, the uniforms, for the most part, distinguish "tops," "dominants" and "daddies" from "bottoms," "submissives" and "pussyboys," respectively.

7. "Gap Gets It," by Nina Munk, *Fortune*, August 3, 1998.

8. Paco Underhill, *Why We Buy*, page 99.

9. In a marketing move to co-opt the more casual dress codes throughout corporate America, consider that Banana Republic is offering discounts to employees of major companies. For instance, employees of Citigroup—the company created when Citicorp and Travelers merged—can enjoy a 20 percent discount by logging onto <www.bananarepublic.com/citigroup>.

10. "Eye candy" in contemporary American homosexual vernacular is an expression for an attractive man, the homosexual equivalent of a straight man saying he's just at the beach watching the babes go by.

11. Alison Lurie, *The Language of Clothes*, page 102.

12. Gump's is a swank retailer not far from the Banana Republic store in San Francisco.

CHAPTER 7

1. America's sustained economic expansion at the end of the nineties created an entirely new market for upscale lines of baby and children's clothing from brands like Giorgio Armani and Bergdorf Goodman.

2. Paco Underhill, *Why We Buy*, pages 103–104.

3. "A New City Rises: A Handful of New and Renovated Buildings Offers a Glimpse into the Future of the Booming South of Market Area," by John King, *San Francisco Chronicle*, November 9, 1999.

4. "Old Navy Brings Gap Earnings Down," by Carol Emert, *San Francisco Chronicle*, August 3, 2000.

5. Carol Emert's article, "Old Navy Brings Gap Earnings Down" (*San Francisco Chronicle*, August 3, 2000, p. C-7) quoted Heidi Kunz, Gap, Inc.'s chief financial officer, as predicting that third-quarter earnings "would likely come in at the low end of analysts' estimates."

6. The criticism was swift. *Fortune* was alarmed; in "A Gap Mishap" on September 18, 2000, it warned that while the Gap was not out of the game, and company claims to the contrary, "[n]one of this suggests an overnight turnaround, of course, and Gap management has been deliberately conservative in its prospects." Rob Walker, writing in *Slate.com* observed on September 7, 2000, in an otherwise empty-headed report that "maybe, after a while even anti-fashion goes out of style." *Business Week* commented on the Gap twice in the same month. Amy Barrett, in "To Reach the Unreachable Teen" (*Business Week*, September 18, 2000) wrote that the Gap's dismal performance was evidence that "even the strongest brands can slip from favor" and be abandoned by Youth Culture. A week before this conclusion, a *Business Week* editorial titled "New Economy, New Social Contract" took the Gap to task, pointing out that "[c]orporations increasingly connect to their customers in a personal, emotional way, and their customers expect more from them. So college students picket Nike Inc. and Gap Inc. to stop sweatshops in Asia."

7. "Isaac Mizrahi: The Fashion Maven Predicts a New Age of Elegance," *Esquire*, March 2000, page 192.

8. Paco Underhill, *Why We Buy*, page 32.

9. Ibid., page 32.

10. These observations, however, are not meant to suggest that the Gap conducts profiling in a systematic way.

CHAPTER 8

1. Alison Lurie, *The Language of Clothes*, pages 158–159.

2. George Marshall, *Spirit of '69: A Skinhead Bible*, pages 17–20.

3. Naomi Klein, *No Logo: Taking Aim at the Brand Bullies*, page 13.

4. Michael J. Wolf, *The Entertainment Economy*, New York: Times Books, 1999, page 261.

5. Alison Lurie, *The Language of Clothes*, pages 79–81.

6. Isaac Mizrahi, *Esquire*, March 2000, page 192.

7. The success of *House of Fashion* spawned *Mission: Makeover*, a play on *Mission: Impossible*'s quest to accomplish impossible feats, where young people—male and female alike—were stripped of their Gap personas and given a complete makeover, such was the sense of desperation that gripped members of Generation Y. "The first thing we are going to do is get rid of those khaki pants," a fashionista says, rolling her eyes in disbelief. "If a guy has a great ass, why can't he wear tight pants to show it off?

8. Alison Lurie, *The Language of Clothes*, page 226.

9. Over the course of the summer, Banana Republic had introduced a virtual tropical fruit stand of colors: mango, hibiscus, guava, watermelon and calypso.

10. "A shirt in the color of kiwi? What kind of gay shit is that?" I was told by a male member of Generation Y whom I interviewed at the Rolling Rock Town Fair featuring the Red Hot Chili Peppers, Filter and Moby in Pittsburgh, Pennsylvania, on August 5, 2000.

11. Alison Lurie, *The Language of Clothes*, page 212.

12. "Gap Gets It," by Nina Munk, *Fortune*, August 3, 1998.

13. In fact, *Reality Bites* marks the first time in pop culture that the dead-end job is represented not by the drudgery of slaving under the Golden Arches at McDonald's but by folding piles of jeans and T-shirts at the Gap.

14. "Gap Gets It," by Nina Munk, *Fortune*, August 3, 1998.

15. "The Beautiful and the Panned: Dot-Com Vulgarities Aside, a Pretty Good 1999 for Ads," by Stuart Elliott, *New York Times*, December 29, 1999.

16. Larry Tye, *The Father of Spin*, page 91.

17. For further information on *Youth Outlook*, visit <www.pacificnews.org>.

18. Of the four teenagers, two were male and two were female. One was Caucasian, one African American, one Asian and one Hispanic. Three were heterosexual and one was homosexual. All were born when Ronald Reagan was president. None had attended a high school prom (as of yet). None had attended or participated in an anti-Gap protest.

19. For the two women, makeovers were included at their request; the two men received new haircuts of their choice. All were given manicures.

20. In San Francisco community standards, "queer" refers to gay, lesbian, bisexual and transgender individuals in a value-neutral manner.

21. "In Search of American Style," by Ted Allen, *Esquire*, March 2000, page 164.

22. Owen Edwards, speaking about Seattle's Gian Decaro, a "sartorial saint," describes as a "miracle" the transformation he achieved in dressing Bill Gates, who has been described as "an adult child lost at the Gap." See "A Tailor Who Upgrades the Computer Class," by Molly Knight, *Daily News Record*, July 1, 1999.

23. *GQ*, July 2000.

24. Ellen Lupton and J. Abbott Miller, *Design Writing Research: Writing on Graphic Design*, Harrisburg, Pennsylvania: Kiosk, 1996, page 177.

25. Naomi Klein, *No Logo: Taking Aim at the Brand Bullies*, page 5.

CHAPTER 9

1. "In Search of American Style," by Ted Allen, *Esquire*, March 2000, page 164.

2. James Gleick, *Faster*, page 75.

3. Naomi Klein, *No Logo*, page 361.

4. Ibid., page 327.

5. Ibid., page 237.

6. Ibid., page 211.

7. Karl Schoenberger, *Levi's Children*, pages. 178–179.

8. Jim Hightower, *If the Gods Had Meant Us to Vote They Would Have Given Us Candidates*, page 256.

9. Ibid., page 257.

10. Naomi Klein, *No Logo*, page 243.

11. Private communication, June 14, 2000.

12. Private communication, June 14, 2000.

13. To receive updates of Global Exchange's efforts to defend labor rights of workers around the world, contact Leila Salazar at Global Exchange, 2017 Mission Street, San Francisco, California 94110, or by e-mail at <leila@globalexchange.org>.

14. "For the first time in years, Gap, Inc.'s annual shareholder's meeting wasn't disrupted by rabble-rousing demonstrators protesting the company's alleged use of sweatshop labor or the logging of redwood forests by its founding family, the Fishers," Carol Emert reported in the *San Francisco Chronicle* on May 6, 2000. "Not coincidentally, the meeting was held in rural Tennessee, 23 miles outside of Nashville, in a newly built Gap distribution center," she wrote in that article, titled "Gap Meets in Rural Tennessee, Avoids Usual Protesters."

15. Her actual statement, in Miami Spanglish, was, "What can I *decirte, chico?* Being beautiful is *más y más dificil* all the time."

16. Alison Lurie, *The Language of Clothes*, pages 226–227.

17. Jennifer Moses, *New York Times*, May 31, 2000, page A31.

18. The absurdity of these fashions, in fact, was mocked in a cartoon in the *New Yorker* magazine (May 29, 2000, page 56), in which a salesman tells a middle-aged, bald man, the "[c]apri pants, capri jacket—the ideal summer suit." The confused client stands bewildered before the mirror, dressed in a ridiculous "capri" business suit.

19. *Marketing Management*, Spring 1994.

CHAPTER 10

1. "Retailers Cite the Weather as April Sales Miss Goals," by Leslie Kaufman, *New York Times*, May 5, 2000, C1.

2. They are Target (Dayton-Hudson), Lane Bryant (The Limited), J.C. Penney and Gap, Inc.

3. Private communication, June 14, 2000.

4. Thorstein Veblen, *The Theory of the Leisure Class*, page 268.

5. Larry Tye, *The Father of Spin*, page 53.

6. Abercrombie & Fitch Spring Break 2000 catalog, page 160.

7. Richard Rodriguez, *Days of Obligation*, page 35.

8. This is how homosexuals have been viewed by society at large according to Dudley Clendinen and Adam Nagourney writing in *Out for Good*.

9. In fact, the emergence of gay aesthetics in mainstream culture is so pervasive that it results in plots in sitcoms and romance movies, where a heterosexual woman mistakenly assumes a man is gay because of the clothes he is wearing, resulting in a comedy of manners. "*Gay?* I'm not gay! What made you *think* I was gay?" a man protests. "Well, look at what you're *wearing!*" That misunderstanding cleared up, the man resolves to never buy "casual clothes" again.

10. Amy Spencer, from Gap, Inc. Corporate Communications, sent me an e-mail dated November 1, 2000, in which she wrote, "I don't have any information about the demographics of our customers. I also wanted to let you know that Gap Inc. strictly prohibits discrimination against applicants, employees, customers, vendors, or other business contacts based on race, color, age, gender, sexual orientation, religion, marital status, national origin/ancestry, or physical/mental disability." This is a peculiar statement insofar as it contradicts pronouncements made by Jenny Ming of Old Navy, Jeanne Jackson of Banana Republic and Robert

Fisher of Gap about the target segments to which they market, not to mention industry authorities, including Michael Wood of Teenage Research Unlimited and Paco Underhill of Environsell.

11. And all the pharmacists are looking to see who's been pilfering their supply of steroids.

12. Interviews with straight young men, between the ages of eighteen and twenty-five, indicated the preferred clothes from companies including Abercrombie & Fitch over the Gap because the Gap was seen as being for "queers."

13. While my informal survey of members of Generation Y is not scientific, the use of the word "pornography" reflects this generation's sentiments; it is not used in either a malicious or inflammatory manner in this context and should not be construed as such.

14. When John Paul II and Fidel Castro—both members of the Matures generation—stand united with Generation Y, something of great social consequence is unfolding.

15. More than one member of Generation Y made the curious observation that the failure of organized religion to reach out to them was substituted by organized social protest.

16. David Brooks, *Bobos in Paradise*, pages 113–116.

17. While "Bobos" combines the first syllables in "bourgeois bohemians," it is often heard in the background of American life, since in Spanish the word means "dummies"—and has long been used by Hispanics to deride inexplicable absurdities of American life.

18. David Brooks, *Bobos in Paradise*, page 111.

19. When Old Navy was introduced into the conversation, the rejoinder was that I was very, very funny man.

20. It is not clear what Miss Manners would have to say about what amounts to a young lady's primer on pissing in public places. The entire article is available in the Yellow Rat Bastard catalog, vol. 1, issue 1.

21. Gertrude Himmelfarb, *One Nation, Two Cultures*, pages 117–118.

22. Michelangelo Signorile's views are found in his national bestseller, *Life Outside: The Signorile Report on Gay Men: Sex, Drugs, Muscles, and the Passages of Life.* New York: Harper Perennial Library, 1998 (reprint edition).

23. The song, "West End Girls," begins with the phrase, "Sometimes you're better off dead." Telling a story about having a gun pointed at one's head, this song catapulted the group to the top of the charts in London before crossing the Atlantic to the gay ghettos of New York and California.

24. An older Hispanic woman said to her daughter, "¿Oíste la letra que están cantando esos maricones?" (Did you hear the lyrics those gays are singing?) before they put down the clothes they had in their hands and proceeded to walk out of the store. The song playing was "I Wouldn't Normally Do This Kind of Thing." The women walked across the corridor and entered the Ralph Lauren Polo Shop within Burdines, an anchor department store.

25. Tracy Chapman, "Telling Stories," Purple Rabbit Music, 1999.

26. In an understatement of how the points of reference have declined, consider that, when asked to define what is "ladylike," a seventeen-year-old member of Generation Y offered, "A lady does not share dental floss."

27. Indeed, magazines, such as *Martha Stewart Living* and *Men's Health*, are more popular because they help Generation X-ers and Generation Y-ers learn the basics of good grooming, proper dressing and gracious manners.

28. In *Fortysomething*, by Ross Goldstein (New York: J.P. Tarcher, 1991), San Francisco psychologist Goldstein explains to male baby boomers what is expected of them in middle age, including how to dress. It is not a coincidence that this book is written by a therapist based in San Francisco, where the Gap's antifashion revolution was unleashed and has had widespread social impact.

SELECTED BIBLIOGRAPHY

Agins, Teri. *The End of Fashion*. New York: HarperCollins, 1999.

Brooks, David. *Bobos in Paradise*. New York: Simon & Schuster, 2000.

Didion, Joan. *Miami*. New York: Vintage Books, 1998.

Gleick, James. *Faster*. New York: Vintage Books, 2000.

Hightower, Jim. *If the Gods Had Meant Us to Vote They Would Have Given Us Candidates*. New York: HarperCollins, 2000.

Himmelfarb, Gertrude. *One Nation, Two Cultures*. New York: Vintage, 2001.

Klein, Naomi. *No Logo: Taking Aim at the Brand Bullies*. New York: Picador USA, 2000.

Levine, Joshua. *The Rise and Fall of the House of Barneys*. New York: William Morrow & Co., 1999.

Lurie, Alison. *The Language of Clothes*. New York: Henry Holt & Company, 1980; paperback, 2000.

Marshall, George. *Spirit of '69: A Skinhead Bible*. London: A.K. Press, 1994.

Rodriguez, Richard. *Days of Obligation*. New York: Viking Penguin, 1993.

Schoenberger, Karl. *Levi's Children: Coming to Terms with Human Rights in the Global Marketplace*, New York: Atlantic Monthly Press, 2000.

Seabrook, John. *Nobrow*. New York: Alfred A. Knopf, 2000.

Tye, Larry. *The Father of Spin*. New York: Random House, 1998.

Underhill, Paco. *Why We Buy*. New York: Simon & Schuster, 1999; paperback, 2000.

Veblen, Thornstein. *The Theory of the Leisure Class*. New York: Dover Publications, Reprinted Edition, June 1994.

INDEX

About the Author

LOUIS E.V. NEVAER is an economist, business entrepreneur, consultant, editor, and former publisher of newsletters on topics in international financial management. His previous books published by Quorum are *Corporate Financial Planning and Management in a Deficit Economy* (1987, with Steven A. Deck), *The Management of Corporate Business Units* (1988), *The Protectionist Threat to Corporate America* (1989), *Strategic Corporate Alliances* (1990), *Strategies for Business in Mexico* (1995), and *New Business Opportunities in Latin America* (1996).